DATE DUE

MALE/FEMALE ROLES

OPPOSING VIEWPOINTS®

MALE/FEMALE
ROLES

OPPOSING VIEWPOINTS®

David Bender & Bruno Leone, *Series Editors*

Neal Bernards & Terry O'Neill, *Book Editors*

OPPOSING VIEWPOINTS SERIES ®

Greenhaven Press, Inc.   PO Box 289009   San Diego, CA 92198-0009

Library of Congress Cataloging-in-Publication Data

Male/female roles : opposing viewpoints / Neal Bernards & Terry O'Neill, book editors.
    p.   cm. — (Opposing viewpoints series)
Includes bibliographical references.
Summary: Various authors debate how sex roles were established and how men and women respond to changes in sex roles. Includes critical thinking skills activities.
    ISBN 0-89908-446-X   (lib. bdg.).—ISBN 0-89908-421-4 (pbk.)
    1. Sex role. [1. Sex role. 2. Critical thinking.]
I. Bernards, Neal, 1963-   . II. O'Neill, Terry, 1944-   .
III. Series.
HQ1075.M35   1989
305.3—dc20   89-23419
                                                              CIP
                                                               AC

"Congress shall make no law ... abridging the freedom of speech, or of the press."

First Amendment to the US Constitution

The basic foundation of our democracy is the first amendment guarantee of freedom of expression. The *Opposing Viewpoints Series* is dedicated to the concept of this basic freedom and the idea that it is more important to practice it than to enshrine it.

Contents

Why Consider Opposing Viewpoints?

"It is better to debate a question without settling it than to settle a question without debating it."

Joseph Joubert (1754-1824)

The Importance of Examining Opposing Viewpoints

The purpose of the Opposing Viewpoints Series, and this book in particular, is to present balanced, and often difficult to find, opposing points of view on complex and sensitive issues.

Probably the best way to become informed is to analyze the positions of those who are regarded as experts and well studied on issues. It is important to consider every variety of opinion in an attempt to determine the truth. Opinions from the mainstream of society should be examined. But also important are opinions that are considered radical, reactionary, or minority as well as those stigmatized by some other uncomplimentary label. An important lesson of history is the eventual acceptance of many unpopular and even despised opinions. The ideas of Socrates, Jesus, and Galileo are good examples of this.

Readers will approach this book with their own opinions on the issues debated within it. However, to have a good grasp of one's own viewpoint, it is necessary to understand the arguments of those with whom one disagrees. It can be said that those who do not completely understand their adversary's point of view do not fully understand their own.

A persuasive case for considering opposing viewpoints has been presented by John Stuart Mill in his work *On Liberty*. When examining controversial issues it may be helpful to reflect on this suggestion:

> The only way in which a human being can make some approach to knowing the whole of a subject, is by hearing what can be said about it by persons of every variety of opinion, and studying all modes in which it can be looked at by every character of mind. No wise man ever acquired his wisdom in any mode but this.

Analyzing Sources of Information

The Opposing Viewpoints Series includes diverse materials taken from magazines, journals, books, and newspapers, as well as statements and position papers from a wide range of individuals, organizations and governments. This broad spectrum of sources helps to develop patterns of thinking which are open to the consideration of a variety of opinions.

Pitfalls To Avoid

A pitfall to avoid in considering opposing points of view is that of regarding one's own opinion as being common sense and the most rational stance and the point of view of others as being only opinion and naturally wrong. It may be that another's opinion is correct and one's own is in error.

Another pitfall to avoid is that of closing one's mind to the opinions of those with whom one disagrees. The best way to approach a dialogue is to make one's primary purpose that of understanding the mind and arguments of the other person and not that of enlightening him or her with one's own solutions. More can be learned by listening than speaking.

It is my hope that after reading this book the reader will have a deeper understanding of the issues debated and will appreciate the complexity of even seemingly simple issues on which good and honest people disagree. This awareness is particularly important in a democratic society such as ours where people enter into public debate to determine the common good. Those with whom one disagrees should not necessarily be regarded as enemies, but perhaps simply as people who suggest different paths to a common goal.

Developing Basic Reading and Thinking Skills

In this book, carefully edited opposing viewpoints are purposely placed back to back to create a running debate; each viewpoint is preceded by a short quotation that best expresses the author's main argument. This format instantly plunges the reader into the midst of a controversial issue and greatly aids that reader in mastering the basic skill of recognizing an author's point of view.

A number of basic skills for critical thinking are practiced in the activities that appear throughout the books in the series. Some of the skills are:

Evaluating Sources of Information   The ability to choose from among alternative sources the most reliable and accurate source in relation to a given subject.

Separating Fact from Opinion   The ability to make the basic distinction between factual statements (those that can be demonstrated or verified empirically) and statements of opinion (those that are beliefs or attitudes that cannot be proved).

Identifying Stereotypes   The ability to identify oversimplified, exaggerated descriptions (favorable or unfavorable) about people and insulting statements about racial, religious or national groups, based upon misinformation or lack of information.

Recognizing Ethnocentrism   The ability to recognize attitudes or opinions that express the view that one's own race, culture, or group is inherently superior, or those attitudes that judge another culture or group in terms of one's own.

It is important to consider opposing viewpoints and equally important to be able to critically analyze those viewpoints. The activities in this book are designed to help the reader master these thinking skills. Statements are taken from the book's viewpoints and the reader is asked to analyze them. This technique aids the reader in developing skills that not only can be applied to the viewpoints in this book, but also to situations where opinionated spokespersons comment on controversial issues. Although the activities are helpful to the solitary reader, they are most useful when the reader can benefit from the interaction of group discussion.

Using this book and others in the series should help readers develop basic reading and thinking skills. These skills should improve the reader's ability to understand what they read. Readers should be better able to separate fact from opinion, substance from rhetoric and become better consumers of information in our media-centered culture.

This volume of the Opposing Viewpoints Series does not advocate a particular point of view. Quite the contrary! The very nature of the book leaves it to the reader to formulate the opinions he or she finds most suitable. My purpose as publisher is to see that this is made possible by offering a wide range of viewpoints which are fairly presented.

David L. Bender
Publisher

Introduction

"In no country has such constant care been taken as in America to trace two clearly distinct lines of action for the two sexes, and to make them keep pace with the other, but in two pathways which are always different."

Alexis de Tocqueville

There is little question that men and women are different, and not only biologically. The big question is *why* are they different? Are gender distinctions caused by innate physiological and psychological differences, or are they caused by the social environment?

Scientists have long studied humans to discover the answers to this question. Their conclusions have sometimes been bizarre. A late nineteenth-century scientist concluded that women's sexual organs disrupted their thinking ability, thus making them less than competent beings and always controversial.

Today's scientists make strong efforts to do tightly controlled and solidly researched studies attempting to determine if hormonal differences affect the basic natures of males and females or if men and women use the two hemispheres of the brain differently. Even with these efforts, their conclusions are not without critics. For example, Steven Goldberg, sociologist and author of the widely read and much-debated book *The Inevitability of Patriarchy*, states that is inevitable that males are in the dominant positions in society because of biological factors—hormones and brain use. He writes, "The central fact is that men and women are different from each other from the gene to the thought to the act." Anne Fausto-Sterling, however, disagrees vehemently with this thesis. Fausto-Sterling, a biologist and author of *Myths of Gender: Biological Theories About Women and Men*, agrees that hormones affect sexual characteristics but concludes that their impact on social behavior is far from proven. For example, she points out that men are frequently said to be naturally dominant because of the extra aggressiveness caused by the male hormone testosterone. However, she argues, the studies that have specifically analyzed the effects of testosterone show no difference in aggression in men with high levels of testosterone and men with low levels. Thus, the link between gender-related hormones and behavior remains uncertain.

13

The same kind of controversy surrounds the question of how much influence society has on male-female differences. On one hand, sociologist Janet Saltzman Chafetz and others conclude from their studies that babies are "neutral" as far as gender identity is concerned. But almost from the moment they are born, their social environment begins to shape them into thinking of themselves as "male" and "female." One kind of baby is dressed predominantly in pink, is given dolls and soft toys to play with, is gently handled, and is encouraged to become docile, cautious, and dependent. The other kind of baby is dressed predominantly in blue, is given boxing gloves and trucks to play with, is played with in a rougher manner, and is encouraged to become active, adventurous, and independent. These distinctive kinds of treatment teach children that what it means to be male is very different from what it means to be female.

Some scientists, however, do not agree that "maleness" and "femaleness" are taught. Regardless of the environment, according to prominent Danish psychoanalyst Erik Erikson and others, there are certain differences between males and females that are innate. Erikson's studies of young children led him to conclude that boys naturally perceive life in an exterior way while girls perceive it in an interior way. Given the same toys to play with, boys build towers and outdoor scenes with active scenarios; girls build enclosures with domestic scenarios. These differences in play, he believes, are due to natural differences, not culturally imposed ones.

Which view of gender distinctions is the true one? Many scientists would say none of these. For example, Cynthia Fuchs Epstein, a sociologist and author of *Deceptive Distinctions: Sex, Gender, and the Social Order*, believes that physiology, psychology, and environment must *all* be taken into account to explain sex differences; there is no one simple answer. Prominent Harvard University paleontologist Stephen Jay Gould agrees. He argues that oversimplification, reducing a complex question to an either-or answer, leads to confusion and deception. The authors in this volume reflect the continuing search for answers, whether simple or complex.

Male/Female Roles: Opposing Viewpoints replaces Greenhaven Press's 1983 book of the same title. This volume contains all new viewpoints and several new topics. The authors in this anthology debate the following questions: How Are Sex Roles Established? Have Women's Roles Changed for the Better? Have Men's Roles Changed for the Better? How Does Work Affect the Family? and What Is the Future of Male/Female Relationships? The editors hope that by participating in these debates, the reader will come away with more questions *and* more answers about what it means to be a man or a woman in today's world.

How Are Sex Roles Established?

MALE/FEMALE ROLES

Chapter Preface

"Nature vs. nurture" is a common phrase heard when discussing the controversy over the origin of male/female roles. "Nature" refers to the argument that a person's gender role is determined mainly by biology, specifically, that one's reproductive role dictates how one acts. According to this theory, women are tender and loving mothers while men are aggressive hunters and the dominant leaders. Advocates of this concept contend that men and women are happiest when fulfilling the roles nature determined for them.

Conversely, the nurture side of the argument asserts that a person's gender role is created mainly through socialization. This theory maintains that one's environment—parents, peers, teachers, and other role models—have the greatest influence on the roles deemed most appropriate for men and women. Supporters of the nurture theory argue that gender roles are not based on biological differences, but on a culture that pressures men to conform to a masculine stereotype and women to conform to a female stereotype.

The authors in the following chapter present their versions of how gender roles originate and the differences between men and women.

"Each sex displays unique emotional characteristics that are genetically endowed."

Biology Determines Gender Roles

James C. Dobson

For centuries people accepted the idea that differences between men and women were biologically determined. With the development of feminism that idea has been challenged. In the following viewpoint, James C. Dobson writes that scientific research proves that men and women differ because of their bodies. Dobson, a well-known television evangelist and Christian family counselor, contends that a woman's menstrual cycle causes her to experience emotional changes that a man does not. He believes that everyday observations prove the biological basis for differing gender roles.

As you read, consider the following questions:

1. Why does Dobson believe that culture cannot fully account for differences in male/female roles?
2. According to the author, how does menstruation make women different from men?
3. In Dobson's opinion, what emotional patterns differ between the sexes?

James C. Dobson, *Straight Talk to Men and Their Wives.* Dallas, TX: Word Books, © 1984. Reprinted with permission.

Iwould like to offer some evidence to show that men and women are biologically unique. The women's movement, in its assault on traditional sex roles, has repeatedly asserted that males and females are identical except for the ability to bear children. Nothing could be farther from the truth.

The Human Brain

Let's begin by discussing the human brain, where maleness and femaleness are rooted. Careful research is revealing that the basic differences between the sexes are neurological in origin, rather than being purely cultural as ordinarily presumed. As Dr. Richard Restak stated in his book, *The Brain: The Last Frontier:*

> Certainly, anyone who has spent time with children in a playground or school setting is aware of the differences in the way boys and girls respond to similar situations. Think of the last time you supervised a birthday party attended by five-year-olds. It's not usually the girls who pull hair, throw punches, or smear each other with food. Usually such differences are explained on a cultural basis. Boys are expected to be more aggressive and play rough games, while girls are presumably encouraged to be more gentle, nonassertive, and passive. After several years of exposure to such expectations, so the theory goes, men and women wind up with widely varying behavioral and intellectual repertoires. As a corollary to this, many people believe that if child-rearing practices could be equalized and sexual-role stereotypes eliminated, most of these differences would eventually disappear. As often happens, however, the true state of affairs is not that simple.
>
> Recent psychological research indicates that many of the differences in brain function between the sexes are innate, biologically determined, and relatively resistant to change through the influences of culture.

Dr. Restak presents numerous studies that document this statement, and then concludes this chapter by quoting Dr. David Wechsler, creator of the most popular intelligence test for use with adults.

> Our findings do confirm what poets and novelists have often asserted, and the average layman long believed, namely, that men not only behave but 'think' differently from women.

Both Drs. Restak and Wechsler are right. Males and females differ anatomically, sexually, emotionally, psychologically, and biochemically. We differ in literally every cell of our bodies, for each sex carries a unique chromosomal pattern. Much is written today about so-called sex-change operations, whereby males are transformed into females or vice versa. Admittedly, it is possible to alter the external genitalia by surgery, and silicone can be used to pad the breasts or round out a bony frame. Hormones can then be injected to feminize or masculinize the convert. But nothing

18

can be done to change the assignment of sex made by God at the instant of conception. That determination is carried in each cell, and it will read "male" or "female" from the earliest moment of life to the point of death. The Bible says emphatically, "Male *and* female created he them." Not one sex, but *two!*

Furthermore, it is my deep conviction that each sex displays unique emotional characteristics that are genetically endowed. Cultural influences cannot account for these novelties. Few psychologists have had the courage to express this view in recent years, because the women's movement has perceived it as insulting. But to be *different* from men does not make women *inferior* to men. Males and females are original creations of God, each bearing strengths and weaknesses that counterbalance and interface with one another. It is a beautiful design that must not be disassembled.

The Menstrual Cycle

Just how do female emotions differ from those of males? Let's consider first the importance of the menstrual cycle. I'm reminded of the late 1960s when hairy young men and women became almost undistinguishable from each other. Two of these hippies, a male and female, were involved in a minor traffic accident and were taken to a local hospital for treatment. The nurse who was completing the intake forms could not determine from their clothing and appearance which sex they represented. After considering the dilemma for a moment she asked, "Okay, which one of you has a menstrual cycle?"

A Powerful Difference

Nature will not be denied. As Yale's Helen Lewis, a committed feminist, was forced to admit to her disappointed fellow ideologues: "The difference between having an XX or an XY as the 23rd chromosome [the genetic distinction between woman and man]*is tremendously powerful.*" Boys and girls, men and women, are and should be behaviorally different, whether as fetuses, newborns, children, or adults.

Allan Carlson, *Persuasion at Work*, March 1986.

The hippie with the bass voice looked at her through his bangs and said,"Not me, man. I gots a Honda."

The question was more significant than merely determining the sex of the patients. Included in this matter of menstruation are many implications for the way females feel about life during the course of the month. It has been said, quite accurately, that the four weeks of the menstrual cycle are characteristic of the four seasons of the year. The first week after a period can be termed the springtime of the physiological calendar. New estrogens (female hormones) are released each day and a woman's body begins to rebound from the recent winter.

The second week represents the summertime of the cycle, when the living is easy. A woman during this phase has more self-confidence than during any other phase of the month. It is a time of maximum energy, enthusiasm, amiability, and self-esteem. Estrogen levels account for much of this optimism, reaching a peak during mid-cycle when ovulation occurs. The relationship between husband and wife is typically at its best during these days of summer, when sexual desire (and the potential for pregnancy) are paramount.

But alas, the fall must surely follow summer. Estrogen levels steadily dwindle as the woman's body prepares itself for another period of menstruation. A second hormone, called progesterone, is released, which reduces the effect of estrogen and initiates the symptoms of premenstrual tension. It is a bleak phase of the month. Self-esteem deteriorates day by day, bringing depression and pessimism with it. A bloated and sluggish feeling often produces not only discomfort but also the belief that "I am ugly." Irritability and aggression become increasingly evident as the week progresses, reaching a climax immediately prior to menstruation.

Psychological Differences

Then come the winter and the period of the menstrual flow. Women differ remarkably in intensity of these symptoms, but most experience some discomfort. Those most vulnerable even find it necessary to spend a day or two in bed during the winter season, suffering from cramping and generalized misery. Gradually, the siege passes and the refreshing newness of springtime returns.

How can anyone who understands this cyclical pattern contend that there are no genetically determined psychological differences between males and females? No such system operates in men. The effect of the menstrual cycle is not only observable clinically, but it can be documented statistically.

The incidences of suicides, homicides, and infanticides perpetrated by women are significantly higher during the period of premenstrual tension than any other phase of the month. Consider also the findings of Alec Coppen and Neil Kessel, who studied 465 women and observed that they were more irritable and depressed during the premenstrual phase than during mid-cycle. "This was true for neurotic, psychotic and normal women alike. Similarly Natalie Sharness found the premenstrual phase associated with feelings of helplessness, anxiety, hostility, and yearning for love. At menstruation, this tension and irritability eased, but depression often accompanied the relief, and lingered until estrogen increased."

I doubt that these facts will come as a great revelation to men or women. Both sexes know that behavior and attitudes are related to the monthly pattern. I receive interesting letters from men who ask, "How can I cope with my wife's irritability during this phase?" Their question reminds me of an incident shared with me by my friend Dr. David Hernandez, who is an obstetrician and gynecologist in private practice. The true story involves Latin men whose wives were given birth control pills by a pharmaceutical company. The Food and Drug Administration in America would not permit hormonal research to be conducted, so the company selected a small fishing village in South America which agreed to cooperate. All the women in the town were given the pill on the same date, and after three weeks the prescription was terminated to permit menstruation. That meant, of course, that every adult female in the community was experiencing premenstrual tension at the same time. The men couldn't take it. They all headed for their boats each month and remained at sea until the crisis passed at home. They knew, even if militant liberationists don't, that females are different from males . . . especially every twenty-eight days.

Innate Biases

Every child is born with innate biases or preferences, predisposed to pay more attention to some sights and sounds than to others, to react to certain happenings more strongly, to learn some things more easily. And we can spot these biases even before babies outgrow their cribs. . . .

By the time he's four to six months old, a boy baby is more interested in looking at objects, geometric patterns, and blinking lights than at people's faces. He may smile for you when you coo and grin at him, but he'll smile just as readily at a brightly patterned mobile hanging over his crib. In contrast, a girl baby saves most of her smiles and baby-noises for faces that smile and make noises back to her.

Kathy Keeton, *Women of Tomorrow*, 1985.

But there are other ways women are unique. Female emotions are also influenced by two other exclusively feminine functions, lactation and pregnancy. Furthermore, the hypothalamus, which is located at the base of the brain and has been called the "seat of the emotions," is apparently wired very differently for males than females. For example, a severe emotional shock or trauma can be interpreted by the hypothalamus, which then sends messages to the pituitary by way of neurons and hormones. The pituitary often responds by changing the body chemistry of the woman, perhaps interrupting the normal menstrual cycle for six months or longer. Female physiology is a finely tuned instrument, being more vulnerable and complex than the masculine counterpart. Why some women find that fact insulting is still a mystery to me.

How do these differences translate into observable behavior? Medical science has not begun to identify all the ramifications of sexual uniqueness. Some of the implications are extremely subtle. For example, when researchers quietly walked on high school and college campuses to study behavior of the sexes, they observed that males and females even transported their books in different ways. The young men tended to carry them at their sides with their arms looped over the top. Women and girls, by contrast, usually cradled their books at their breasts, in much the same way they would a baby. Who can estimate how many other sex-related influences lie below the level of consciousness?

Admittedly, some of the observed differences between the sexes *are* culturally produced. I don't know how to sort out those which are exclusively genetic from those which represent learned responses. Frankly, it doesn't seem to matter a great deal. The differences exist, for whatever reason, and the current cultural revolution will not alter most of them significantly. At the risk of being called a sexist, or a propagator of sexual stereotypes, or a male chauvinist pig (or worse), let me delineate a few of the emotional patterns typical of women as compared with men.

Emotional Patterns

The reproductive capacity of women results in a greater appreciation for stability, security, and enduring human relationships. In other words, females are more *future*-oriented because of their concern for children.

Related to the first item is a woman's emotional investment in her home, which usually exceeds that of her husband. She typically cares more than he about the minor details of the house, family functioning, and such concerns. To cite a personal example, my wife and I decided to install a new gas barbecue unit in our backyard. When the plumber completed the assignment and departed, Shirley and I both recognized that he had placed the appliance approximately six inches too high. I looked at the device and said, "Hmmm, yes sir, he sure made a mistake. That post is a bit too high. By the way, what are we having for dinner tonight?" Shirley's reaction was dramatically different. She said, "The plumber has that thing sticking up in the air and I don't think I can stand it!" Our contrasting views represented a classic difference of emotional intensity relating to the home.

Anyone who doubts that males and females are unique should observe how they approach a game of Ping Pong or Monopoly or dominoes or horseshoes or volleyball or tennis. Women often use the event as an excuse for fellowship and pleasant conversation. For men, the name of the game is *conquest*. Even if the setting is a friendly social gathering in the host's backyard, the beads of sweat on each man's forehead reveal his passion to win. This aggressive competitiveness has been attributed to cultural influences. I don't believe it. As Richard Restak said, "At a birthday party for five-year-olds, it's not usually the girls who pull hair, throw punches, or smear each other with food."

Males and females apparently differ in the manner by which they develop self-esteem. Men draw the necessary evidence of their worthiness primarily from their jobs—from being respected in business, profession or craft. Women, however, *especially those who are homemakers*, depend primarily on the romantic relationship with their husbands for ego support. This explains why the emotional content of a marriage is often of greater significance to women than men and why tokens of affection are appreciated more by wives, who obtain esteem from these expressions of love and generosity.

Instinct and Preferences

A maternal instinct apparently operates in most women, although its force is stronger in some than others. This desire to procreate is certainly evident in those who are unable to conceive. I receive a steady influx of letters from women who express great frustration from their inability to become mothers. Although culture plays a major role in these longings, I believe they are rooted in female anatomy and physiology.

Perhaps the most dramatic differences between males and females are evident in their contrasting sexual preferences. He is more visually oriented, caring less about the romantic component. She is attracted not to a photograph of an unknown model or by a handsome stranger, but to a *particular* man with whom she has entered into an emotional relationship. This differing orientation is merely the tip of the iceberg in delineating the sexual uniqueness of males and females.

These items are illustrative and are not intended to represent a scientific delineation of sexual differences. The reader is invited to add his own observations to the list and to make his own interpretations.

"The limited number of proven biological differences among the sexes has been vastly exaggerated by cultural interpretations."

Biology Does Not Determine Gender Roles

Gerda Lerner

Research concerning male/female differences has often been criticized because many women scientists contend that male researchers observed the phenomena from a biased perspective. In the following viewpoint, Gerda Lerner, a professor of history at the University of Wisconsin at Madison, writes that many popular biological theories concerning gender roles have been disproven. She argues that biology does not preordain roles for men and women; rather, social customs dictate their roles.

As you read, consider the following questions:

1. How does the author discredit the "man-the-hunter" theory for differing gender roles?
2. Why does Lerner not accept sociobiology as an explanation?
3. According to the author, if biology does not explain gender differences, what does?

Traditionalists, whether working within a religious or a "scientific" framework, have regarded women's subordination as universal, God-given, or natural, hence immutable. Thus, it need not be questioned. What has survived, survived because it was best; it follows that it should stay that way.

Scholars critical of androcentric assumptions and those seeing the need for social change in the present have challenged the concept of the universality of female subordination. They reason that if the system of patriarchal dominance had a historic origin, it could be ended under altered historical conditions. Therefore, the question of the universality of female subordination has, for over 150 years, been central to the debate between traditionalists and feminist thinkers.

For those critical of patriarchal explanations, the next important question is: if female subordination was not universal, then was there ever an alternative model of society? This question has most often taken the form of the search for a matriarchal society in the past. Since much of the evidence in this search derives from myth, religion, and symbol, there has been little attention given to historical evidence.

Female Subordination

For the historian, the more important and significant question is this: how, when, and why did female subordination come into existence?

Therefore, before we can undertake a discussion of the historical development of patriarchy, we need to review the major positions in the debate on these three questions.

The traditionalist answer to the first question is, of course, that male dominance is universal and natural. The argument may be offered in religious terms: woman is subordinate to man because she was so created by God. Traditionalists accept the phenomenon of "sexual asymmetry," the assignment of different tasks and roles to men and women, which has been observed in all known human societies, as proof of their position and as evidence of its "naturalness." Since woman was, by divine design, assigned a different biological function than man was, they argue, she should also be assigned different social tasks. If God or nature created sex differences, which in turn determined the sexual division of labor, no one is to blame for sexual inequality and male dominance.

The traditionalist explanation focuses on woman's reproductive capacity and sees in motherhood woman's chief goal in life, by implication defining as deviant women who do not become mothers. Woman's maternal function is seen as a species necessity, since societies could not have survived into modernity without the majority of women devoting most of their adult lives to child-

25

bearing and child-rearing. Thus the sexual division of labor based on biological differences is seen as functional and just.

Biological Factors

A corollary explanation of sexual asymmetry locates the causes of female subordination in biological factors affecting males. Men's greater physical strength, their ability to run faster and lift heavier weights, and their greater aggressiveness cause them to become hunters. As such they become the providers of food for their tribes and are more highly valued and honored than women. The skills deriving from their hunting experience in turn equip them to become warriors. Man-the-hunter, superior in strength, ability, and the experience derived from using tools and weapons, "naturally" protects and defends the more vulnerable female, whose biological equipment destines her for motherhood and nurturance. Finally, this biological deterministic explanation is extended from the Stone Age into the present by the assertion that the sexual division of labor based on man's natural "superiority" is a given and therefore as valid today as it was in the primitive beginnings of human society.

No Biological Origin

Even if early gender differences did occur regularly and consistently, this would not necessarily indicate that they were of biological origin. Adults differentiate between baby boys and girls from birth onward, so that we cannot tell whether a particular behavioral gender difference observed during infancy is produced by different parental reactions or by different biological maturation. We are also skeptical of the assumption that later masculine and feminine characteristics can be traced to early gender differences, since there is little evidence for such continuity in psychological development. In view of these criticisms, we do not support the view that gender differences found early in life are necessarily biological in origin.

John Archer and Barbara Lloyd, *Sex and Gender*, 1985.

This theory, in various forms, is currently by far the most popular version of the traditionalist argument and has had a powerful explanatory and reinforcing effect on contemporary ideas of male supremacy. This is probably due to its "scientific" trappings based on selected ethnographic evidence and on the fact that it seems to account for male dominance in such a way as to relieve contemporary men of all responsibility for it. The profound way in which this explanation has affected even feminist theoreticians is evident in its partial acceptance by Simone de Beauvoir, who takes as a given that man's "transcendence" derives from hunting and warfare and the use of the tools necessary for these pursuits.

Quite apart from its dubious biological claims of male physical superiority, the man-the-hunter explanation has been disproven by anthropological evidence concerning hunting and gathering societies. In most of these societies, big-game hunting is an auxiliary pursuit, while the main food supply is provided by gathering activities and small-game hunting, which women and children do. Also, it is precisely in hunting and gathering societies that we find many examples of complementarity between the sexes and societies in which women have relatively high status, which is in direct contradiction to the claims of the man-the-hunter school of thought.

Challenging Male Dominance

Feminist anthropologists have challenged many of the earlier generalizations, which found male dominance virtually universal in all known societies, as being patriarchal assumptions on the part of ethnographers and investigators of those cultures. When feminist anthropologists have reviewed the data or done their own field work, they have found male dominance to be far from universal. They have found societies in which sexual asymmetry carries no connotation of dominance or subordination. Rather, the tasks performed by both sexes are indispensable to group survival, and both sexes are regarded as equal in status in most aspects. In such societies the sexes are considered "complementary"; their roles and status are different, but equal.

Another way in which man-the-hunter theories have been disproven is by showing the essential, culturally innovative contributions women made to the creation of civilization by their invention of basketry and pottery and their knowledge and development of horticulture. Elise Boulding, in particular, has shown that the man-the-hunter myth and its perpetuation are social-cultural creations which serve the interest of maintaining male supremacy and hegemony.

Traditionalist defenses of male supremacy based on biological-deterministic reasoning have changed over time and proven remarkably adaptive and resilient. When the force of the religious argument was weakened in the nineteenth century the traditionalist explanation of women's inferiority became "scientific." Darwinian theories reinforced beliefs that species survival was more important than individual self-fulfillment. Much as the Social Gospel used the Darwinian idea of the survival of the fittest to justify the unequal distribution of wealth and privilege in American society, scientific defenders of patriarchy justified the definition of women through their maternal role and their exclusion from economic and educational opportunities as serving the best interests of species survival. It was because of their biological constitution and their maternal function that women were considered unsuited for higher education and for many vocational pursuits. Menstruation and menopause, even pregnancy, were regarded as debilitating, as diseased or abnormal states which incapacitated women and rendered them actually inferior.

Biology Is Not Destiny

Our newly-acquired knowledge on biological factors and gender differences in human behavior is so far very preliminary and fragmentary, and it behooves us to be cautious in interpretation and reporting. But it is clear now that we have no support for the notion that biology is destiny.

Anke A. Ehrhardt, *Science for the People*, July/August 1986.

Similarly, modern psychology observed existing sex differences with the unquestioned assumption that they were natural, and constructed a psychological female who was as biologically determined as had been her forebears. Viewing sex roles ahistorically, psychologists had to arrive at conclusions from observed clinical data which reinforced predominant gender roles.

Sigmund Freud's theories further reinforced the traditionalist explanation. Freud's normal human was male; the female was by his definition a deviant human being lacking a penis, whose entire psychological structure supposedly centered on the struggle to compensate for this deficiency. Even though many aspects of Freudian theory would prove helpful in constructing feminist theory, it was Freud's dictum that for the female "anatomy is destiny" which gave new life and strength to the male supremacist argument.

The often vulgarized applications of Freudian theory to child-rearing and to popular advice literature lent new prestige to the old argument that woman's primary role is as child-bearer and child-rearer. It was popularized Freudian doctrine which became the prescriptive text for educators, social workers, and the general audiences of the mass media.

Sociobiology

E.O. Wilson's sociobiology has offered the traditionalist view on gender in an argument which applies Darwinian ideas of natural selection to human behavior. Wilson and his followers reason that human behaviors which are "adaptive" for group survival become encoded in the genes, and they include in these behaviors such complex traits as altruism, loyalty, and maternalism. They not only reason that groups practicing a sex-based division of labor in which women function as child-rearers and nurturers have an evolutionary advantage, but they claim such behavior somehow becomes part of our genetic heritage, in that the necessary psychological and physical propensities for such societal arrangements are selectively developed and genetically selected. Mothering is not only a socially assigned role but one fitting women's physical and psychological needs. Here, once again, biological determinism becomes prescriptive, in fact a political defense of the status quo in scientific language.

Circular Reasoning

Feminist critics have revealed the circular reasoning, absence of evidence and unscientific assumptions of Wilsonian sociobiology. From the point of view of the nonscientist, the most obvious fallacy of sociobiologists is their ahistoricity in disregarding the fact that modern men and women do not live in a state of nature. The history of civilization describes the process by which humans have distanced themselves from nature by inventing and perfecting culture. Traditionalists ignore technological changes, which have made it possible to bottle-feed infants safely and raise them to adulthood with care-takers other than their own mothers. They ignore the implications of changing life spans and changing life cycles. Until communal hygiene and modern medical knowledge cut infant mortality to a level where parents could reasonably expect each child born to them to live to adulthood, women did indeed have to bear many children in order for a few of them to survive. Similarly, longer life expectancy and lower infant mortality altered the life cycles of both men and women. These developments were connected with industrializaion and occurred in Western civilization (for whites) toward the end of the nineteenth century, occurring later for the poor and for minorities due to the uneven distribution of health and social services. Whereas up to 1870 child-rearing and marrriage were co-terminus—that is, one or both parents could expect to die before the youngest child reached adulthood—in modern American society husbands and wives can expect to live together for twelve years after their youngest child has reached adulthood, and women can expect to outlive their husbands by seven years.

Outdated Roles

Traditionalists expect women to follow the same roles and occupations that were functional and species-essential in the Neolithic. They accept cultural changes by which men have freed themselves from biological necessity. The supplanting of hard physical labor by the labor of machines is considered progress; only women, in their view, are doomed forever to species-service through their biology. To claim that of all human activities only female nurturance is unchanging and eternal is indeed to consign half the human race to a lower state of existence, to nature rather than to culture.

The qualities which may have fostered human survival in the Neolithic are no longer required of modern people. Regardless of whether qualities such as aggressiveness or nurturance are genetically or culturally transmitted, it should be obvious that the aggressiveness of males, which may have been highly functional in the Stone Age, is threatening human survival in the nuclear age. At a time when overpopulation and exhaustion of natural resources represent a real danger for human survival, to curb women's procreative capacities may be more "adaptive" than to foster them.

Further, in opposition to any argument based on biological determinism, feminists challenge the hidden androcentric assumptions in the sciences dealing with humans. They have charged that in biology, anthropology, zoology, and psychology such assumptions have led to a reading of scientific evidence that distorts its meaning. Thus, for example, animal behavior is invested with anthropomorphic significance, which makes patriarchs of male chimpanzees. Many feminists argue that the limited number of proven biological differences among the sexes has been vastly exaggerated by cultural interpretations and that the value put on sex differences is in itself a cultural product. Sexual attributes are a biological given, but gender is a product of historical process. The fact that women bear children is due to sex; that women nurture children is due to gender, a cultural construct. It is gender which has been chiefly responsible for fixing women's place in society.

"Parents, media, teachers, and peers are important socializing agents for teaching the young their gender roles."

Culture Influences Gender Roles

James A. Doyle

Many sociologists and anthropologists explain the differences in gender roles as being the product of various cultural influences. In the following viewpoint, James A. Doyle writes that parents, the media, teachers, and peer groups all contribute to a person's understanding of sex roles. Doyle, a teacher at Roane State Community College in Harriman, Tennessee, argues that while certain factors may be more important at different stages in people's lives, their overall view of male/female roles is a product of many influences.

As you read, consider the following questions:

1. How does Doyle define the term "socialization"? What are socializing agents?
2. According to the author, what experiment proves that adults treat boys and girls differently?
3. Why does Doyle believe that an adolescent's peer group is a powerful socializing agent?

Passing by a hospital nursery, one can observe just how similar most newborn babies really are in their appearance and, more important, in their behaviors. If it weren't for the pink and blue blankets scattered among the bassinets, one would not know a female from a male. . . .Even to the casual observer, it is apparent that most infants spend most of their first few weeks sleeping with only short periods of wakefulness. Then why is it that so many people earnestly see male infants as being so different from female infants? An answer may be simply that most parents see their children through "gender-colored" glasses that focus on presumed gender differences where few exist. Because parents see their infants differently, there may be a tendency to treat each gender differently. Treating male and female infants differently is just the first step in the long process called socialization which, among many things, leads to the creation of two very different gender roles.

But what do we actually mean by the term socialization? *Socialization* is the process by which all people (i.e., children, adolescents, adults, and senior citizens alike) learn what is expected of them through their interactions with others. Socialization can be thought of as a social mold that shapes each person to fit into a group. A child, for example, learns certain basic feeding skills, including which utensil to use with which type of food. Depending on the society, a child may be taught to use a spoon and fork or a set of chopsticks. Children and others must learn the ways, traditions, norms, and rules of getting along with others, and socialization is the process by which everyone learns the lessons that others deem necessary for them to fit into their group.

Socializing Agents

When a mother tells her daughter to pick up the dishes on the kitchen table, when a little girl sees a picture in the Christmas catalog of little girls playing with a miniature stove, or when a young boy recites the Boy Scout oath that he should be "physically strong, mentally awake, and morally straight," we can see different *socializing agents* at work. Any person or social institution that shapes a person's values, beliefs, or behaviors is a socializing agent. Socializing agents are especially effective during a person's early years, when one is most impressionable. An effective socializing agent usually is respected by the person being socialized.

Some of the most important lessons a child learns and those that are reinforced throughout a child's early years and beyond are her or his gender roles. Let's examine some of the different socializing agents (i.e., parents, different media, teachers, and peers) that combine to shape a child's gender role.

Parents are one of the more important agents. But just how early in their children's lives do parents begin to teach their children what is expected of them in terms of their gender label?

In a fascinating study, Jeffrey Rubin and his associates found that first-time parents saw their one-day-old infants in terms of gender differences. Typically, fathers saw their newborn sons "as firmer, larger featured, better coordinated, more alert, stronger, and hardier," while other fathers saw their daughters "as softer, finer featured, more awkward, more inattentive, weaker, and more delicate." These fathers saw gender-related differences when actually none were obvious. More than likely, these fathers' notions of gender stereotypes played an important role in why they saw their newborn infants so differently. Other researchers have found similar patterns where parents see their children in terms of gender stereotypes rather than their children's actual behaviors. As infants grow older, their parents' notions about gender stereotypes continue to influence how parents treat their children. Various studies have reported that parents treat each gender differently.

Environmental Influences

Most of our knowledge of the biological basis for differential behavior in human males and females is very rudimentary. . . . Rather than invoking fundamental biological differences as being at the root of differences between achievements of women and men, it would be wiser to examine and accept numerous data available that indicate that societal, cultural, and environmental influences may be of paramount importance.

Susan Abbott, M.B. Nikitovitch-Winer, and Judith Worell, *Society*, September/October 1986.

Parents know their infant's sex, and some may suggest that they are reacting to real gender differences and not to something they have preconceived in their minds. What about adults who don't have first-hand knowledge of an infant's sex (i.e., they have not examined the infant's genitals)? Do they also treat male and female infants differently? The answer is most emphatically yes. Research shows that one of the more important factors influencing how an adult interacts with an infant is the infant's gender label. For instance, a helpful toy salesperson (a stranger) will select toys for a child according to a child's gender. To highlight just how important a child's gender is for an adult, let's examine one study to see how adults use gender to guide their play with an infant.

Treated Differently

Jerrie Will, Patricia Self, and Nancy Datan asked eleven mothers to play with a six-month-old infant. Five of the mothers played with the infant who was dressed in blue pants and named "Adam."

Later, the other six mothers played with the same infant who was then wearing a pink dress and being called "Beth." (Actually, the infant was a six-month-old male.) Placed in a room with the infant, the mothers were given several toys to entertain the child with, specifically, a plastic fish, a doll, and a train. When asked to play with either "Beth" or "Adam," the respective mothers generally offered Adam the train and Beth the doll. Not only did these mothers offer different toys on the basis of the "perceived" gender of the infant, they even interacted differently with the infant. The mothers who thought they had Beth smiled more and held her closer to themselves than did the mothers who had Adam. After the observations were completed, the mothers were interviewed, and all stated that mothers should not treat male and female infants differently. However, as found here, and in other studies, parents and nonparents alike do interact with and treat infants differently on the basis of the perceived gender of the infant, and this differential treatment continues as children grow older.

Gender and Play

Besides providing gender-related toys for their children, parents also play with boys and girls differently. Parents are more likely to interact and talk more with their daughters, while parents with sons are more apt to "roughhouse" and play more actively with them. Female infants are usually seen as more fragile by both mothers and fathers alike. There are many reasons for this differential treatment, but we can suggest that parents want their sons to be rough and tough, or "masculine," and daughters are encouraged to be neat and orderly, or "feminine," in their behaviors.

Even a child's bedroom doesn't escape the parents' concern over what is expected of little boys and girls. When the decors of preschoolers' bedrooms are examined, obvious touches of "masculine" and "feminine" motifs are likely to be found. In boys' bedrooms, the prevalence of sports' equipment, trucks, and military paraphernalia is common; in girls' rooms, dolls, and household items are more often included in the decors parents furnish.

Household Chores

Parents also continue shaping their children's gender roles through the kinds of jobs they assign them around the house. In a state-wide sample (Nebraska) of 669 boys and girls between the ages of two and seventeen, researchers Lynn White and David Brinnerhoff found distinctive gender differences in the kinds of jobs young people did. Basically, boys did "men's work": mowing the lawns, shoveling snow, taking out the garbage, and other general yard-work chores. Girls, on the other hand, did "women's work": cleaning up around the house, doing the dishes, cooking, and as we might expect, babysitting for younger siblings. Others have also found similar divisions of labor along gender lines in their studies of task assignments. . . .

Obviously, parents are not the only socializing force in a child's life. There are also other forces present in the child's early life that shape the content of the gender role.

Culture and Gender Identification

Whether we are conscious of it or not, we treat boys (and men) differently than we treat girls (and women) and have different expectations for how males and females are supposed to behave in certain situations. We define who we are in terms of our gender.

Culture plays a critical role in shaping the gender identification process. What is practically universal is the significance that gender has in defining who an individual is in society, and virtually all children strive to acquire an appropriate gender role.

David F. Bjorklund, *Parents*, February 1987.

The mass media—books, magazines, comics, radio, television, films, and records—play a significant role in people's lives. The hours of entertainment they provide are beyond calculation. But mass media provide more than mere entertainment; they teach, persuade, and shape people's lives. A recurrent theme in much of the media is how the genders should live. When we see an advertisement in a magazine, listen to popular songs, read a romance novel, or watch a soap-opera, the message is often decidedly traditional in content—males should act "masculine," and females "feminine." Let's examine some of the more important media and focus on just what messages they emphasize in terms of gender roles.

Children's books with their stories of human-like animals and real people provide both countless hours of enjoyment and a powerful vehicle for the socialization of gender roles. Sociologist Lenore Weitzman writes:

Through books, children learn about the world outside their immediate environment: they learn what other boys and girls do, say, and feel, and they learn what is expected of children their age. Picture books are especially important to the preschool child because they are often looked at over and over again at a time when children are in the process of developing their own sex role identities. In addition, they are read to children before other socialization influences (such as school, teachers, and peers) become important in their lives.

The gender roles presented in children's books often offer a biased and narrow portrayal of the female's role. To learn more about the not-so-subtle gender messages contained in these early primers, we need to examine how the genders and their roles are portrayed. Lenore Weitzman, along with several of her colleagues, conducted a content analysis of several prize-winning children's books (i.e., the Caldecott Medal winners between 1967-1971). A majority of the books told stories about males, but a few females were present in the stories. The gender-bias in these books becomes striking when we note that human male characters out-numbered human female characters by eleven to one. The bias becomes even more obvious when animal characters (e.g., rabbits, horses, puppies) are added. The ratio of male to female animals is a whopping 95 to 1. As for the stories themselves, males per-formed a variety of different and exciting activities and roles that portrayed them as acting competently and in charge of the stories' action. When females did enter the stories, they usually did so in a rather limited and, for the most part, quite passive way. The message in these primers is rather clear: Boys live exciting and independent lives, whereas girls are primarily auxiliaries to boys. (To put it more bluntly: It's a man's world, kids!) . . .

Television

Without a doubt, television plays a significant role in the socialization process for young and old alike. When it comes to children's television and its commercials, we find considerable gender biases and sexism in its content. An early study of the highly acclaimed "Sesame Street" even found its presentation of the gender roles relatively biased in traditional ways.

But children do not limit their viewing habits to children's fare only. It's prime-time television that draws the largest numbers of every age group. Let's begin with those TV segments that pay for the shows, the commercials. Katharine and Kermit Hoyenga studied some 300 prime-time television commercials with an eye to how the gender roles were presented. Overall, their research found:

> There are more exclusively male than exclusively female oc-cupations. . . . In only three cases was the product expert a female when a man also appeared in the commercial, and two of these commercials were for medical products. Overall, females are more often pictured using medical products (64 percent were females) and products designed to enhance the user's appearance or smell (75 percent). Only a few commercials included any type of sexual interaction (kissing, caressing), but the male was always the aggressor. If commercials were the only basis for inferring behavior and role assignments, the person watching them would conclude that women must stay at home, that they are allowed out of the house only in the company of men, and, rarely, of children, and that they are rarely allowed to drive cars.

In general, TV commercials portray women almost solely in the helping role, waiting on others and living out their lives in service to others, never really taking charge of their own lives. Such a view perpetuates traditional views of women's role in society.

TV Ads

However, a few television sponsors have made an effort to introduce counterstereotypic gender presentations. For example, we occasionally see Josephine the Plumber tackling a stopped up drain and showing a man what needs to be done. But do such commercials have an effect other than being novel? Joyce Jennings and several colleagues found that women who watched counterstereotypic TV commercials were more self-confident and less likely to conform to group pressure in other situations. Portraying women in counterstereotypic ways may have positive effects for women in the TV audience in terms of their building self-confidence as self-determining and achievement-oriented individuals.

For the most part, however, advertisers present the genders in traditional and stereotypic ways. Males celebrate the end of another day at the office or plant by stopping at a local bar with the gang to throw down a few beers. If not in a bar, a man is out in a distant woods or by a remote stream all because he chose the right kind of four-wheel drive vehicle. In contrast, women in most commercials seem interested only in stemming the telltale signs of age, marveling over the softness of bathroom tissue, bemoaning the waxy buildup on their kitchen floors, or standing seductively by some car as a male describes the power under the hood. . . .

Teachers as Socializers

The stated purpose of formal education is to teach the young the basics: "readin', writin', and arithmetic." However, the educational system teaches far more than the basics. Social values like conformity, competition, achievement, discipline, cooperation with others, and orderliness are only a few of the values taught and reinforced in school. The teacher is a key element in the educational system. What and how students learn and also how the students see themselves and define their roles are influenced by the teacher's expectations and behavior and by the effects of the teacher being a role model for them. The impact of a teacher's expectations shouldn't be taken lightly. In one study, a teacher was told that the class was divided between bright students and average students on the basis of some test results. Later in the school year, the "bright" students actually did better on standardized tests than those who had been labeled average. Surprisingly, the only difference between these two groups was the teacher's knowledge of the earlier purported test results which the researchers had actually made up. Although not every teacher is susceptible to biased information about students, many teachers hold traditional gender stereotypes about their students that can affect their students' views of what is expected of them.

Teachers treat the genders differently. Psychologist Lisa Serbin and several of her colleagues studied how teachers treat preschool children and how this treatment influenced the children in learning their gender roles. In the classroom, Serbin found that preschool boys generally acted more aggressively, whereas girls behaved more dependently. Clearly, these behaviors mirror the commonly accepted gender stereotypes for each gender. Serbin also found that the teachers' behaviors toward their students helped reinforce these gender-specific behaviors. Specifically, when boys acted aggressively, their teachers were more likely to reprimand them than they were to reprimand girls who acted in a similar manner. Research has shown that reprimanding a child for a particular behavior may have the same effect as reinforcing that behavior and, consequently, that behavior is more likely to continue. Thus, the teachers' reprimands may have reinforced the boys' aggressive behaviors. When girls behaved dependently, the teachers' interactions with them can be seen as a type of rein-forcement for their dependent behaviors. When girls needed assistance, their teachers often required that the girls come to them for help, which reinforced the girls' dependency on an adult. Boys, however, weren't required to come to their teachers for assistance. In summary, Serbin found that teachers play a decisive role in their students' acquisition of behaviors associated with traditional gender stereotypes. . . .

As we can see, students learn more than the three R's from their teachers. Besides being a place where students learn the basics, school is also a place where students interact with others of their own age, or what most people refer to as a peer group. However, the time the young spend in school does not equal the amount of time they spend with their friends just hanging out at the local fast-food place or driving around together.

Peers as Socializers

By definition a *peer group* is made up of those individuals with whom we share a similar status as well as many similar values and behaviors. One of the main functions of a peer group is to be a sounding-board where a person can try on new behaviors and perfect those already learned. During adolescence, the peer group is probably the most powerful socializing agent in a young person's life. During the transition from childhood to early adulthood, or that period called adolescence, most teen-aged boys and girls strive more for the approval and acceptance of their peers that they do for that of their own families. The importance of the peer group is summarized best in the following statement by Paul Henry Mussen:

> The peer group provides an opportunity to learn how to interact with age-mates, how to deal with hostility and dominance, how to relate to a leader, and how to lead others. It also performs a psychotherapeutic function for the child in helping him deal with social problems. Through discussions with peers the child may learn that others share his problems, conflicts, and complex feelings, and this may be reassuring. . . . Finally, the peer group helps the child develop a concept of himself. The ways in which peers react to the child and the bases upon which he is accepted or rejected give him a clearer, and perhaps more realistic, picture of his assets and liabilities.

The next time you are strolling around a shopping mall or walking down a crowded street, notice the groups of young people who are interacting together. What do you notice about the groups? Probably one of the first impressions that will strike you is the similarity in dress and behavior. One area where peers influence their members is that of appearance. Young people generally dress to impress their friends. Much of the interaction that takes place between adolescent peers helps to reinforce their conceptions of gender roles. Young boys show off their "masculine" behaviors for girls, and girls act as if they find the boys' "masculine" behaviors quite appealing. Girls coach each other on the "ways" of boys, and vice versa. . . .

Relationships and Gender Roles

Neither born in isolation nor raised in seclusion, we all need others to become fully human. Sociology studies the relationships among and between people. Sociologists are especially interested in the positions or statuses that people occupy within various groups. Each person has numerous statuses; some we have no control over (ascribed status), while others we must do something to earn (achieved status). Each status carries with it a set of prescriptive behaviors, called norms, that make up a particular role. Our gender norms and roles are some of the most important features of our lives.

The norms associated with being female encompass the prescriptions that a female should have children and marry in order to fulfill herself as a female. The norms for males usually prescribe that a male should shun acting feminine, be a success, be aggressive when the occasion warrants it, be the initiator in sexual relations, and be self-reliant and tough.

Most sociologists emphasize the importance of socialization as the primary means a group uses to teach the young what is expected of them. Parents, media, teachers, and peers are important socializing agents for teaching the young their gender roles.

39

"When men are the providers while women specialize in childbearing and homemaking, the latter tend to be viewed as dependents."

Economics Determines Gender Roles

Francine D. Blau and Marianne A. Ferber

Francine D. Blau and Marianne A. Ferber are professors of economics at the University of Illinois at Champagne-Urbana. In the following viewpoint, Blau and Ferber contend that the work status of women has more influence on sex roles than does biology. They cite examples from colonial times to the present of women's roles in the family and in society. They argue that changes are due to women's participation, or lack thereof, in the work world. Dependence on the male's income, they argue, results in women's role as housewife and caretaker. When working outside the home, women's roles become more equal to men's.

As you read, consider the following questions:

1. Why do the authors discount animal research when determining the origin of sex roles?
2. According to Blau and Ferber, what happens to sex roles when women enter the work force in great numbers?
3. In the authors' opinion, why is it important that women share in "productive" work?

Blau/Ferber, *The Economics of Women, Men, and Work,* © 1986, pp. 15, 16, 17, 18, 25, 26, 27, 28, 30, 31, 34, 35. Reprinted by permission of Prentice-Hall, Inc., Englewood Cliffs, NJ.

As recently as the 1970s, a common interpretation of the behavior of, and relation between, men and women emphasized the importance of the biological maternal function of the female in determining the nature and content of her being. In this view, a woman's early life is a preparation for becoming, and her later life is devoted to being, a successful wife and mother. Accordingly, her nature is compliant, not competitive, nurturant, not instrumental. Her activities, while not necessarily confined to the home at least center around it, for her primary mission is to be a helpmate to her husband and to provide a warm and safe haven for her family. If she does work for pay, she will do best in jobs compatible with her household responsibilites and her "feminine" personality. Men, on the other hand, are not constrained by their paternal function from fully entering the world outside the home. On the contrary, their natural role as provider and protector spurs them on to greater efforts.

The popular perception based, to an extent, on the work of earlier researchers has often been that investigations of male and female roles among nonhuman species provided support for the view that biology is destiny. Therefore, we too begin with a brief look at animals and their behavior. . . .

There are extreme variations in male and female behavior by species and often within species depending on their environment. Some are highly male-dominant, some female-dominant, others rather egalitarian. Furthermore, how groups are characterized depends on the type of dominance being measured. In general, males tend to be aggressive about acquiring and defending territory, but females are often extremely ferocious about protecting the young.

No Uniform Behavior

Even when it comes to care of their offspring, behavior is far from uniform. In lower animal forms, such as fish, it is common for the young not to receive any care from either parent, while both father and mother birds generally participate in caring for their infants. Female mammals, of course nurse the newborn, but there are species where the mothers hardly bother beyond that. Among many primates, on the other hand, there is at least some "fathering" and the marmoset father carries the infant at all times except when it is feeding.

Much of the research on sex roles among animals has concentrated on primates because they are closer to humans than the others. Even there, however, sweeping generalizations are rarely justified. The behavior of these animals is typically dimorphic (that is, certain types of behavior are more typical of one sex than the other). But these differences are generally a matter of degree, not of kind, and there is much overlap. Only among some species, such as rhesus monkeys, are males far more aggressive and belligerent than females. Nor do differences in behavior necessarily mean that females are socially inferior. Only among some species, especially baboons and rhesus monkeys, is there a rigidly hierarchical social structure dominated by highly aggressive males. It is particularly interesting that among chimpanzees, the most socially advanced nonhuman primates, females do not appear to occupy a subordinate position. Harem-like groups with dominant males are entirely unknown.

"Okay...Heads, *I* hunt animals and you raise the kids. Tails..."

These examples should suffice to make anyone cautious about the argument that any attribute or behavior is always male or female, even if generalizing from animals to humans were otherwise acceptable. But this is, itself, a debatable point. An alternative approach suggests that what distinguishes "homo sapiens" from other species is that, for humans, it is primarily the norms and expectations of their societies, not blind animal instincts, that are important in shaping their actions and their relations. In this view, biology constrains, but does not determine, human behavior. Human gender roles are no more limited to those of animals than is human behavior otherwise limited to that of animals. . . .

In Colonial America, as in other pre-industrial economies, the family enterprise was the dominant economic unit, and production was the major function of the family. Most of the necessities for survival were produced in the household, though some goods were generally produced for sale, in order to be able to purchase some market goods and to accumulate wealth. Cooking, cleaning, care of the young, the old, and the infirm, spinning, weaving, sewing, knitting, soap and candle making, and even simple carpentry were carried on in the home. Much of the food and other raw materials were grown on the farm. All members of the family capable of making any contribution participated in production, but there was always some specialization and division of labor.

Among the nonslave population, men were primarily responsible for agriculture and occasionally trade, while women did much of the rest of the work including what would today be characterized as "light manufacturing" activity. But this sex-role specialization was by no means complete. Slave women were used to work in the fields. Widows tended to take over the enterprise when the need arose, and in very early days, single women were on occasion given "maidplots." Even though men and women often had different tasks, and the former were more often involved in production for the market and generally owned all property, everyone participated in productive activity. Even aged grandparents would help with tasks that required responsibility and judgement, perhaps also supervise children in carrying out small chores they could adequately perform from a very early age.

All family members, except for infants, had the same economic role. They either contributed goods and services directly or earned money by selling some of these in the market. The important economic role of children, as well as the plentiful availability of land, encouraged large families. High infant mortality rates provided a further incentive to bear many children. In the eighteenth century, completed fertility may have averaged as many as eight to ten births per woman.

Productive Members

Wealthy women were primarily managers, not just workers, within the household. This was, no doubt, a less arduous and possibly a more rewarding task but one no less absorbing. For these women, as for the more numerous less affluent ones, there was little role conflict. The ideal of the frugal, industrious housewife, working alongside all her family, corresponded closely to reality. The only women for whom this was not true were very poor women, who often became indentured servants and, of course, black women, who were generally slaves. The former were, as a rule, not permitted to marry during their years of servitude, the latter might potentially have their family entirely disrupted by their owners' choice. Both had to work very hard, and slaves did not even have the modest legal protection of rights that indentured servants enjoyed.

The one thing all these diverse groups had in common was that they were productive members of nearly self-sufficient households. While there was some exchange of goods and services, chiefly barter, it was only well into the nineteenth century that production outside the home, for sale rather than for direct use, came to dominate the economy.

Industrial America

During the early period of industrialization in the late eighteenth and early nineteenth centuries, women in the United States, like elsewhere, worked in the textile mills and other industries that sprang up in the East. Initially, primarily young farm girls worked in the factories, often contributing part of their pay to supplement family income and using some to accumulate a "dowry" that would make them more desirable marriage partners. The employment of these young women in factories may have appeared quite natural to observers at the time—the same people (women) doing much the same type of work they had done in the home, only in a new location and under the supervision of a foreman rather than the head of the household. Once married, women would generally leave their jobs to look after their own households, which would soon include children.

Work and Equality

Male dominance is minimized when women and men share status and power; when the work of a society is interchangeably male or female; when gender is irrelevant to what the sexes do; when men and women work together. Such integration is rare, however.

Carol Tavris and Carole Wade, *The Longest War: Sex Differences in Perspective*, 1984.

The earliest available data show that at the end of the nineteenth century, when the labor force participation rate for men was 84 percent, only 18 percent of women were in the paid labor force, and the percentage of married women was 5 percent. The situation was different for black women. Around 25 percent of black wives were employed. Most of these worked either as domestics or in agriculture in the rural South. While such early industries as textiles, millinery, and cigars did employ women, mainly young single ones, the new, rapidly growing sophisticated industries relied from the beginning almost entirely on male workers.

Among some immigrant groups, however, who in the course of the nineteenth century increasingly replaced American-born workers in factories, it was not uncommon even for married women to be employed. Most of these people came to the "New

World" determined to improve their economic condition and particularly to make sure that their children would get a better start than they did. At times, the whole family worked. Often if a choice could be made between the children leaving school to supplement family income, or the mother seeking employment, even among groups traditionally reluctant to have women work outside the home, the latter choice was made. By the same token, maternal employment was associated with dire need and was viewed as a temporary expedient to give the family a better start. Few wives remained in the labor force once the husband earned enough for an adequate living. The immigrants' goal of achieving the desired standard of living included what by then was widely considered the American ideal of the family—the male breadwinner who supported his family and the female homemaker who cared for his domestic needs.

The Traditional Family

As an ever larger segment of the population began living in urban centers rather than on farms, and family shops were replaced by factories, women found that their household work increasingly came to be confined to the care of children, the nurturing of the husband, and the maintenance of the home. There were no longer a garden or farm animals to take care of, no need for seasonal help with the crops, and no opportunity to participate in a family business. As husbands left the home to earn the income needed to support their families, there came to be a new division into a female domestic sphere and a male public sphere.

Thus, along with industrialization arose the concept of the *traditional family*, which lingered to a greater or lesser degree well into the twentieth century. The family shifted from a production unit to a consumption unit, and the responsibility for earning a living came to rest squarely on the shoulders of the husband. Wives (and children) grew to be dependent on his income. Thus, redistribution of income became a more important function of the family, as it provided a mechanism for the transfer of income from the market-productive husband to his market-dependent wife and children. Not only did specific *tasks* differ between men and women, as was always the case, but men and women now had different *economic roles* as well.

If the wife also entered the labor market, it was assumed that she was compensating for her husband's inadequacy as a breadwinner. It was sometimes viewed as necessary for the wives of poor people, immigrants, or blacks to work. But for the middle-class, white wife, and even for the working class wife whose husband had a steady income, holding a job was frowned upon as inconsistent with her social status, or, in some instances, as selfishly pursuing a career at the expense of her household responsibilities. . . .

As the economic role of women changed within the family, so too did the image of the ideal wife. While the colonial wife was valued for her industriousness, the growing *cult of true womanhood* that developed with industrialization in the nineteenth century equated piety, purity, domesticity, and submissiveness with the femininity to which all women were expected to aspire. Their role was in the now consumption-oriented home—as daughter, sister, but most of all as wife and mother. This ideal particularly extolled the lifestyle of affluent middle- and upper-class women who were to a great extent freed even from their domestic chores by the servants their husbands' ample incomes could provide. Understandably, over-burdened, working class women might come to look longingly at such a more leisurely existence as something to hope for and strive toward. For men of all social classes, it came to be a mark of success to be the sole wage earner in the family.

Changing Attitudes

This image of the family was fostered not only by the example of the middle and upper middle classes, the envy of the poor woman bearing the double burden of paid and unpaid work or toiling at home to make ends meet on a limited budget, but also by male workers and their trade unions. Initially, the availability of women and children for work in industry was welcomed by national leaders, because they provided cheap, competitive labor, while agricultural production could be maintained by men. However, attitudes changed as workers became more plentiful with the growing influx of immigrants. Male workers and their unions were particularly eager to get wives out of the labor force and women out of all but the lowest paid jobs. Their goals were to reserve the better positions for themselves, make sure they would not be underbid, and give greater force to the argument that a "living wage" for a man had to be sufficient to support a dependent wife and children. Thus, women received little, if any, support from organized labor in trying to improve their own working conditions and rewards.

This was the genesis of the traditional family, once accepted as the backbone of American society. As we have seen, it is in fact comparatively recent in origin, dating back only to the mid-nineteenth and early twentieth centuries. Even in its heyday, it was never entirely universal. Many poor, black, and immigrant married women worked outside their homes and others earned income at home, taking in boarders or doing piece work. Throughout this period, market work was quite common among single women, and a relatively small number of women chose careers over marriage as a lifelong vocation. Nonetheless, exclusive dedication to the role of mother and wife was widely accepted as the only proper and fulfilling life for a woman. It was not long however, before this orthodoxy was challenged for increased modernization brought about dramatic changes in conditions of production and in the economic roles of men and women. . . .

Conclusion

The roles of men and women and the social rules that prescribe appropriate behavior for each are not shaped by biology itself. Rather they are determined by the interaction of biology with the technology of production—the way goods and services are produced under given circumstances. When men are the providers while women specialize in childbearing and homemaking, the latter tend to be viewed as dependents, to some extent even as possessions. They may be put on a pedestal, protected, and sheltered, and the affluent may be permitted to enjoy luxuries and leisure. But they tend not to achieve any significant degree of independence or status apart from their family.

When, on the other hand, "productive" work is shared by women, they are less likely to be primarily defined in terms of their maternal and family role. They are not excluded to the same extent from the public sphere and lead far more autonomous and less subordinate lives. Participating in productive activities beyond housekeeping has tended to bring women a greater measure of equality, but they have also generally worked very hard under these conditions, since they have always been responsible for household and children, no matter what else they did.

While the roles of men and women are influenced by the technology of production, it is entirely likely that gender roles that develop as a rational response to conditions at one time in the course of economic development continue their hold long after they have ceased to be functional. Among tribes where men did the hunting while women looked after planting and harvesting, women continued to do most of the horticultural work long after hunting ceased to be a major economic activity. The view that women should devote themselves entirely to homemaking, once a full-time occupation when life was short, families large, and housekeeping laborious, lingered long after these conditions changed substantially. Jobs originally allocated to men, because they required great physical strength, often continued as male preserves when mechanization did away with the need for musclepower. The possibility that such lags in adjustment are not uncommon should be kept in mind when we come to analyze the current situation.

"The brain . . . differs anatomically in men and women in ways that may underlie differences in mental abilities."

Brain Structure Explains Male/Female Differences

Daniel Goleman

In the following viewpoint, Daniel Goleman writes that new findings in brain research point to small but significant differences between men's and women's brains. Goleman, a science writer for *The New York Times*, presents the findings of brain researchers who believe that women excel in verbal skills while men dominate in spatial skills because of physical differences in male and female brains. He argues that such findings may lead to a better understanding of differences between men and women.

As you read, consider the following questions:

1. According to the author, what physical differences are there between men's and women's brains?
2. What reason does Goleman give for women's superior verbal skills?
3. How do researchers explain the fact that women recover from strokes better than men, according to Goleman?

Researchers who study the brain have discovered that it differs anatomically in men and women in ways that may underlie differences in mental abilities.

The findings, although based on small-scale studies and still very preliminary, are potentially of great significance. If there are subtle differences in anatomical structure between men's and women's brains, it would help explain why women recover more quickly and more often from certain kinds of brain damage than do men, and perhaps help guide treatment.

The findings could also aid scientists in understanding why more boys than girls have problems like dyslexia, and why women on average have superior verbal abilities to men. Researchers have not yet found anything to explain the tendency of men to do better on tasks involving spatial relationships.

Sex Differences

The new findings are emerging from the growing field of the neuropsychology of sex differences. Specialists in the discipline met at the New York Academy of Sciences to present their latest data.

Research on sex differences in the brain has been a controversial topic, almost taboo for a time. Some feminists fear that any differences in brain structure found might be used against women by those who would cite the difference to explain "deficiencies" that are actually due to social bias. And some researchers argue that differences in the brain are simply due to environmental influences, such as girls being discouraged from taking math seriously.

The new research is producing a complex picture of the brain in which differences in anatomical structure seem to lead to advantages in performance on certain mental tasks. The researchers emphasize, however, that it is not all that clear that education or experience do not override what differences in brain structure contribute to the normal variation in abilities. Moreover, they note that the brains of men and women are far more similar than different.

Still, in the most significant new findings, researchers are reporting that parts of the corpus callosum, the fibers that connect the left and right hemispheres of the brain, are larger in women than men. The finding is surprising because, over all, male brains—including the corpus callosum as a whole—are larger than those of females, presumably because men tend to be bigger on average than women.

Because the corpus callosum ties together so many parts of the brain, a difference there suggests far more widespread disparities between men and women in the anatomical structure of other parts of the brain.

"This anatomical difference is probably just the tip of the iceberg," said Sandra Witelson, a neuropsychologist at McMaster University medical school in Hamilton, Ontario, who did the study. "It probably reflects differences in many parts of the brain which we have not yet even gotten a glimpse of. The anatomy of men's and women's brains may be far more different than we suspect."

The part of the brain which Dr. Witelson discovered is larger in women is in the isthmus, a narrow part of the callosum toward the back. . . .

Dr. Witelson's findings on the isthmus are based on studies of 50 brains, 15 male and 35 female. The brains examined were of patients who had been given routine neuropsychological tests before they died.

"Witelson's findings are potentially quite important, but it's not clear what they mean," said Bruce McEwen, a neuroscientist at Rockefeller University. "In the brain, bigger doesn't always mean better."

Convincing Findings

In 1982 a different area of the corpus callosum, the splenium, was reported by researchers to be larger in women than in men. But that study was based on only 14 brains, five of which were female. Since then, some researchers, including Dr. Witelson, have failed to find the reported difference, while others have.

Since such differences in brain structure can be subtle and vary greatly from person to person, it can take the close examination of hundreds of brains before neuroanatomists are convinced. But other neuroscientists say the findings are convincing enough to encourage them to do tests of their own.

Both the splenium and the isthmus are located toward the rear of the corpus callosum. This part of the corpus callosum ties together the cortical areas on each side of the brain that control some aspects of speech, such as the comprehension of spoken language, and the perception of spatial relationships.

"The isthmus connects the verbal and spatial centers on the right and left hemispheres, sending information both ways—it's a two-way highway," Dr. Witelson said. The larger isthmus in women is thought to be related to women's superiority on some tests of verbal intelligence. It is unclear what, if anything, the isthmus might have to do with the advantage of men on tests of spatial relations.

The small differences in abilities between the sexes have long puzzled researchers.

On examinations like the Scholastic Aptitude Test, which measures overall verbal and mathematical abilities, sex differences in scores have been declining. But for certain specific abilities, the sex differences are still notable, researchers say.

Gender Advantages

While these differences are still the subject of intense controversy, most researchers agree that women generally show advantages over men in certain verbal abilities. For instance, on average, girls begin to speak earlier than boys and women are more

51

fluent with words than men, and make fewer mistakes in grammar and pronunciation.

On the other hand, men, on average, tend to be better than women on certain spatial tasks, such as drawing maps of places they have been and rotating imagined geometric images in their minds' eye—a skill useful in mathematics, engineering and architecture.

Of course, the advantages for each sex are only on average. There are individual men who do as well as the best women on verbal tests, and women who do as well as the best men on spatial tasks.

A More Diffused Brain

Woman's verbal and spatial abilities are more likely to be duplicated on both sides of the brain, more dispersed as it were, and hence an insult to either side of the brain (for example, tumor, stroke, trauma, surgery) is not likely to incapacitate a woman as seriously. The clinical findings from large series of patients therefore suggest that woman uses the recessive (less dominant) side of the brain to greater advantage, or at least to greater functional advantage, than the male, whose hemispheric brain function seems to be an all-or-none type of activity for that locus of brain tissue. Again, woman is more diffused.

James C. Neely, *Gender: The Myth of Equality*, 1981.

One of the first studies that directly links the relatively larger parts of women's corpus callosums to superior verbal abilities was reported at the meeting of the New York Academy of Sciences by Melissa Hines, a neuropsychologist at the University of California at Los Angeles medical school.

Dr. Hines and her associates used magnetic resonance imaging, a method that uses electrical fields generated by the brain, to measure the brain anatomy of 29 women. They found that the larger the splenium in the women, the better they were on tests of verbal fluency.

There was no relationship, however, between the size of their splenium and their scores on tests of spatial abilities, suggesting that differences in those abilities are related to anatomical structures in some other part of the brain or have nothing to do with anatomy.

Language Abilities

"The size of the splenium," Dr. Hines said, "may provide an anatomical basis for increased communication between the hemispheres, and perhaps as a consequence, increased language abilities."

Researchers now speculate that the larger portions of the corpus callosum in women may allow for stronger connections between the parts of women's brains that are involved in speech than is true for men.

"Although we are not sure what a bigger overall isthmus means in terms of microscopic brain structure, it does suggest greater interhemispheric communication in women," Dr. Witelson said. "But if it does have something to do with the cognitive differences between the sexes, it will certainly turn out to be a complex story."

Part of that complexity has to do with explaining why, despite the bigger isthmus, women tend to do less well than men in spatial abilities, even though the isthmus connects the brain's spatial centers, too.

"Bigger isn't necessarily better, but it certainly means that it's different," Dr. Witelson said.

Other Differences

A variety of other differences in the brain have been detected by the researchers.

For instance, Dr. Witelson found in her study that left-handed men had a bigger isthmus than did right-handed men. For women, though, there was no relationship between hand preference and isthmus size.

"How our brains do the same thing, namely use the right hand, may differ between the sexes," Dr. Witelson said.

She also found that the overall size of the callosum, particularly the front part, decreases in size between 40 and 70 years of age in men, but remains the same in women.

Several converging lines of evidence from other studies suggest that the brain centers for language are more centralized in men than in women.

One study involved cerebral blood flow, which was measured while men and women listened to words that earphones directed to one ear or the other. The research, conducted by Cecile Naylor, a neuropsychologist at Bowman Gray School of Medicine in Winston-Salem, N.C., showed that the speech centers in women's brains were connected to more areas both within and between each hemisphere.

Recovering from Strokes

This puts men at a relative disadvantage in recovering from certain kinds of brain damage, such as strokes, when they cause lesions in the speech centers on the left side of the brain. Women with similar lesions, by contrast, are better able to recover speech abilities, perhaps because stronger connections between the hemispheres allow them to compensate more readily for damage on the left side of the brain by relying on similar speech centers on the right.

In the *Journal of Neuroscience*, Roger Gorski, a neuroscientist at U.C.L.A., reported finding that parts of the hypothalamus are significantly bigger in male rats than in female ones, even though the size of the overall brain is the same in both sexes.

And Dr. McEwen, working with colleagues at Rockefeller University, has found a sex difference in the structure of neurons in part of the hippocampus that relays messages from areas of the cortex.

Brain Function

Dr. McEwen, working with rat's brains, found that females have more branches on their dendrites, which receive chemical messages to other neurons, than do males. Males, on the other hand, have more spines on their dendrites, which also receive messages from other neurons. These differences in structure may mean differing patterns of electrical activity during brain function, he said.

"We were surprised to find any difference at all, and, frankly, don't understand the implications for differences in brain function," Dr. McEwen said. "But we'd expect to find the same differences in humans; across the board, findings in rodents have had corollaries in the human brain."

"There are no convincing data for sex-related differences in cognition or cerebral lateralization."

Brain Structure Does Not Explain Male/Female Differences

Anne Fausto-Sterling

In the following viewpoint, Anne Fausto-Sterling writes that research done on how men and women think is inconclusive. Fausto-Sterling, an assistant professor of medical science at Brown University in Providence, Rhode Island, argues that explaining gender differences through biology is simplistic.

As you read, consider the following questions:

1. Why does the author think it is irrelevant whether or not men and women use different parts of their brains?
2. In Fausto-Sterling's opinion, does research support the brain lateralization theory? Why or why not?
3. According to the author, how do biological explanations for gender roles fail?

Functionally, humans have two brains. The idea has become sufficiently commonplace to appear even in the daily newspaper cartoons. While the left hemisphere of the brain appears specialized to carry out analysis, computation, and sequential tasks, in the right half resides artistic abilities and an emotional, nonanalytic approach to the world. As originally developed, the idea of brain hemisphere differentiation said nothing about sex differences. But it didn't take long for some scientists to suggest that left-right brain hemisphere specialization could "explain" supposed male/female differences in verbal, spatial, and mathematical ability. The development, dissemination, and widespread acceptance of such ideas provides a second and still very active example of science as social policy.

Humans, like all vertebrates, are bilaterally symmetrical. Although our left and right sides represent approximate anatomical mirror images of one another, they are not equally competent at the many daily activities in which we engage. Each of us has a particular hand and foot preference, using one side of the body more skillfully than the other to, among other things, kick a football, throw a baseball, write, or eat. Such functional asymmetry provides one tangible measure of a complex and poorly understood division of labor between the two sides of the brain. Looking down on the brain from above, one sees the convoluted folds of the right and left halves of the cerebral cortex connected by an enormous mass of nerve fibers, the corpus callosum. Each brain hemisphere controls movements executed by the opposite side of the body. Most people are right-sided, that is, they perform most major activities with the right side of the body, and can thus also be thought of as left-brained. The common scientific belief is that the left hemisphere controls the right side of the body's activities. The converse is probably true for many but not all left-siders. . . .

Theories on Brain Differences

Not long after the discovery of hemispheric specialization, some scientists began using it to explain both the supposed female excellence in verbal tasks and the male skill in spatial visualization. In the past, at least four different theories on these skills have appeared, the two discussed here having received the most attention although, interestingly enough, they are mutually incompatible. The first, put forth in 1972 by two psychologists, Drs. Anthony Buffery and Jeffrey Gray, now suffers disfavor. The other, elaborated by Dr. Jerre Levy—who during and after her time as Dr. Roger Sperry's student, played an important role in defining the modern concept of hemispheric specialization—is still in fashion. The pages of *Psychology Today, Quest,* and even *Mainliner* magazine (the United Airlines monthly) have all enthusiastically described her theory. Speculation also abounds that sex differences in hemispheric specialization result from different prenatal and pubertal hormonal environments. Since a number of psychologists have pointed to a substantial body of experimental evidence that renders Buffery and Gray's hypothesis untenable, we will consider only Levy's views.

Levy hypothesizes that the most efficiently functioning brains have the most complete hemispheric division of labor. Women, she suggests, retain a capacity for verbal tasks in both hemispheres. In other words, they are less lateralized for speech than are men. When verbal tasks in women "spill over" to the right side of the brain, they interfere with the right hemisphere's ability to perform spatial tasks. Men, in contrast, have highly specialized brain halves—the left side confining its activities solely to verbal problems, the right side solely to spatial ones.

Let's suppose for a moment that male and female brains do lateralize differently and ask what evidence exists to suggest that such differences might lead to variations in performance of spatial and verbal tasks. The answer is, quite simply, none whatsoever. Levy derives the idea not from any experimental data but from a logical supposition. In her later work she takes that supposition and "reasons" that "a bilaterally symmetric brain would be limited to verbal or spatial processing. . . ." Psychologist Meredith Kimball reviewed the small number of studies that might act as tests of Levy's logical supposition and came up empty-handed, concluding that there is no evidence to support the key assumption on which Levy builds her hypothesis.

Little Proof and No Progress

The research field of sex differences in brain asymmetry owes its existence to the search for sex differences and the belief that sex is a fruitful category for understanding cognitive function in people. The variation in cognitive function between the sexes is small compared with the variation in the overall population. Because we have no theory of brain function which would enable us to analyze the small intersex variation, the focus on sex differences cannot lead to significant scientific progress.

Joe Alper, *Science for the People*, September/October 1985.

Nevertheless, the proposal that men and women have different patterns of brain lateralization has provoked enormous interest. Scientists have published hundreds of studies, some done on normal subjects and others derived from subjects with brain damage due to stroke, surgery, or accident. The idea that verbal function might operate differently in male and female brains came in part from a long-standing observation: among stroke victims there appear to be more men than women with speech defects serious enough to warrant therapy. There may be a number of explanations for why men seek speech therapy more frequently than do women. To begin with, more males *have* strokes. Also, it is possible that males seek remedial therapy after a stroke more frequently than do females. And strokes may affect speech less severely in females because females have better verbal abilities before the illness.

Some researchers have attempted to sort out these possibilities, but a controlled study of stroke victims is extremely difficult. One reason is that there is no way of knowing for sure whether male and female victims under comparison experienced exactly the same type of brain damage. Even comparisons of individuals who had surgery performed on similar parts of their brains are probably quite misleading because of variation in brain morphology from individual to individual. It would be possible to ascertain the exact regions of the brain affected only by looking at microscopic sections of it, a practice that is routine in animal experiments but would of course be impossible with live human beings. Extensive reviews of clinical studies reveal a great deal of controversy about their meaning, but little in the way of strong evidence to support the idea that women have bilateralized verbal functions. Consider the statement of Jeanette McGlone, a scientist who believes her work to *support* the differential lateralization hypothesis:

> Neither do the data overwhelmingly confirm that male brains show greater functional asymmetry than female brains. . . . One must not overlook perhaps the most obvious conclusion, which is that basic patterns of male and female brain asymmetry seem to be more similar than they are different.

If this is the kind of support the proponents of sex differences in laterality put forward, then it is amazing indeed that the search for sex-related differences in brain lateralization remains such a central focus of current research in sex-related cognitive differences.

Inconclusive Tests

In addition to looking at patients with brain damage, researchers have tested Levy's hypothesis using normal individuals. The most common way of measuring hemispheric specialization in healthy people is by the dichotic listening test. To look for language dominance, experimenters ask the subject to don a set of headphones. In one ear the subject hears a list of numbers, while in the other he or she simultaneously hears a second, different list. After hearing the two lists, the subject (if not driven nuts) must remember as many of the numbers as possible. Usually subjects can recall the numbers heard on one side better than those heard on the other. Some experimenters believe that right-ear excellence suggests left-hemisphere dominance for verbal abilities and vice versa, but this conclusion ignores other possibilities. Individuals who take the tests may develop different strategies, for instance, deciding to try to listen to both sets of numbers or to ignore one side in order to listen more closely to the other.

Lack of Supporting Data

The argument that hemispheric differences account for different abilities in women and men is rapidly becoming dated among brain researchers. The objections of the scientists are reinforced by reviews of research literature that indicate a lack of data to support the relationship between brain lateralization and behavioral differences of the sexes.

Cynthia Fuchs Epstein, *Deceptive Distinctions*, 1988.

Some scientists have reported sex differences in performance on dichotic listening tests, but three reviews of the research literature indicate a lack of solid information. Many studies show no sex differences and, in order to show any differences at all, large samples must be used, all of which suggests that same-sex disparities may be larger than those between the sexes. One reviewer, M.P. Bryden, ends her article with the following comments:

> Any conclusions rest on one's choice of which studies to emphasize and which to ignore. It is very tempting to . . . argue that there are no convincing data for sex-related differences in cognition or cerebral lateralization. . . . In fact, what is required is better research.

Analogous methods exist for studying visual lateralization. Tests utilize a gadget called a tachistoscope, through which a subject looks into a machine with an illuminated field. The machine flashes different items in front of either the right or the left eye, and the subject tries to identify as many as possible. Nonverbal images such as dots (as opposed to words or letters) suggest some left-field (right-hemisphere) advantages for men, but here too the data vary a great deal. For example, many (but not all) studies show male left-eye advantages for perception of photographed faces, scattered dots, and line orientations, but no sex differences for the perception of schematic faces, depth, or color. In addition, the fundamental question of whether such tests have anything at all to do with brain lateralization continues to cloud the picture. . . .

Misconstruing Biology

Are men really smarter then women? The straightforward answer would have to be no. Early in this century, scientists argued that there might be more male than female geniuses because male intelligence varied to a greater extent than did female intelligence. This "fact" provided proof positive of the overall superiority of the male mind. Hypotheses in defense of this position still pop up from time to time. They consist of old ideas in modern dress and are unacceptable to most mainstream psychologists. In apparent contrast Eleanor Maccoby and Carol Nagy Jacklin believe that males and females are equally intelligent while entertaining the possibility that the two sexes have somewhat different cognitive skills; they suggest a biological origin for such differences. Although the possibility is admissible, I have tried to show both that any such differences are very small and that there is no basis for assuming a priori that these small variations have innate biological origins.

Inaccurate Understanding

This viewpoint bears witness to the extensive yet futile attempts to derive biological explanations for alleged sex differences in cognition. Although these efforts all have a certain social wrongheadedness to them, they do not stand or fall on their political implications. Rather, such biological explanations fail because they base themselves on an inaccurate understanding of biology's role in human development. Roger Sperry suggests this when he writes that each person's brain may have more physical individuality than do the person's fingerprints. His statement is radical because it implies that attempts to lump people together according to broad categories such as sex or race are doomed to failure. They both oversimplify biological development and downplay the interactions between an organism and its environment. As a result of doing research, I arrived at the same conclusion. My feelings come from having thought carefully about the present state of our knowledge about the genetics of behavior, the embryological development of the sexes, and the ways in which hormones act as physiological controllers and evocators in males and females. By coming to understand these aspects of human development, we can see more clearly why simple, unidirectional models of biological control of human behavior misconstrue the facts of biology.

Recognizing Statements That Are Provable

From various sources of information we are constantly confronted with statements and generalizations about social and moral problems. In order to think clearly about these problems, it is useful if one can make a basic distinction between statements for which evidence can be found and other statements which cannot be verified or proved because evidence is not available, or the issue is so controversial that it cannot be definitely proved.

Readers should be aware that magazines, newspapers, and other sources often contain statements of a controversial nature. The following activity is designed to allow experimentation with statements that are provable and those that are not.

The following statements are taken from the viewpoints in this chapter. Consider each statement carefully. *Mark P for any statement you believe is provable. Mark U for any statement you feel is unprovable because of the lack of evidence. Mark C for any statements you think are too controversial to be proved to everyone's satisfaction.*

If you are doing this activity as a member of a class or group, compare your answers with those of other class or group members. Be able to defend your answers. You may discover that others will come to different conclusions than you. Listening to the reasons others present for their answers may give you valuable insights in recognizing statements that are provable.

P = *provable*
U = *unprovable*
C = *too controversial*

1. Psychological research indicates that many of the differences in brain function between the sexes are innate, biologically determined, and resistant to change.

2. The man-the-hunter explanation has been disproven by anthropological evidence concerning hunting and gathering societies.

3. Men not only behave but think differently than women.

4. Longer life expectancy and lower infant mortality rates have altered the life cycles of both men and women.

5. Among chimpanzees, the females do not appear to occupy a subordinate position.

6. Female emotions are influenced by two exclusively female functions, lactation and pregnancy.

7. Women often play games as an excuse for fellowship. For men, the name of the game is conquest.

8. The gender roles presented in children's books often offer a biased and narrow portrayal of females' roles.

9. The aggressiveness of males, once needed in the Stone Age, is threatening human survival in the nuclear age.

10. The mass media play a significant role in modeling acceptable human behavior.

11. The social roles of men and women are not shaped by biology itself.

12. Parents influence their children's gender roles through the jobs they assign around the house.

13. Men are more aggressive than women. Men commit 75 percent of all violent crimes.

14. Mothering is not only a socially assigned role but one fitting women's physical and psychological needs.

15. There are extreme variations in male and female behavior within animal species.

16. Most people are comfortable with their assigned gender roles.

17. What distinguishes humans from other species is that the norms and expectations of society, not animal instincts, shape their actions.

18. Fathers' notions of gender stereotypes play an important role in why they treat male and female infants differently.

Periodical Bibliography

The following articles have been selected to supplement the diverse views presented in this chapter.

Matt Clark	"Cherchez la Difference: Hormones, Verbal Skills and Needlepoint," *Newsweek*, November 28, 1988.
James P. Comer	"The Effects of Changing Gender Roles," *Parents*, June 1988.
Geoffrey Cowley	"How the Mind Was Designed," *Newsweek*, March 13, 1989.
Lydia Denworth	"Heirs of Uncertainty," *Ms.*, December 1988.
Helen Fisher	"A Primitive Prescription for Equality," *U.S. News & World Report*, August 8, 1988.
Elizabeth Hall	"All in the Family," *Psychology Today*, November 1987.
Janet L. Hopson	"Boys Will Be Boys, Girls Will Be . . ." *Psychology Today*, August 1987.
Julia Kagan	"Taking Charge of Change," *Working Woman*, August 1987.
Lilian G. Katz	"Boys Will Be Boys and Other Myths," *Parents*, March 1986.
Judith Kelman	"Boys, Toys . . . Joys," *McCall's*, December 1987.
Merrill McLoughlin	"Men vs. Women," *U.S. News & World Report*, August 8, 1988.
Gail F. Melson and Alan Fogel	"Learning To Care," *Psychology Today*, January 1988.
Ethel S. Person	"Some Differences Between Men and Women," *The Atlantic Monthly*, March 1988.
Dava Sobel	"Mother's Moment," *Ladies' Home Journal*, December 1987.
Society	"Patriarchy and Power," September/October 1986.
Georgia Witkin-Lanoil	"Boys Will Be Boys," *Health*, August 6, 1987.

Have Women's Roles Changed for the Better?

MALE/FEMALE
ROLES

Chapter Preface

The resurgence of the women's movement in the 1970s had a powerful impact on many people's lives. Many women credit the women's movement with giving them opportunities and choices not available a few decades ago, when gender roles dictated that women defer to men, stay home, and care for children. More women than ever before are acquiring advanced educations, working, and supporting and heading families. Approximately 56 percent of women with children under the age of six are working outside the home, and the numbers are even greater for mothers of older children. Many of these women feel personally fulfilled and challenged by having roles both outside and in the home. These women are working at all kinds of jobs, from construction to office work, from clerk to executive. And women are continuing to enter the upper echelons of business and the professions, according to Sarah Hardesty and Nehama Jacobs, authors of *Success and Betrayal*. As of 1986, women outnumbered men for the first time in the white-collar professions.

But some women believe that along with the advances have come heavy burdens. Many women who work outside the home no longer find it economically or psychologically possible to stay at home, and find that they must work to survive. Yet they still perform the major part of child and household care, often working twelve or more hours a day. Studies such as Arlie Hochschild's, reported in her book *The Second Shift*, show that in dual-career households, women do 75 percent or more of the housework and child care. Finally, and ironically, many women have found that liberalized laws relating to divorce and family support left them alone and financially struggling.

Have women's roles changed for the better? The authors in the following chapter debate this question.

"American women have made remarkable and magnificent strides."

Women's Lives Have Improved

Stella G. Guerra

In the following viewpoint, Stella G. Guerra points to advances women have made in their professional lives. She believes that these advances show that women have made significant strides in today's society. She also contends these advances prove women's lives have changed for the better. Guerra is the acting deputy assistant secretary of the Air Force, Civilian Personnel Policy, and Equal Employment Opportunity. This viewpoint is an excerpt from a speech she presented at a training program for women employed by the federal government.

As you read, consider the following questions:

1. List some of the accomplishments Guerra believes American women have achieved.
2. What three factors have contributed to American women's success, according to the author?
3. List some of the positive expectations Guerra has for American women in the future.

Stella G. Guerra, "Women in America Shooting for the Stars," a speech presented to the Federally Employed Women 17th National Training Program on July 23, 1986.

Let me begin by telling you what an honor it is for me to be participating in the opening session of the Federally Employed Women (FEW) 17th National Training Program. . . .

I decided to talk about women—the progress we've made in the past and the strides we are making today. . . .

The Past

First, let's take a trip back to the past and take a brief glimpse at the road we have traveled. Rocky, and at times filled with a pothole or two, our path has been similar to a newborn baby. Like a newborn struggling to focus with blurry vision on those admiring parents that hold her aloft for all to see, we have strived to focus on our personal objectives as well as worked to help America achieve its present day global status as the most prosperous country in the world.

Dating back to our forebears who first stepped foot on American soil, we have been a part of our nation's progress. In what some have called the toddler years of our country—the 1800's, we helped America take its first steps toward world prominence. We moved west, we worked in the fields tilling the soil, and in the factories to produce the food and goods that our country needed to prosper and grow.

Moving on—in the 1900's, during what some have affectionately referred to as "the Rosie the Riveter period," working in shipyards and steel mills, we helped our nation meet labor shortages in a time of national crisis. Afterwards, many of us who had entered the workforce returned home—but not for long. By the mid-point of the 20th century, virtually no aspect of American society had been left untouched by our eager rush into the labor force.

Like a child that is anxious to learn about the world and all its opportunities, we began to stretch, to grow and expand our horizons. In a span of less than 50 years, our numbers in the labor force doubled. Our unbridled innocence and energy altered forever the way we lived and worked in this country. In the second half of the 1970's more of us were enrolled in college than ever before, and we began to move rapidly into business, industry, the federal sector, the teaching fields and other professions such as law and medicine.

The early years of America were indeed a time of challenge and a time of change. As women, we were a "spitting image" of that challenge and change. When America dreamed—we dreamed. When our nation stretched to achieve, we stretched. When America laughed, we shared in that laughter. Collectively, like that great universal symbol that stands off the shores of New York—*Lady Liberty*—we too stand as clear examples that in this country our dreams are achievable because we have the freedom to work toward change and to pursue our success-oriented goals. Yes, relying on inner strength, American women have made remarkable and magnificent strides.

Today, we are in a time like no other period in our nation's history. . . . We are moving ahead with great vigor and a national commitment not experienced in quite some time. Today we see a spirit of accomplishment and a sense of pride seldom seen on the national level.

With that same belief in achievement and success, we have moved with America from the so-called "smoke stacked" industries of years past to an economy where three out of every four jobs are located in the service industry. In this industry, on an average, we've created one million new jobs each year for the past 20 years; of these, two out of every three have gone to women. Right now more than 54 percent of our country's women are working and our percentage in the overall workforce has increased to 44 percent. In short, we are continuing to help America forge an environment that says—opportunities are abundant.

Women Are Reaching the Top

For the first time in history, women are beginning to reach a critical mass within the business community. According to futurist John Naisbitt, the balance of power is rapidly shifting in favor of women, making life for them "a new seller's market." Women already out-number men at 52 percent in the nation's colleges; at the elite business schools—Harvard, Yale, and Stanford—they constitute 50 percent of the student body. As of February, 1986, women professionals outnumbered men for the first time: the nation's pool of 13.8 million professional workers had 29,000 more women than men, according to the U.S. Bureau of Labor Statistics. The issue is no longer whether corporations will hire women but how many women they must hire to get the top graduates.

Sarah Hardesty and Nehama Jacobs, *Success and Betrayal*, 1986.

In this environment of prosperity we've seen many firsts:
The first female brigadier general
The first female astronaut
The first female sky marshall
The first female ambassador to the United Nations
The first female justice of the Supreme Court
The first female director of Civil Service
The first female U.S. Customs rep in a foreign country
The first female to graduate at the very top of the class in a service academy—Navy '84; Air Force '86
The list goes on and on—and this same progress can be seen in all sectors of our society.
In business there's been a sharp increase in the number of

women who own their own businesses. The number of self-employed women from 1980-1984 alone jumped 22 percent to 2.6 million people.

Three key factors have contributed to this significant upswing.

Leadership Experience

First, we are gaining experience in positions of leadership in both corporate America and the federal sector. We are moving into middle and upper level management at a record pace. . . .

The second factor pushing us on and upward has been education. Across the land, numbers increased twofold in the past 21 years for those of us entering the halls of higher education.

—In the same period, our numbers in law, medicine, and architectural schools have gone from 5 to 32 percent. Now we account for more than half of all college enrollment, earn one-third of all PhD's, and

—We are awarded 50 percent of all bachelors and masters degrees.

—Today more of us are going to college than ever before.

Our search for knowledge and quest for excellence has certainly opened up the doors of opportunity.

These opportunities have led us down paths previously untraveled. As our visions were broadened, women began to move into non-traditional areas—the third major factor for our success. Federal women were on the cutting edge of this movement. As Betty Harragan pointed out in her book, *Games Mother Never Taught You,* "Women have the potential to stagger the imagination." Our movement into presidential cabinet level positions, into missile silos as crew commanders, aircraft mechanics and into the officer and enlisted ranks have indeed staggered the imagination. It also serves as a glistening example that in the past and in the present our hopes and dreams are interwoven into the very fiber of America. A fiber that will preserve opportunities and chart the course for a new generation of achievers.

The Future

During the next decade, almost two-thirds of the female population will enter the work force and stay longer. Like the population at large in the teen years of America, we'll see our life span increase. At the start of the 20th century, we were expected to live on an average of 48 years; now it's 72 years. And as remarkable as it seems, children born today are expected to live into their eighties.

As attitudes toward working careers change, so too will the structure of jobs. People like Patricia Aburdene and John Naisbitt, author of *Reinventing the Corporation,* tell us—an increase in knowledge power will create major changes in the way we work, live and relax. It's expected that by 1990 our work week will average 32 hours and by year 2000, it will be 25 hours. Flexible work schedules will be the norm with two or three people sharing jobs.

The great impact of high technology will shape and mold the jobs of tomorrow. Advances in technology, attitudes about work, and the increase in life spans will demand a change in the way we are educated and trained. More people will have college degrees or have had some sort of on-the-job training. . . .

Women Are Achieving Power

Women have quietly taken over in business, industry and the professions; they are distinguishing themselves in civil and public service; they are scientists and spacepersons; they are making their mark on the media not as pretty-face performers but as professional power-houses. . . .

All women are implicitly women of power. Today's top female leaders are pioneering on behalf of us all, leading the way forward to a future in which all women will more and more claim not only their rights, but their own souls.

Rosalind Miles, *Women and Power*, 1985.

Job performance and pay for performance will continue to provide opportunities for our professional growth and financial gain. Various alternate personnel systems both in and outside of the federal government will be developed that specifically address pay for performance. In conjunction with these changes, in demographics and values, Federally Employed Women will do much to help continue to close the gap for America.

Shooting for the Stars

With vision and a sense of direction, we will continue to do what's right for America. We will continue to discuss and help explore ways to resolve concerns such as paternity leave and the use of sick leave to care for our families at times of illness. Like the years of "Rosie the Riveter" we'll continue to do our part to keep America strong, prosperous and upward bound.

Whether we are in the home rearing children or soaring towards the stars in outer orbit—women—and especially Federally Employed Women will help set a standard that will be hard to surpass. We will do this by helping to answer the tough questions and by facing the critical challenges ahead. James Baldwin once said, "Not everything that is faced can be changed; but nothing can be changed until it is faced."

"The plain truth is that modern American women . . . have little economic security."

Women's Lives Have Not Improved

Sylvia Ann Hewlett

Sylvia Ann Hewlett believes that American women have not made the great advances often publicized in the popular press. In fact, she believes American women are still greatly handicapped, particularly in the area of economics. Rising divorce rates and the lack of laws to provide child support and equal pay have hurt women financially. Hewlett is vice-president for economic studies at the United Nations Association and a member of the Council on Foreign Relations.

As you read, consider the following questions:

1. In what ways does the author believe American women are more vulnerable economically than their mothers were?
2. According to Hewlett, what are some of the benefits European women have that American women are lacking?
3. Does Hewlett believe it is possible for women to "have it all"?

Excerpts from pp. 11-17, 402-403 of *A Lesser Life: The Myth of Women's Liberation in America* by Sylvia Ann Hewlett. Copyright © 1986 by Sylvia Ann Hewlett. By permission of William Morrow and Co., Inc.

"How'm I doing?" is the question New York City's Mayor Ed Koch uses as a battle cry in his campaigns. Ask it about American women—how're we doing?—and the answer is likely to be a reworking of the old cigarette ad: We've come a long way, baby, but we still have a long way to go. Broaden the question a little, and ask how American women are doing compared with European women, and the response is likely to be a touch smug: Maybe things aren't perfect here, but we're certainly light-years ahead of women in Europe.

But are we? I once thought so. I grew up in Britain, and, like most Europeans, viewed American women with awe and respect. They were, after all, the most powerful and liberated women in the world. . . .

Trying To Have It All

When I arrived at Harvard University as a graduate student at the end of the 1960s, I felt doubly lucky. Not only had I come to America—to immigrants always the land of opportunity—but I felt that I was destined to be part of that golden generation of women who were going to find a place in the sun. By the early 1970s the women's movement was maturing, doors were being flung open, and the barriers to professional achievements for women were falling. I felt confident I could have it all: career success; marriage; children. A few years later, when I actually dealt with the problems of bearing and raising children while building a career, I learned what most women learn: It's damn tough. In fact, it was (and is) much tougher than I had expected given the popular image of the new superwoman—strong, efficient, cheerful, working, raising her kids, having it all.

While living here, I stayed in close touch with my sisters in Britain, two of whom were also working and having children around the same time I was. They didn't seem to have as hard a time as I. At first I thought this was most likely due to differences in type of job, career ambitions, life-styles, and so on. But as time went on, I began to wonder.

Economic Vulnerability

So I decided to look into it. And the more I looked, the more shocked—and dismayed—I became. For despite all those new female M.B.A.'s, M.D.'s, astronauts, and TV anchorpersons, modern American women suffer immense economic vulnerability. They have less economic security than their mothers did and are considerably worse off than women in other advanced countries.

Way back in the 1950s a traditional division of labor gave women a substantial degree of financial security. Maybe many were stuck in bad marriages, but the man did go out every day and earn enough to support his family. In exchange the woman ran the home and brought up the children. With the sexual revolution and liberation this all changed. Divorce became common—in fact, it became three times more common—and women could no longer count on marriage to provide the economic necessities of life.

This, of course, is a worldwide trend, but the rate of divorce in the United States is now two to twenty times higher than in other rich nations, and the degree of financial insecurity and injury women suffer as a result of divorce is far higher in America than anywhere else in the world.

Accompanying the breakdown of traditional marriage in the late sixties and seventies was a dramatic rise in the proportion of women who worked. This was part cause, part consequence. The weakening of traditional roles forced women into the labor force, while the fact of working and earning salaries enabled more women to free themselves of the bonds of traditional role playing.

Again, this was part of a larger trend; throughout the advanced world women have entered the labor force at an extremely rapid rate in recent years. How have they fared in the workplace? It is fairly well known that working women in the United States earn approximately 64 percent of the male wage and that this earnings gap holds true for corporate executives as well as for retail clerks. But it is less well known that the United States has one of the largest wage gaps in the advanced industrial world and is one of the few countries where the gap between male and female earnings hasn't narrowed over the course of the last twenty years.

SALLY FORTH By Greg Howard

Reprinted with special permission of NAS, Inc.

The plain truth is that modern American women, liberated or not, have little economic security as wives and mothers, or as workers. They are squeezed between the traditional and modern forms of financial security to an extent which is unknown in other societies.

Our mothers sought, and the majority of them found, economic security in marriage, but that avenue no longer offers any such guarantee. Because of stagflation, higher rates of unemployment, and much higher rates of divorce, men can no longer be relied upon to be family breadwinners—at least not over the long haul. The escalating divorce rate is a critical factor because with divorce men generally relinquish responsibility for their wives and often for their children. Thus the breakdown of marriage massively increases the disparity between male and female incomes.

In *The Divorce Revolution*, Stanford sociologist Lenore Weitzman shows that after divorce the standard of living of the ex-husband rises 42 percent while that of the ex-wife (and her children) falls 73 percent. Since alimony is paid in only 5 to 10 percent of divorces, and since two-thirds of custodial mothers receive no child support from ex-husbands, millions of women end up bearing complete financial responsibility for raising the children of divorce. Partly because of this economic fallout of divorce, 77 percent of this nation's poverty is now borne by women and their children.

Unequal Rewards for Men and Women

But perhaps modern women neither need nor want the security of traditional marriage. After all, conventional wisdom tells us that today's liberated women should be able to find their economic salvation in the marketplace. Yet in the workplace there continue to be highly unequal rewards for men and women. American women earn 64 percent of the male wage, this despite the fact that they have had as much education as their male counterparts—unlike women in other countries, who generally lag behind men in educational attainment. The earnings gap between men and women has not narrowed in five decades and shows no sign of doing so in the future. A female wage is often inadequate to provide a woman, let alone a family, with the bare necessities of life. Getting a job does not necessarily lift a single woman or a divorced mother out of poverty.

In Western Europe, by contrast, women have a much better shot at economic viability. Marriage remains a considerably more dependable institution than in America, and therefore, traditional forms of economic security mean more. The divorce rate in the United States is now double that in Sweden, Britain, and Germany; triple that in France; and twenty times as high as in Italy. On the work front, wage gaps in Europe have been closing, and women's wages relative to men's are now 2 to 30 percent higher than in the United States.

But that's not all. These other advanced democracies have also instituted family support systems, such as paid maternity leaves, child allowances, subsidized day care, and free health services, all of which considerably ease the lives of working parents. In contrast, more than 60 percent of working mothers in the United

States have no right to maternity leave, and recent social spending cutbacks have reduced even further the low level of public support for child care. These problems of childbearing and child rearing are critical as 90 percent of women have children at some point during their lives.

In other words, while women in other countries have better maintained the security of marriage and have steadily improved the material conditions of their lives—by narrowing earnings differentials between men and women and increasing the scope of family support systems—women in this country are becoming more and more vulnerable. Despite their legendary claims to power and privilege, American women actually face a bad and deteriorating economic reality.

Women Still Earn Low Pay

Although many occupational barriers have fallen, the U.S. work force is still almost entirely sex-segregated; most occupations are either predominantly female or predominantly male in composition. Women are clustered primarily in low-status and low-paying clerical, retail sales, and service jobs often termed the "pink-collar ghetto." Women are severely underrepresented at the other end of the occupation spectrum. At least 75 percent of the jobs in the higher-paying professions are held by men.

Julie Kuhn Ehrhart and Bernice R. Sandler, "Looking for More Than a Few Good Women in Traditionally Male Fields," report from the Project on the Status and Education of Women, January 1987.

The *Wall Street Journal* put its finger on the nub of the problem when it described my generation of American women in the following terms: "Aglow with talent and self-confidence, young women who came of age in the early 1970s breezed through college, picked up their law degrees and MBA's and began sprinting up the corporate ladder." There was only one snag: These same women found their careers "sabotaged by motherhood." Although most of these women chose joyfully to become mothers and would have a hard time seeing their babies as saboteurs, the *Journal* hit the nail on the head.

The problem centers on a clash of roles. Those of us who reached maturity in the 1970s were expected to clone the male competitive model in the labor market while raising our children in our spare time. Compounding this double burden were gratuitous psychological pressures, because we were also expected to raise these children according to wildly inflated notions of motherhood. In essence, I belonged to that "lucky" generation of superwomen who got to combine the nurturing standards of the 1950s with the strident feminism of the 1970s. But as many of us discovered when we struggled to bear and raise children mid-career, the rigid standards of the 1950s "cult of motherhood" are impossible to combine with the equally rigid standards of our fiercely competitive workplaces. Mere mortals such as I end up trapped between the demands of the earth mothers and the hard-nosed careerists, and because these demands are incompatible and contradictory, we are ultimately unable to satisfy either. Neither hired help nor supportive husbands can insulate working mothers from these antagonistic pressures. . . .

Why Should It Be So Hard?

The problems of contemporary American women are not the result of some massive or inevitable conflict between work and family life. Rather, they result because the United States does less than any other advanced country to make life easier for working mothers. We have less maternity leave, less subsidized child care, less job flexibility. And partly due to this deficit in our public policies, women in America earn less, proportionately, than their counterparts in other nations. . . .

Which brings me back full circle. The impetus to write this came from my own experience, prompted by the difficulties and frustrations I encountered when attempting to bear two children mid-career. Why should it be so hard? I wondered. Now I know. It shouldn't.

"A woman might wisely choose the fulfillment of making a peanut butter and jelly sandwich and watch her child enjoy it."

Women Should Be Able To Choose Motherhood Without Guilt

Anna Quindlen and Suzanne Fields

Many women who choose motherhood over a full-time career feel that society does not respect them. In the following viewpoint, Anna Quindlen and Suzanne Fields argue that women should be able to choose motherhood with pride. Motherhood is both fulfilling and essential, they argue. Quindlen, the author of Part I, is a feminist and a writer who chose to give up a full-time career to raise her two young sons. Fields, the author of Part II, is a columnist for *The Washington Times*.

As you read, consider the following questions:

1. According to Quindlen, why did she formerly not have much respect for mothers?
2. Why is Quindlen happy that she left her career to become a full-time mother?
3. Why does Fields think the "new praise of motherhood" is occurring?

Anna Quindlen, "Mother's Choice," *Ms.*, February 1988. Reprinted with the author's permission. Suzanne Fields, "Rediscovering Motherhood's Rewards," *The Washington Times*, December 17, 1985. Reprinted with permission.

I

I am a mom. It's not all I am. But it's the identity that seems to cling to me most persistently right now, like ivy on the walls of an old stone house. Perhaps this is because, just over two years ago, I ditched a perfectly good full-time job in the office for two perfectly good part-time jobs at home, one writing, the other making Tollhouse cookies with assistants who always get eggshell in the batter and praising people who manage to go in the toilet one time out of three. It's a terrific life, but that's not how it's perceived by the outside world. When I quit the job that did not include eggshells and toilet training there was a kind of solemn attitude toward what I was doing, not unlike the feeling people have about Carmelite nuns. People thought I was Doing the Noble Thing. They also thought I was nuts.

There are valid and complicated reasons why they were wrong, but they haven't been ventilated enough. There has always been a feeling on the part of moms that the Women's Movement has not taken them seriously, has in fact denigrated what they do, unless they do it in a Third World country or do it while running a Fortune 500 company and the New York marathon.

The Shame of Being a Mom

I once felt this same way about moms. Like almost everything else, this feeling had to do with the past. When I was growing up, motherhood was a kind of cage. The moms I knew had more children than they probably would have chosen, spaced closer together than they probably would have liked. Smart, dumb, rich, poor—as soon as you started throwing up in the powder room at parties and walking around in those horrible little pup-tent dresses your life was over. Your husband still went out every day, talked to other adults about adult things, whether it was the Red Sox bullpen or the price of steel. And you stayed home and felt your mind turn to the stuff that you put in little bowls and tried to spoon into little mouths and eventually wound up wiping off of little floors.

By the time I was a grown-up, the answer, if you were strong and smart and wanted to be somebody, was not to be a mom. I certainly didn't want to be one. I wanted my blouses to stay clean. I wanted my plants to have leaves. And I wanted to climb unencumbered up to the top of whatever career ladder I managed to cling to. The Women's Movement was talking about new choices. Being a mom was an old one, and one that reeked of reliance on a man and loss of identity. What kind of choice was that? So I exchanged one sort of enforced role for another, exchanging poor downtrodden mom, with Pablum in her hair, for tough lonely career woman, eating take-out Chinese from the cardboard container. I was neither imaginative nor secure enough to start from scratch. So my choice wasn't about choice at all, only about changing archetypes.

I suppose I only really learned about choice when I chose to devote more of my time to a life I had previously misunderstood and undervalued: that is, when I became a mom. I was finally strong and smart enough to do something that left me vulnerable but made me feel terrific, too. I should say that it's challenging and invigorating, that the future of the next generation is in my hands. But that doesn't have much to do with my real life. About half of being a mom is just like being a mom was for my mother. It's exhausting and grungy and chaotic and there's an enormous amount of sopping things up with paper towels and yelling things like "Don't you ever stick something like that in his ear again or I will throw you out the window!" It has nothing to do with Doing the Noble Thing.

(Here is the Noble Thing part, at least from a feminist perspective: I am raising boys here. I am teaching them to cook. I am making a game out of putting dirty clothes in the hamper. I am refusing to create Princes. If it kills me, I am going to make at least two sensitive, caring, honest individuals who know what to do with a wire whisk and what wash temperature permanent-press shirts require. Whose idea of the average woman is someone smart, aggressive, and mouthy, with her own surname and checking account.)

Shaping Lives

There is an honor and legitimacy about being home raising children that parents—mostly mothers—know exists. I am not talking about hollow words like "raising children is such a hard job" or polite comments about the "patience and stamina it takes to raise kids" that are spoken to fill space, without much understanding or concern. I'm talking about a sense that a parent has that for each child there is a life to help shape and that there is no one else who can do as good a job as she—or he—can.

Deborah Fallows, *A Mother's Work*, 1985.

I wanted to be somebody, and now I am—several somebodies, to be exact. And one of them is Mom, who has job responsibility for teaching two human beings much of what they will know about feeling safe and secure, about living comfortably with other people, and with themselves. It's a job I'm good at, but that's not really why I chose it. I chose it because, while half of it is exhausting and maddening and pretty horrible, the other half is about as fun as anything has ever been in my life. Going to the playground, picking people up at school, reading "Curious George," a hundred thousand times, building castles at the beach, watching barbershop haircuts in the mirror, making Tollhouse cookies, praising people who go in the toilet: for me, this is about as good as it gets. One of the reasons I became a feminist is because I really believe that, at some level, women are better. And lots of women realize that work is great and work is money and work is ego enhancing. But, at a certain point, it's simply work—no more, no less. They realize that when men are still developing strategies for their careers, along with clogged arteries.

I love my work. Always have. But I have another job now and it's just as good. I don't need anyone to validate me anymore with a byline or a bonus, which is a good thing, because this job still doesn't get much validation, at least until it's over and you've helped raise someone who isn't a cheat or a con man. I don't need validation. I'm having fun instead.

That's why I did what I did. I didn't do it for the kids. I did it for me. Isn't that what we feminists were supposed to be supporting, a little healthy selfishness? I didn't feel guilty about being away all day at work. I just knew I was missing the best time of my life. Like today. Two guys asked me to have pizza and watch *Sleeping Beauty* with them. Do you remember how terrific *Sleeping Beauty* is, with those three fat little fairies named Flora, Fauna, and Merryweather? I could have been at the office, but instead I Did the Noble Thing: two slices with extra cheese and a long discussion of the difference between enchanted sleep and death.

II

In the space that fills the pendulum between the public and the private worlds of women, something strange is happening. Women—even some feminists, sheepishly—are singing praises of motherhood.

Statistics continue to show increasing numbers of women entering the full-time work force, but personal stories among middle class women (the anecdotal evidence that we all trust most), are taking another turn. Women who become mothers are talking about quitting work, or cutting back.

"I'm not a right-wing nut," the woman says defensively, "but those pro-family women had something right when they said how important it was to be a mother to your child. Not just to give them 'quality time,' but to be able to give them different kinds of time."

The woman, aged 40, a neighbor, said she was an "activist-feminist" on the West Coast for 10 years until she had a baby, a daughter, three years ago. She still works full-time as a business consultant, but she's quitting next year to "enjoy" her daughter.

"She's growing up so fast, I don't want to miss everything. Feminism was wrong in not pointing out what *we*—mothers— would miss by pursuing the feminist agenda. I hope I'm not too old to have another child." . . .

A Lack of Respect for Moms

In her book *A Mother's Work*, Deborah Fallows . . . comes down hard on the women's movement for its lack of respect and understanding of mothers who stay at home. Those of us who know what we like, rather than just "think we like," can find a mother's loving and common-sense concern for her children in Mrs. Fallows's defense of full-time motherhood.

Like my neighbor (who recommended *A Mother's Work*), Mrs. Fallows points out the flaw inherent in the "quality time" theory. It doesn't count all those little moments that lack quality, like trips to the market (with the warfare at the candy shelves), stops at the post office, the bank, the cleaners, those unexciting events that help to inculcate a sense of responsibility and sometimes even elevate to ritual those commonplace, everyday chores of domesticity.

Prejudice Against At-Home Mothers

"Right now there is real prejudice against women who don't work," says Marjorie Hansen-Shaevitz, a La Jolla, Calif., psychologist who has studied women's changing roles. Women at home, she says, often feel like failures. "They can't be only a perfect mother, wife and homemaker," she says. "They have to be a perfect worker too."

Barbara Kantrowitz et al., *Newsweek*, March 31, 1986.

Such moments help her, she writes, to get to know her children "as well as I possibly can, and see them in as many different environments and moods as possible in order to know best how to help them grow up. . . . What I need is *time* with them—in quantity, not quality."

Mothers have been elevated, celebrated, as well as denigrated through the centuries, but it wasn't until this century that mother was thought to be the cause of most adult neuroses.

Freud—or at least his followers—placed a powerful psychological burden on Mother. Small wonder that many women relished the notion of leaving the care of their children to others. What had been the *natural* care of a loving mother became "Momism," in Philip Wylie's biting and ugly sarcasm, a malevolent smothering force of attention.

Those days seem to be over.

Chic cocktail-party conversations about "what mother did to

me'' have given way to the happy recollections of peanut butter sandwiches and hot Cream of Wheat on cold mornings, the honest recognition and appreciation of emotional and financial sacrifices women may have made to take care of their families. Rarely do men *or* women complain about how awful it was that dear old Mom couldn't have been a brain surgeon, particle-beam physicist, or ABC-TV anchorwoman.

In Praise of Moms

Some of the new praise of motherhood seems to grow out of the sad observation that many women today—most of them single parents—who would spend more time with their children if they could, cannot.

Phone Friend, Washington's hotline for frightened and lonely children, receives hundreds of calls every week from youngsters who have no one else to talk to and who hear strange noises rattling through their empty houses.

Those who push most recklessly for desirable social change envision only utopian outcomes (you may remember the fervor on behalf of communes), and so it was with feminism. For a brief decade, it was thought women could have it all. Few women believe that now. Feminism helped women to make independent choices, which is all to the good, but those choices have inevitably led now to a greater appreciation for what necessarily had to be left behind.

The redemption of everyday life is not as heady, nor as exciting, as running for Congress, writing the Great American Novel, or arguing a case before the Supreme Court. But as Deborah Fallows discovered . . ., later may be the time for all that, when the children are older.

In the meantime, a woman might wisely choose the fulfillment of making a peanut butter and jelly sandwich and watch her child enjoy it.

"I have often wanted a baby. I don't want to be made to feel a second-rate person because I don't have one."

Women Should Be Able To Remain Childless Without Guilt

Paula Weideger

For the past several years, women who are full-time mothers have complained that they have been unappreciated and even despised. Paula Weideger believes that now the reverse is happening—society is finding a new respect for mothers and denigrating those women who are not mothers. Weideger argues that there is room and need for both kinds of roles in our society. Weideger, the author of *History's Mistress*, wrote this article for *Ms.* magazine.

As you read, consider the following questions:

1. How does the author believe the women's movement shaped her view of her choice not to be a mother?
2. What does the author mean when she writes that she fears a return to a "motherhood hierarchy"?
3. Why did the Whitehead case make Weideger particularly concerned that women who are not mothers are not respected?

Paula Weideger, "Womb Worship," *Ms.*, February 1988. Reprinted with permission.

I am not a mother. I have maternal feeling enough to know I have missed a lot and will go on with this missing, this yearning, as long as I live. But I don't feel victimized. It is because of choices I have made as well as those fate has made for me that I am not a mom. Nor do I feel bitter or brittle because mine is not a mother's life. I say this with accuracy, I hope, and with relief. It so easily might have gone another way. For an awfully long time a woman who made my choice would have been thought incomplete to a warping degree—a shriveled-up old maid. It would have been hard, in the end, not to be convinced this was true.

Now, in part because of what the Women's Movement accomplished, I just feel like me. Rotten sometimes, terrific once in a while. The history of what has and has not taken place inside my uterus is the cause of neither mood nor of any of the others in between. That I am nulligravida is of importance to my gynecologist, of course, but outside her office it does not define me. This is what I thought at least. But I found out I have been wrong.

Thinking Less of Nonmothers

I am speaking up about this business of having babies because I have learned that people other than doctors—female other people—not only catalog me as a "nulli," but think of me as being less on that account.

Ironically, nonmothers are in the situation many housewives said they were in during the late 1960s and into the 1970s. Then feminism was so vital and had so much impact that women who stayed at home said they felt devalued. Left out. Now it is I who do. Yet it was an aim of the Women's Movement to give women more choices than they had had and to make it easier for a woman to choose to be no man's wife or any child's mother without having to pay a scorching price. How has this reversal come about? Or is it a reversal in fact? Were feminists of 10 and 15 years ago lying when they talked so much about autonomy? And so little about mother love?

Some may have been, surely. But mostly I think feminists were telling the truth insofar as they could get a look at it. The desire to have children, along with good feelings about motherhood, were buried because women were so scared. They were afraid they would turn out like their own mothers, most of whom were housewives and housewives only. Women like me who grew up in the 1950s had been made edgy and claustrophobic by the narrowness of the life laid out for them from birth. To give mother-feeling any place in your heart might mean being lost to mothering forever—or at least "till the kids are grown."

Today a woman is more likely to feel exhausted by the breadth of life she is expected to live. Certainly the desire for children is now being acknowledged and acted upon. This could mean that now women feel more confident and less trapped. And surely that is welcome. What is not so wonderful about the return of giving motherhood a place is that it seems to have returned in partnership with the old hierarchy. The one in which mothers perch at the top and nonmoms huddle down below.

Mind you, mothers are not asserting they are better people. You could say many feel it in their bones along with other intuitions. Or elsewhere in the place where bigotry rests. It all depends on your point of view. For sure, I was slow to catch the return of this prejudice. But during the trial in New Jersey about the custody of a baby known in court as "M," I began to see it plainly. And to discover that even veteran women warriors can be riddled with it, too.

Defending the Old-Fashioned Mother

I'd been out of the country when the trial began and when I got home I wasn't sure who was who in the cast of characters. I was filled in, fast. Impatient and furious, women around me were talking about the case, about how horribly one of the principals was being treated by the lawyers for the opposition and the press.

Childlessness Is a Rational Decision

"There are people who are not cut out to have children," says Robert A. Brown, a family therapist at the University of Maryland. "Some people see the overall trend of childlessness as a reflection of the Me Generation, people only interested in their own happiness. But from what I've seen, I don't see this as a great narcissistic revolution. They're making a reasonable and rational decision."

Barbara Kantrowitz et al., *Newsweek*, September 1, 1986.

The women who were doing all the impassioned talking were feminists and I, therefore, assumed the person they were championing was Dr. Elizabeth Stern. Dr. Stern, after all, had done what many feminists advised doing. She'd waited until she was well placed in her career before having a family. But during this "postponement" her health had declined and having a baby would be too risky, she thought. Instead, her husband provided the sperm, both came up with the money, and they decided to employ a mother surrogate. Mary Beth Whitehead, a housewife, was picked for the job.

It was Mary Beth Whitehead and not Dr. Stern who the feminists I heard talking were rallying around. Mary Beth Whitehead who changed her mind when the baby was born and was fighting to keep it for herself. The reasons given when I asked why they were

rushing to Whitehead's support pretty much amounted to one—
Mary Beth Whitehead had carried and delivered the baby;
therefore the child was rightfully hers.

Motherhood Is Sacred

Disturbed by what I was hearing, I thought I might write about
this issue and phoned several notable feminists asking what they
thought. I spoke to Betty Friedan out in California where she was
teaching, and to Marilyn French at her home in Florida; both
seemed to share the belief expressed by Erica Jong. "Motherhood
is sacred" Jong told me when I reached her in Connecticut. There
is no higher law, they seemed to be saying. On television and in
the papers I saw Phyllis Chesler put this belief into action. She
seemed to be out in New Jersey almost every day acting as if Mary
Beth Whitehead were the reincarnation of the sainted Joan of Arc.

All this was about the stature of biological mothers, of course,
but there were implications about what it meant for those who
have mothered not. And these were not left only to inference.
"Selfish" and "narcissistic" were some of the more run-of-the-
mill adjectives I heard used to describe women who are not moms.

If feminism has helped women by creating more choices than
they sometimes feel they can gracefully manage, biomedical
engineers have added still more, and women, including some
prominent feminists, seemed to be suffering from an overdose.
Yet new possibilities do now exist and retreating to notions of the
sanctity of the womb will not make them go away. Nor help
women solve their moral and practical problems.

Is Only One Choice Wise?

Just as professional women sometimes decide to stay at home
so they can see their children learn to walk, other women
sometimes decide to carry a baby for financial reward rather than,
say, clean out offices at 3 A.M. Is the one choice invariably wise
and the other inevitably foolhardy? Some women may think that
"hiring" another woman's womb is a way to curb the tyranny
of ovaries that go into retirement too soon. Are these women more
self-indulgent than those who have babies so they can buy
designer outfits for three? Or more shallow? Are they less
"deserving" of a child than every woman who bears one?

Enough. This is not about the weird, exciting, unnerving
possibilities created by biological tinkering. Or the difficult-to-
answer questions they bring. It is about motherhood and you and
me.

Nonmothers are not really important to those who are bringing
back the mother hierarchy, except for the occasions when baby
is used as the trump card in the old woman against woman game.
The real reason for the reappearance of so much vanity, sentimen-

tality, and even arrogance about the wonderfulness of mothering has to do with men.

Not even the possibilities offered by surrogate technology even the score when it comes to the ticking away of the biological clock. Men who want children are no longer limited by the fertility of their partners. As for custody fights, even successful professional women have found that their husbands usually have more money and, therefore, more clout when it comes to battles about the fate of their children in the divorce court.

Childless Women Are Happy

A study of over 2,000 women and men conducted at Vanderbilt University in Nashville revealed that married, childless women who work are the happiest people of all—happier than men *and* happier than women with children.

Lynne S. Dumas, *Health*, January 1988.

Asserting the divine rights of mothers is a way for moms to try and get back. To get the power they want. But it will not do. It is picking the wrong target and dividing women. We all lose.

What was so exciting about those days when lots of women were going off to consciousness-raising groups was that women found out how much they had in common when at first it seemed they led such very different lives. I do not believe that motherhood has to be the one uncrossable divide.

This baby business is far too crucial to be the victim of so much hyperbole. The strong maternal feelings of many mothers should not be ignored, but I would not be so quick to sweep away all thought of the laws made by human beings. Custody, adoption, foster care, abortion, child abuse—all of this needs to be looked at good and hard, and plenty of earthly laws and many earthly assumptions need fiddling with in order to make a better life for children and for the rest of us. They have rather an enormous effect on the results of the baby-making enterprise. The kids, that is. It is their fate, as well as that of their parents, that makes the whole subject so critically important, isn't it? Not every woman will care to pay attention to this, of course. But among those who do will be women who do not have a child of their own. Just as among those whose minds will be elsewhere are many who are mothers.

The reappearance of the old mother hierarchy damages us all. I am vulnerable to the attitudes of superiority some biological mothers express in a way I never was when men used to lord it over us. I have often wanted a baby. I don't want to be made to feel a second-rate person because I don't have one.

"Women do face real choices, each of which
exerts its price and bestows its rewards."

Women Are Free To Choose
the Life Roles They Want

Nicholas Davidson

Nicholas Davidson believes that today's women have a world of
choices available to them. They can be mothers or career women
or both. No one role is perfect for all women, he writes. Davidson
has a degree in history and is the author of *The Failure of Feminism*,
from which this viewpoint is excerpted.

As you read, consider the following questions:

1. Davidson believes women's lives are divided into three
   stages. What are they?
2. Davidson contends that women have basically three life
   paths from which they are free to choose: "the careerist,
   housewife, and superwoman." What does he see as the
   advantages and disadvantages of each?

Reprinted from Nicholas Davidson's *The Failure of Feminism* with permission of
Prometheus Books, Buffalo, New York.

If the experience of the past generation has taught us anything, it is that one cannot simply extrapolate present trend lines into the future. . . .

It would thus be much too easy to assume that American women will continue indefinitely in the same directions as those of the past fifteen years. The current work environment in America is mixed in results and highly uncomfortable to many. The tensions it generates, not purely a result of "the conditioning" we are encouraged to fear and distrust, seek a resolution. These dynamic, continuing tensions will inevitably have societal consequences—exactly which, remains to be seen.

What has changed is well known: the occupational barriers that kept men and women from doing the same jobs have been breached. What has yet to be worked out is a comfortable accommodation to this fact in the lives of individuals. . . .

Stages of Change

The new life plan for American women will be distinguished, not by the steady sweep of the male career and family paths, but by its division into distinct stages. The first third of a woman's life (roughly speaking) will typically be spent in educational and maturational experiences of various sorts. The next third will be characterized by intense involvement in family life, which will be the major locus of both affectional and work life for most women. If a career is pursued, it will be downplayed relative to the demands and fulfillments of family life. In either case, paid work will not be the primary determinant of identity or the most powerful source of fulfillment for most women. The following third, after children are grown, will see an increase in women's extrafamilial activities, which will in many cases involve a full or part time return to the world of paid work. The numbers of middle-aged women in the work force will be further swelled by the greater numbers of widowed and divorced women at this time in life.

This tripartite model confounds the nearsighted careerist track of the Myth of Independence and, unlike the feminine mystique, allows time for maturation in early adulthood before marriage and for meaningful and remunerative activity after children have left the nest. It is compatible with both interdependence and individuation, and is the only conceivable realistic model for the majority of women under the conditions of current civilization.

Women's characteristic needs will differ from stage to stage, and will at every stage differ from men's. Any viable female advocacy must address these concrete realities of women's lives.

Older women will need opportunities beyond the family, but it's not as if all twenty-year-old women were going into careers. It's a different type of problem than if that were the case. For instance, relatively few women in the post-child-rearing years will compete for executive positions in banking, law, and so forth.

Women in Business

Some feminists have taken to pointing out that "Women are not cloning the male model." While this statement is intended as an attack on maleness, it does contain a grain of truth. Women really are not duplicating men's approaches to work—quite apart from the allegedly determinative issue of housework. For instance, the numerous businesses women have started in recent years tend to be small, personal affairs which, it can be expected, will give many women a work environment more congenial to them, will permit women greater economic security, and will increase the diversity of our culture, but will not compete with the world of large corporations.

Blessed with Options

Many things in today's world are in short supply. But the woman of the 1980s and beyond has been blessed with two things in abundance: options and choices.

With little fear of social stigma or unfavorable repercussions, a woman today is able to choose to be single or married, to pursue a career or to stay at home, to raise a family or to remain childless, to combine motherhood with a career or to make raising her children a full-time commitment.

Kaye Lowman, *Of Cradles & Careers*, 1984.

American women are presented with three life paths: the careerist, housewife, and superwoman models. Each of these has its characteristic difficulties. Day care is not a panacea, for the high octane professions that the feminist mystique prescribes as the acme of female fulfillment inherently require unreasonable amounts of effort over a period of years. These years of flat-out effort usually coincide with the period in which a woman is raising a family. Even if her husband is among the few who are willing and able to contribute fifty percent or more of child care, she makes an extreme sacrifice—the experience of raising her own children—in return for a problematic reward, namely the sort of professional recognition whose value many *men* (who have no choice) came to question in the sixties. The superwoman must cram all her personal relationships into the few exhausted hours left over from work, commuting, shopping, making appointments, and so forth. The result may be worth the price this exerts on her relationships, but it is necessary to recognize that there is a price. Too, unless this life-style is a mutual decision, it seems likely that many men will be severely frustrated by a wife who is rarely home, and is constantly exhausted or busy when she is. Because modern fields change so fast, the strategy of educating oneself for a profession and then putting it on hold for five, ten, or twenty years to raise a family often doesn't work out or, if it does, mandates a lower status position than would have been the case had there been no interruption. And it is not possible to cut back work effort beyond a certain level without falling behind others. There is no way a person working eight hours a day, and subject to interruptions, can compete with a person working fourteen hours a day without interruptions. Prestige professions are inherently the most difficult form of paid employment to integrate into women's life cycles.

Yet the price of sacrificing family life to job is one that most women shy away from in horror. Most people, men and women, will in the long run make almost any sacrifice necessary to marry and have children, both for the positive reason that they wish to participate in love relationships and to avoid loneliness. As the Me Generation discovered the hard way, singleness is a miserable way to live for most people once they find themselves beyond the communal settings of youth culture.

Choosing Housewifery with Open Eyes

In comparison with the careerist and superwoman tracks, the housewife alternative offers real advantages. But in any case, women are not "going back" to the fifties. To be a housewife in the late eighties is not the same thing it was in the late fifties. Women who choose the housewife option today are doing so with their eyes open, not because they have no other choices. Because they are making an informed, self-affirming choice, very few of them will be prone to the sense of entrapment against which Betty Friedan revolted. In addition, the whole cultural context has changed, and we may expect that they will reinvent many aspects of the housewife role to their personal benefit and that of their families. The end result of the fifties and seventies excesses—if we can learn the lessons of each—is that at long last women will be free to follow their own lights, and that in consequence the misdirection of vast numbers of women into uncongenial life tracks will finally come to an end.

Indeed, the dividing line between women who "work" and women who "stay at home" may be blurred. It would be an advantage to all concerned if more jobs became available that would not require a forty-hour work week. The productivity of women who work, say, only twenty hours a week is probably far higher on average than those who work full time. It is mostly a timorous clinging to a misunderstood work ethic that delays the development of more such jobs, like that of the employers who once felt that to oblige any worker to toil for less than fourteen hours a day, six days a week, would sap the national character. Flexible work hours, which have gained considerable favor in some quarters, are another useful innovation.

Having Children and a Career

The question is no longer whether women prefer motherhood to a career. According to the Department of Labor, 65 percent of new mothers return to the work force within a year of childbirth. Studies of female college graduates indicate that a majority of young women are training for a career they plan to pursue the rest of their lives.

Sharon Nelson and Karen Berney, *Nation's Business*, May 1987.

The housewife role does have its pitfalls. It can be wearing to be constantly attending to others' needs. Housewives are subject to isolation from other adults. Above all, they must at the present time function in a culture that still retains a good deal of misogyny. The old view that women's roles must be second-rate persists, aggravated by the newer feminist disparagement of female activities and values, the feminist devaluation of the feminine. Housewives are in a position of vulnerability with regard to difficult husbands, which can sometimes be reduced with the bargaining power of a separate paycheck. In addition, there comes a point during her children's adolescence when the demands on a mother radically diminish. What women do at this point will be a matter of personal inclination and initiative, but for many the best solution will be to reenter the world of paid employment on one basis or another. But all the potential difficulties that beset housewives are matched or exceeded by the difficulties facing women in other life tracks, and each problem housewives face has a potential solution—unlike the superwoman model, which tends to require that women (and their husbands and children) cease to be made of flesh and blood.

Real Choices

The important point is that women do face real choices, each of which exerts its price and bestows its rewards. We must stop pretending that any one of these three paths presents a panacea for all women, as surely as we must resist efforts to close the door on any one of them. A more realistic life plan than those of fifties or seventies women must be made available to the girls who are now growing up, one that offers real choices, without obscuring or exaggerating either the difficulties or the fulfillments of any one of these paths.

Panaceas do not exist. Every life-style has its drawbacks and dangers. Masculinity and femininity impose their difficult aspects along with their advantages and pleasures. Masculine separateness exerts its price. Feminine connectedness is inseparable from feminine vulnerability. The careerist and wife-mother life orientations both present real, though differing, problems to women—and the attempt to combine these two life tracks is usually even more fraught with pain, anxiety, and missed nights' sleep. Even the most comprehensive day care is a very inadequate solution for a woman or her children if she must put in the kind of hours required of aspiring investment bankers, professors seeking tenure, or medical interns. And to somehow force competitive men to slow down would pose insuperable problems of oppression, anomie, and civilizational decay.

The Nature of Life's Choices

But we cannot go back to some balanced, related world of the prehistoric past, for life has always had its areas of difficulty. Even if we could go back to the Neolithic village or yet further back to the camps of the mammoth hunters, we would find sources of joy and difficulty equivalent to those that confront people in our own culture. We must recognize that life presents certain imperatives and certain choices. The nature of both the imperatives and the choices has been almost impenetrably obscured for the past twenty years, under the prevailing influence of cultural determinism, unisexism, and feminism. It is time for Americans to start educating themselves about these matters, unlike the sixties generation which crashed through life like a blindfolded driver trying to negotiate a twisting road with a guide shouting false directions in his ear.

"I enjoy the idea of being single. . . . I have the whole world to explore."

Single Women Are Fulfilled

Shere Hite

Shere Hite, a historian and former model, is the author of a trio of controversial books that report on Americans' sexual philosophies and mores. These books, *The Hite Report*, *The Hite Report on Male Sexuality*, and *The Hite Report: Women and Love* are based on responses to lengthy questionnaires Hite mailed to thousands of people. The format of these books includes brief interpretive material and several quotations taken from the surveys' respondents. *Women and Love* surveys women's attitudes on a variety of love-related issues, including marriage and romance. In the following viewpoint, excerpted from *Women and Love*, Hite reports that many women view being single as a fulfilling and enjoyable way of life.

As you read, consider the following questions:

1. List what seem to you to be the three most common reasons the quoted women give for enjoying being single?
2. Why do the women the author interviews think marriage is overrated?
3. Why do the women dispute the belief that being alone is lonely?

I like being single. Being single you have time to putter, ponder, read, take classes, go to movies—you see more of the world, instead of having to learn about another person. You can be closer with friends. Sure, it's got its ups and downs—but as they say, "No pain, no gain—no guts, no glory!"

My experience of being single and having relationships is that first I am consumed twenty-four hours a day. This goes on for about three months of agonizing and craziness, with intense emotional involvement. Then I have something like a nervous breakdown and we break up. Then I talk to great girlfriends on the phone about it all until I am myself again. Until the next time.

Women of all ages enjoy being on their own. Most like having a wide circle of friends and open avenues to meeting and relating to others, taking any job they want, and following a multitude of interests. On the other hand, in a couple, one may relate more narrowly, and there is often not time for all one's friends. Women like being in charge of their lives—whether this includes deciding to marry or remain "single." . . .

Women Who Don't Want To Marry

26 percent of single, never-married [heterosexual] women between the ages of twenty and thirty say they are not interested in marriage:

"The idea of marriage scares me right now. I am sure in time the fear will subside and I will see a different side to it. I think it is important for some individuals, but not all. I do not think I am monogamous by nature!" . . .

"Marriage seems overrated—people reaching for a type of security that just doesn't exist anymore. It is based on assumptions that aren't realistic. As a contract, it's very unfair and inequitable. I hope I never get married." . . .

18 percent of never-married women [heterosexual] between the ages of thirty and fifty say they are not interested in getting married:

"I am forty-eight. I like being single. It is nicer to be yourself than less than a person with someone else. The men I have seen, and still see on occasion, all tend to treat women traditionally . . . as less than equals. I would rather be the fifth wheel with other couples and content alone than be part of a couple and discontent a lot of the time."

"I believe in loving as intensely as possible whenever it happens to you, whomever you find to love—for as long as it lasts. I do not believe in finding the 'one' and considering that that is the end of loving anyone else. This would deaden the original choice also."

"I am thirty-eight. I have not come this far along to give up now and get married, just for the sake of the thing. I am too proud of my life. I have put too much into it. As I've become older, I have a stronger sense of myself. I'm less and less willing to settle for an inadequate love relationship. I'm glad I have finally reached this stage. Like too many women (and maybe men too), I used to settle for men that used me for their own sexual purposes just to gain a little affection. The rewards weren't worth the grief.''

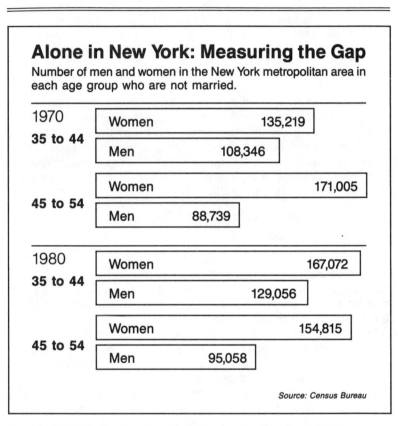

Alone in New York: Measuring the Gap

Number of men and women in the New York metropolitan area in each age group who are not married.

1970		
35 to 44	Women	135,219
	Men	108,346
45 to 54	Women	171,005
	Men	88,739
1980		
35 to 44	Women	167,072
	Men	129,056
45 to 54	Women	154,815
	Men	95,058

Source: Census Bureau

46 percent of women who are divorced (and 59 percent who are widowed) do not want to marry again—at least any time soon:

''I am alone by choice. I am trying to sort my feelings out, get to know what it is that I really want in life and in a partner before I get involved again. I'm going to school, enjoying time with my children, seeing movies, reading, and living the way I want to live. I don't have the time right now to devote the energy a relationship takes.'' . . .

''I thought, after my husband died, that I would like to get married again, but now I find I enjoy being single and living by myself. I like the freedom—the chance to come and go as I please without being accountable to anyone. I enjoy going to parties by myself. It is difficult to find someone I like enough to prefer being with them—part of the problem is that there aren't as many men around who have as good an education as I have, and intellectual conversation is something I care for a great deal."

"I like raising my children without any interference. I do miss someone to give me a break from the kids, someone to talk to—but I talk to my kids, so that isn't a biggie. My friends don't envy me, because they know what being a single parent on a limited income is like." . . .

Why Women Like Being Single

93 percent of single, never-married women say, no matter what the problems, they love the freedom and independence of being on their own, the fun of meeting and knowing different people, calling their lives their own:

"I enjoy the idea of being single, especially at my age. I have the whole world to explore."

"I love doing what I want, when I want—and it forces me to reach out to others."

"Traveling and going places on my own, unencumbered by a partner—I enjoy it. I am free to go about as I please without having to defend my actions, or report to anyone. I have the option of doing all kinds of things! I haven't yet found anyone I love and respect enough to commit the rest of my life to."

"It's great to be responsible for no one but yourself. I love being able to flirt with anyone I please, not being tied down, having an apartment exactly the way I want it, not having to answer to anyone." . . .

Most women who become single after a divorce also love being on their own, independent:

"It's heaven to be single. No matter what problems the day brings, I look back, and by comparison the day is a fantastic success!"

"How do I feel? Good! I like to feel free, not tied down emotionally, because it always seems to engulf me. I never thought I could survive on my own, but I now realize I can spread my love among many people and have many fulfilling relationships."

"After living with my husband for four years, I discovered that I couldn't ever again stand the thought of living for a long time with another grown-up person. They sooner or later try to boss me, or I become the boss, and I can't bear it. Children (I have two) don't boss you around, and besides they grow and want to have homes and lives of their own. But a husband—to make him move you must start a catastrophe! Also, when I was married, I felt unwanted by everybody: men, employment managers, and working female friends."

"I definitely prefer being single to being a part of an even moderately unhappy couple! Sometimes I miss having someone I can count on to do things with, but marriage never provided that anyway." . . .

Another woman, age sixty-two, describes how after leaving her marriage, the only job she could get was in a photocopy shop for minimum wage, with a young, "snotty" male boss—but she is still glad of her decision, and proud:

"My first job after I became single was in a quick-copy shop at just over minimum wage. When I asked for a ten-cent raise after three months, the owner/boss kept me for two hours going over all my defects—while through a plate-glass window we could see his wife waiting to pick him up and probably not knowing what the hell the conversation was about. He made me wait another month for my ten-cent raise. I was about fifty-six at the time. I'd like to kill him.

"Nevertheless, I don't have a vocabulary to tell the pleasure of sleeping alone after sharing a bed with the same man for thirty years. It was heaven. It took months to get used to the sheer joyous ecstasy. I realized when he left that whenever I approached my home while he lived there, a tension of fear would build up. He's been gone about ten years and I still approach home late at night feeling an exultation that I no longer feel fear when I approach my house, but just pleasure. I exult daily in having won. . . .

Discouraging Marriage

One out of every eight women born in the mid-1950's will never marry, compared to only one in 25 women in the preceding generation. Nearly one of five college-educated white women born in the 1950's will never marry. Among young black women, whether college-educated or not, almost three in 10 will never marry. Simply put, the extent to which young women today are not marrying is making modern demographic and social history. . . .

Although record numbers of women are active in the labor force, many husbands are unwilling to make the sacrifices that wives made in the past. Most men simply do not do their fair share of child care and house work. Further, husbands are often unwilling to move for the sake of their wives' careers. This lack of male cooperation confronts women with an obvious disincentive to marry.

Neil G. Bennett and David E. Bloom, *The New York Times*, December 13, 1986.

"After raising five children to adulthood and independence, I entered the job market for the first time at fifty-six and I am surviving— 'making it'! I need most now instances, occurrences, in which my intelligence is reaffirmed. My goals are to retain my home, remain financially independent, and start making enough money to do things like go to shows and concerts, travel and take vacations. I can see it's all within my grasp now—in just a year or two, I will have it all—and I can be proud of having done it myself." . . .

Most Women Love To Spend Time Alone

Although living alone is supposed to be lonely, most women love to spend time alone, have time to themselves. Many women can be themselves when alone in a more complete way than at any other time.

More women mention feeling lonely inside a non-close relationship than they ever do being single (almost no women mention feeling alone because of being single). Women say, over and over, that they have many good women friends, sometimes friends of a lifetime, and that their communication with them is the closest of their lives. Being single and trying out different relationships can be "lonely" because of the ups and downs, the lack of stability, and the constant "starting over." While breaking up or being in a bad relationship can be depressing, actually being "alone" is not, according to women here.

Most women in this study, single or married, say they would like to have *more* time alone. When asked, "What is your favorite activity for yourself, your favorite way to waste time?" the overwhelming majority of women chose activities that were solitary—such as taking a bath, reading a book, going for a long walk, perhaps with their dogs, having time to just sit and have a cup of tea, etc. . . .

Being "alone" is not "sad" and "bad," but often very refreshing, restoring the spirit, allowing feelings to come to the surface, recentering in oneself. It also allows time for creativity and planning/dreaming future thoughts. However, being single rarely means "living alone"; in fact, it means living *less* alone for many women.

One woman states memorably the case for being single:

"Being single, you have the opportunity to, in fact, change the world—as male thinking patterns are quite stuck and it is difficult to debrief yourself while involved with them. You have no one controlling or discounting you as a single (hopefully, anyway). Your life is more flexible. The disadvantages to being single I think mainly rest largely in one's security and affirmation needs. At our present stage of development, women are more defined by love relationships than men. Women want to be substantiated because this is an area of poverty for women—they don't usually substantiate themselves adequately, so they look for men to do it—and put themselves in jeopardy thereby. I think women are desperate for affirmation from the power group. But we don't have to be."

And another, who was married for twenty-five years, and now wouldn't trade her independence for anything, sums it all up:

"I was a wife and mother for twenty-five years, my work was basically homemaking. My greatest achievement is my four years of college. I didn't graduate, but I still see it as my greatest achievement, beyond mothering, beyond wifing, beyond anything else. Also—my divorce and entry into the world, because I don't feel like I was in the world or in any way in charge of my own life until I got divorced. I've been divorced for nine years. I prefer it.

"The best job I could get when I left the marriage was as a cleaning woman—that's my experience, what I did for twenty-five years. It's worth it to be on my own. Being in control of my life. Independence! Absolute independence. I love doing what I want to do, being with whom I want to be with, staying out as late as I want, changing my mind if I want, living the way I want, listening to the music I want.

"The divorce was like death and rebirth. I never had any regrets. I felt relieved that I could start living again. I still feel that relief nine years later. It took me six years to come out of my divorce, six years of emotional turmoil. I talked to my friends, and went to college in those years, which was very, very helpful.

Benefits Available to Singles

The benefits that people seek in marriage have become widely available to single people in socially acceptable ways. Chief among them: sex for men and financial security for women.

Laura Mansnerus, *The New York Times*, June 15, 1988.

"I remember crying over problems with my husband. Why? Because I could never reach him, I could never really communicate with him, never share with him. I had two semi-nervous-breakdowns during my marriage and felt very low immediately following my divorce. But I was the loneliest when I was married and my husband didn't share my life. I was lonelier married, when he was with me but I couldn't reach him emotionally. That made me feel very, very lonely.

"Was there a time that I gave up on love as not being very important? Oh, definitely. Relationships are still not very important to me. People always say, don't give up, don't give up. I don't see it as giving up, I see it as a preference.

"What is my sex life like? Oh, boy. Sometimes there is no sex life. I have nothing on a regular basis. But I enjoy periods of either no sex or being sexual with just myself. Taking care of my own needs. I was very shy when I married my husband. I relate more

100

aggressively the older I get. I have branched out. I used to be strictly heterosexual, now I get a great deal of pleasure making love to women occasionally too. What I like best about sex with women is that women give, women are touchers, there is much more touching and caressing with a woman. They just don't go for 'the act' of sex. What do I like best about making love to men? I guess I like feeling feminine or like a woman maybe.

Happiness

"When was I the happiest with someone? I'm trying to think—in a relationship recently, in the last two years—I only saw him under certain circumstances, we just got together and went out and danced and had a few drinks, went to a café or something. I was happiest when I was sharing with him, doing something, dancing. I don't know that I was ever deliriously happy about being in love.

"My most important relationship with a woman in my life has been my relationship with my daughter. She is my best friend. She is a ray of light in my life. I love her dearly, dearly, dearly, she is a beautiful human being. Have I talked to her about menstruation? Oh yes, years ago, she's older now. I told her that she was a human and her body was hers and that she should always take pleasure in her body and never feel guilty about it, and she thanked me profoundly, she still thanks me, she still remembers that.

"I'm white, ethnic Italian. Schooling—high school and four years of college. The approximate total income in my household—hold on—about $5,000. What kind of work do I do? As I said, I do cleaning work, it was what I did for twenty-five years, it's my best expertise. I obtained this questionnaire at my church.

"To women I say—you can be who you want to be. Look how I've changed! I've revised, I'm like T.S. Eliot. There will be time for a hundred more revisions. Oh, a thousand revisions."

"These women enter treatment in order to better understand . . . why they have not been able to get into 'a stable relationship with a man.'"

Single Women Are Frustrated

Elizabeth Mehren

Elizabeth Mehren, a staff writer for the *Los Angeles Times*, reports in the following viewpoint that many of today's highly successful single women are unhappy with their unmarried status. They may appear to have it all, but they feel as though they are failures as people. Mehren interviewed numerous psychologists who say that these women find that a career cannot compensate for the lack of a spouse and children.

As you read, consider the following questions:

1. What are some of the reasons given in this viewpoint to explain why large numbers of successful women in their thirties go to therapists to help them cope with being single?
2. According to the viewpoint, why are few eligible men available to today's woman in her thirties?
3. What myths encourage single women to feel unhappy, according to the viewpoint?

Not long ago, Manhattan psychotherapist Renee Goldman called a colleague, wanting to refer a client. Barely were the words out of Goldman's mouth when her associate thundered her reply.

"If this is another single woman over 30 wanting to get married," the second psychotherapist railed, "don't even think about it."

The description was a precise fit, and Goldman's colleague made it entirely clear she did not need to add another husband-seeker to her client roster. It was an epidemic of sorts, they agreed, this seeking to make sense of the single status. Never married or long divorced, a growing number of single women are taking their turmoil to psychologists and psychiatrists.

"It is a phenomenon of this era, it really is," Los Angeles psychologist Annette Baran said. "I would suspect that the great majority of any psychotherapist's practice—maybe two-thirds of anybody's practice—is single women who have relationship problems."

Dwelling on the Odds

To help explain the trend, mental health professionals cite media reports spotlighting a so-called man shortage and dwelling on the purportedly dismal odds of marriage for women over 30. A widely publicized study by two Yale sociologists and a Harvard economist, for example, asserted that only 20% of white, college-educated women who reach age 30 without marrying can be expected to do so. After age 35, the figure dropped to 5%. For those over 40, the researchers said "perhaps 1%" would marry.

Other social scientists have since questioned the findings, stressing that the Census Bureau figures show that the nation's marriage rate has actually been increasing since 1980. Moreover, Census data indicate that median ages for first marriages have climbed from 20.5 in 1964 to 23.0 in 1984—a significant change in the parlance of demographers. Marriages for highly educated women between the ages of 27 and 39, the figures demonstrate, rose between 1970 and 1980, a time when the marriage rate for the population at large was in decline.

But numbers are scant consolation to women who feel they are unwitting players in some great game of coast-to-coast Old Maid and who share a collective sense of terror about their prospects of marriage. . . .

Those in the mental health field point to certain common elements among these women clients: highly successful careers, high incomes and, often, family backgrounds that are almost baroque in their complexity. But they fail to pinpoint a pathology that characterizes these women, agreeing only that it is a major concern.

"It's happening more and more," said Kenneth Druck, a psychologist with a large practice of single men and women in

San Diego. The unmarried, over-30 woman, he said, "is coming in because she thinks something is wrong. She has an underlying sense of failure, a nagging suspicion that perhaps she has missed the boat somewhere. The fact is, she doesn't have a relationship. She's not part of a family." . . .

The issue itself was subjected to analysis when New York psychoanalyst Janice Lieberman presented a paper, "Issues in the Psychoanalytic Treatment of Single Women Over 30," at the annual conference of the American Psychological Association. Wrote Lieberman, "These women enter treatment in order to better understand themselves and why they have not been able to get into 'a stable relationship with a man,' meaning marriage. Usually this affect-laden word, 'marriage,' is not used in the first sessions. 'Being single' is occasionally raised as the presenting problem, but more often than not, it is mentioned after several sessions have elapsed. . . .

"I was not threatening—in fact, I was very consciously and aggressively pursuing a policy of not seeming threatening—and next thing I know, he marries a little tramp in my marketing department."

Hamilton. Reprinted by permission.

"The casual way in which the problem appears," Lieberman continued, "belies the fact that many of these patients bring to treatment a hidden agenda: *to find a husband.*"

Certainly the issue of confusion, if not outright discomfort, over marital status is not exclusive to women in this age bracket. "You see it with men, too, by the way," Druck said. "There are more and more men who come in and say they want a wife and a family."

But traditionally, women have sought psychological help in far greater numbers than have men. Men are less likely to consult a psychological professional at all, and when they do, the questions they raise are apt to be of a different nature entirely. They may complain of difficulty in sustaining a relationship, but their focus is likely to differ dramatically from that of their female age peers.

As Druck pointed out, "While men may have some of the same concerns, there aren't a thousand books out about women who hate men, or about men who love too much."

For Carla, a 38-year-old officer for a foundation in Boston, "This is the issue: I don't have a role model. The old role model is mother—the grow-up, get married and have babies role model. What I did was go to graduate school and become a quote, un-quote success in my scholarly field. I'm going in a direction that is absolutely dark. There's nobody guiding me, no role model for a woman who has a series of relationships, but not marriage.

"A lot of women are looking to therapy for this," she said, "so they can make up their own goals. I think we are all confronting the old ways on one hand, and the unknown on the other."

Carla said she sees her therapist on a weekly basis "because I want to be able to get to a point where I can nurture myself." But sometimes, she said, "I feel like you're going to a therapist and you're just paying him to be your pal."

She would like to be married, and though her child-bearing days are numbered, Carla said she still thinks about having children. But the realities of the marital marketplace do not fill her with optimism. "Life is just a free fall, it really is," Carla said. "I figure the only safety net you have is, you know, your IRA."

Bloodied in the Trenches

Her lament is a familiar one to Mill Valley's Pierre Mornell. "I see a lot of women who've made it in the trenches, and they're bloodied. They've got a right to say 'Is this all there is?'"

Mornell, a member of the clinical faculty at UC San Francisco and author of "Thank God It's Monday" (Bantam, 1985) and "Passive Men, Wild Women" (Simon & Schuster, 1979), said single women in therapy often express the need for family, for children. "Whether that is due to estrogen and progesterone or it's the reality that you've been out in the trenches and you're bloodied and battered, there's something rather profound in terms of genes and wanting to nurture and raise children, and have a quieter, simpler life, or simply a withdrawal from the (professional) battle-field."

Virtually uncharted, this mid-life, male-female psycho-emotional territory is also convoluted and confusing, Mornell said. "What you're touching on is the tip of a very complicated iceberg which I know I don't completely understand."

Particularly among women patients, Mornell often encounters a series of symptoms: poor concentration; eating or drinking too much; sleep disruption; a general blue view of the world. Taken together, the symptomatology points to depression. "When you start taking a history," said Mornell, "men or the lack of men are one aspect of that history."

In the Wrong Office

But that issue, he said, is seldom what sends them to the therapist's office in the first place. "If somebody came to me and said they wanted to find a man, I would say you're in the wrong office." In any case, said Mornell, in treatment, "I think, you get off how-do-I-find-a-man very quickly, and touch upon what kind of men have been there—and therefore what kind you want."

Among many successful women he has treated, "one theme that often emerges," Mornell said, "is that they've often had alcoholic fathers. What they grew up doing was learning to be perfect, to be successful, to be in control. Control becomes an important theme because somebody in the family was wildly out of control.

Only Her Hairdresser Knows

Several studies over the years have concluded that single women are happier than their married sisters. But, this flies in the face of experience for Nancy Stapleton, a hairdresser, who listens to the stories that women reserve for their psychiatrists and the people who snip or curl their hair.

"They seem to feel they're missing something and they're very distracted by looking for a man," Ms. Stapleton said of her single clients. "You remind them that they're very successful and they say, 'Yeah, but. . . .' Married women don't have as many 'Yeah, buts'—or at least they don't verbalize them."

Jane Gross, *The New York Times*, April 28, 1987.

"It becomes very complicated," he said, "as you take it down from attraction to unavailable men into what you can control. And in any good relationship, one party or the other is at some point going to have to give up control."

In various forms, control is an issue that often surfaces in psychotherapy. For single women vexed by their status, Janice Lieberman suggests, the control question can be particularly confounding.

"If there is something wrong with me, then I can change it, and it is a controllable thing," Lieberman said. "If it's out there, and you can't change it, then it's not controllable." An actual shortage of available men, she reasons, is not controllable.

Women become desperate, Lieberman said, grabbing at the nearest available male straw. "You heard about the woman who moves into an apartment, and meets the guy next door?" she asked. The man calmly tells his new neighbor about his sordid past as a bank robber, a murderer, an embezzler and a tax evader. "'So,' she says, 'are you single?'"

Among women longing for a satisfying relationship, Robin Norwood's giant best-seller, "Women Who Love Too Much" (Tarcher Press), seems to have ignited a nationwide brush fire. On any evening of the week, women across the country gather in homes, classrooms, church halls to examine the phenomenon of excessive—and what they call addictive—love.

Therapy Groups

Though she has adapted the term slightly, calling her groups Women Who Give Too Much, Hermosa Beach psychotherapist Myrna Miller now has well over 50 such women meeting in weekly and bi-weekly groups. Recently, she filled a classroom in a Manhattan Beach adult school with 23 women (and one man) eager to understand the "too much" phenomenon, anxious to build a solid relationship. "I've never had turnouts week after week like I do now," Miller said. "It's become almost like a movement."

Santa Barbara psychotherapist Norwood takes a cautious view of the proliferation of groups ostensibly inspired by her book. "The book is misunderstood a lot," she said. "There are therapists out there teaching classes where the bottom line is how to find a man, and it's not about that." Norwood's book, as well as most of her practice, she said, deals primarily with "women who are in relationships with men who are addictive."

Still, Norwood in no way disputes the distress, even despair and desperation, that sends these women into such gatherings. "We pursue relationships the way people used to pursue religion," she said. "The irony is that women who don't have a man think they'd be fine if they had one, and vice versa."

In "Too Many Women" (Sage Publications, 1983), a book he co-wrote with his late wife Marcia Gutentag, University of Houston professor of psychology and education Paul Secord called attention to "The fact that sex ratios have changed dramatically in the

United States from 1960 to 1970, from having an adequate supply of men to an inadequate supply."

He attributes this phenomenon to what he calls "the marriage squeeze," or the fact that women have tended to marry men several years their senior. As divorce rates have climbed and birth rates have dropped, the practice has continued, leaving fewer men in the so-called "eligible" category. Soaring incomes have narrowed the marital choices for these women still further, since the same tradition that condones a man's right to choose a partner of a lower social and economic status essentially forbids the same practice by a woman.

According to Secord's sex-ratio thesis, "when you have a surplus of men, then relationships between men and women are very different. Men court women, and are willing to make a long-term commitment. Women are also apt to be relatively content with the marital role, and you have a moral tradition that expresses strong sanctions against things like adultery or premarital sex, especially for women."

But a surplus of women, he said, means that "everything changes. Men tend to have more alternative relationships with women. They are less likely to make commitments to women, and more apt to have higher divorce rates.". . .

Psychotherapist Diana Adile Kirschner, co-director of the Institute for Comprehensive Family Therapy in Spring House, Pa., says her single female clients are "highly motivated," commuting from as far as Boston and New York to undergo treatment.

"These are women who have master's degrees and Ph.D.'s," she said. "They are lawyers, they are women who are into management-level stuff in corporations, and they are doing quite well. At this point in their life, they could care less about career. They don't want to hear about advancing."

Many, Kirschner said, "have opted for a career, then turn around and find themselves devoid of eligible men, and in a position where they haven't developed certain skills and arenas in order to pursue men and connect to them."

The Return to Traditional Values

Kirschner focuses her treatment in the context of cultural norms. "We are returning to a traditional value system," she said, "and at the same time, I really believe that to a certain degree there are actual biologically based yearnings to reproduce and so forth." Exploring her clients' histories, she said "generally, what you do find is that there is something wrong psychologically."

During therapy she strives for a "corrective relationship," or "reparenting," that includes homework, directives and role-modeling from women who have combined marriage and career. Kirschner also concentrates on confidence, a quality she contends "goes back to earlier programming in the family. These women don't have it. They can be confident handling difficult business interplay, they can be brilliant in the courtroom, and you put them in a social situation with a man and they are absolutely terrified."

Kirschner is optimistic. She emphasizes that "the reality is that there are very, very few men statistically," but adds, "the other side of that is that there are some."

Janice Lieberman is less sanguine. "You've got to realize it's a needle-in-the-haystack thing," the New York psychoanalyst said. "If you keep getting caught in the hay, then you can't go on."

Her paper for the American Psychological Association confronted this question head-on, then went on to upbraid some members of her profession for failing to acknowledge this condition adequately. Wrote Lieberman: "The male shortage is a fact that is commonly denied by society and by psychoanalysts. I believe that this denial stimulates self-image difficulties in single females."

In her New York office, Lieberman is more forceful still. "I'm so sick of all this 'Smart Women, Foolish Choices' stuff. The therapists throw it back to these women. They say, it's your fault, you're making the wrong choices." Indeed, said Lieberman, "One therapist even told me, 'If I acknowledge the male shortage, my patients will give up on therapy."

Single herself, Lieberman maintains that too many of her professional colleagues are simply unaware of the horrors of midlife dating and mating. "We tend to deny unpleasant things," she said. "If people are dying at the age of 80, it's a horrible thing, but we can accept it. We do not accept the fact that beautiful, bright women may be very sad because they are never going to find somebody. It argues with a fundamental part of our culture: the promise we have all had that you're going to find somebody."

No Magic Solution

To the dismay of the unmarried woman who would like a prescription, whether for a husband or for a happy life alone, no magical elixir is known to exist. "Therapy is a catalyst, but it's definitely not the panacea," said Ken Druck's wife and fellow psychotherapist, Karen Druck.

"Therapy is a lot of work," she added. "If you really want to make changes, it takes a lot of getting in touch with what basically made you the way you are."

Distinguishing Between Fact and Opinion

This activity is designed to help develop the basic reading and thinking skill of distinguishing between fact and opinion. Consider the following statement as an example: "Working women in the US earn approximately 64 percent of the male wage." This statement is a fact which can be verified. But consider a statement which expresses an opinion about working women: "Women are not appreciated in the work world." Such a statement is clearly an opinion. Many people would agree, but many others would not.

When investigating controversial issues it is important that one be able to distinguish between statements of fact and statements of opinion. It is also important to recognize that not all statements of fact are true. They may appear to be true, but some are based on inaccurate or false information. For this activity, however, we are concerned with understanding the difference between those statements which appear to be factual and those which appear to be based primarily on opinion.

Most of the following statements are taken from the viewpoints in this chapter. Consider each statement carefully. *Mark O for any statement you believe is an opinion or interpretation of facts. Mark F for any statement you believe is a fact.*

If you are doing this activity as a member of a class or group, compare your answers with those of other class or group members. Be able to defend your answers. You may discover that others will come to different conclusions than you. Listening to the reasons others present for their answers may give you valuable insights in distinguishing between fact and opinion.

If you are reading this book alone, ask others if they agree with your answers. You will find this interaction valuable.

O = *opinion*
F = *fact*

1. Women are moving ahead with great vigor and a national commitment not experienced in quite some time.

2. Sally Ride was the first female astronaut to go into space.

3. The divorce rate in the US is now two to twenty times higher than in other rich nations.

4. After divorce, the standard of living of the ex-husband rises 42 percent while that of the ex-wife (and her children) falls 73 percent.

5. The problems of contemporary American women result because the US does less than any other advanced country to make life easier for working mothers.

6. American women are presented with three life paths: the careerist, the housewife, and the superwoman.

7. The price of sacrificing family life to the job is one that most women shy away from in horror.

8. Panaceas do not exist; every lifestyle has its drawbacks and dangers.

9. I really believe that women are better than men, and so I became a feminist.

10. Statistics continue to show increasing numbers of women entering the full-time work force.

11. Women who choose not to become mothers do so out of selfishness and narcissism.

12. Because of the new technologies, men who want children are no longer limited by the fertility of their partners.

13. Women don't want to be made to feel second-rate because they don't have children.

14. The responses to Shere Hite's survey show that most women who become single after a divorce love being on their own.

15. Being alone is not "sad" and "bad," but often very refreshing and enjoyable.

16. Never married or long divorced, a growing number of single women are taking their turmoil to psychologists and psychiatrists.

17. The Harvard study concluded that only 20 percent of white, college-educated women who reach age thirty without marrying can expect to do so.

Periodical Bibliography

The following articles have been selected to supplement the diverse views presented in this chapter.

Mary Anne Dolan "When Feminism Failed," *The New York Times Magazine*, June 26, 1988.

Barbara Ehrenreich "The Next Wave," *Ms.*, July/August 1987.

Leslie Garis "Suburban Classic," *Ms.*, July/August 1987.

Barbara Gruzzuti Harrison "Can *Anyone* Really Have It All?" *Mademoiselle*, December 1988.

Brett Harvey "Childlessness in the 80s," *Cosmopolitan*, October 1986.

Linda Lehrer "More Than She Bargained For," *Ms.*, January/February 1989.

Ed Marciniak "The Impact of the Women's Movement on the Family: A Father's Perspective," *America*, March 7, 1987.

Mary O'Connell "Isn't That Just Like a Woman," *Salt*, March 1988. Available from Claretian Publications, 205 W. Monroe, Chicago, IL 60606.

Jeannie Ralston "When a Woman Does a Man's Job," *McCall's*, October 1988.

Eloise Salholz, et al. "Feminism's Identity Crisis," *Newsweek*, March 31, 1986.

Martha Smilgis "The Dilemmas of Childlessness," *Time*, May 2, 1988.

Ann Snitow "Pages from a Gender Diary," *Dissent*, Spring 1989.

Gloria Steinem "Is a Feminist Ethic the Answer?" *Ms.*, September 1987.

Ruth R. Wisse "Living with Women's Lib," *Commentary*, August 1988.

Georgia Witkin "Woman to Woman," *Health*, July 1988.

Pamela Wong "No Babies!?" *Eternity*, June 1987.

Have Men's Roles Changed for the Better?

Chapter Preface

In putting together this chapter, the editors confronted a problem that characterizes the study of men's roles: There is comparatively little material available about the nature and status of men. In contrast, bookstores and libraries have entire sections devoted to women—their psychology, physiology, and social roles. Magazine stands have rows of magazines devoted to both men's and women's interests. While most women's magazines contain articles about women's roles and women's relationships with other people, only a few men's magazines include these types of articles.

Nevertheless, it is clear that over the past thirty years, many men have been reexamining their roles in society and in their relationships with other people. Men's support groups, first popularized in the 1970s as a response to the women's movement, are found in most large cities, and many more men openly discuss their feelings and their relationships. In recent years, men have also been taking on a more active parenting role, whether from desire or necessity is debated in the following viewpoints.

The authors of the viewpoints in this chapter debate whether men have made significant changes in their lives and whether such changes are beneficial.

"As men loosen up, the rigid self-destructive compulsions . . . will diminish. Men will reconnect with themselves and others."

Men Have Changed for the Better

Herb Goldberg

Herb Goldberg is a well-known psychologist and professor of psychology at California State University in Los Angeles. He is the author of several books, including *The Hazards of Being Male* and *The New Male-Female Relationship*. In the following viewpoint, Goldberg describes the way men can move from destructive traditional roles to more open, relaxed, and balanced roles that will enhance their personal lives and their relationships with other men and women.

As you read, consider the following questions:

1. Near the beginning of this viewpoint is a lengthy quotation from an admired companion of the author. In what ways does this man's account reflect the positive changes Goldberg sees in men?
2. According to many commentators, the "old man" was macho; the "new man" was wimpy. What qualities does Goldberg see in the evolving man he describes in this viewpoint?
3. What behaviors will be discarded with the emergence of the new man, in the author's opinion?

I mentioned to a friend that I was writing a book on "the new hazards of being male." He is a person I admire for his openness and ability to stay rooted and successful in the "real world" while still remaining in touch with and true to his deeper sensibilities and feelings. I am comforted by the way he laughs at the seemingly endless contradictions and paradoxes involved in the business of *being a man*, which often distress me, and by the way he expresses with an easy self-acceptance his sensitivity as well as his crass macho and ego-centered side. . . .

Reviewing a Life of Change

His response, I felt, eloquently captured the experience of many men who have made the matter of exploring and changing their experience as men a central focus in their lives.

Looking at my own life over those ten years, and my struggle to break away from the rigid and deadening patterns I observed in older men and many of my peers, and also to avoid the endless and compelling illusions and images that are the bait for most of us, has given me a keen appreciation of the phrase "the razor's edge"—because that's exactly where I feel I've lived much of that time.

Working to make sure that my personal and inner life is as fully alive and important as the outer one, I often wondered whether I was deluding myself; just trying to be different, superior, or one step ahead—which is classic macho motivation—or if I was unknowingly trying to distance and disconnect, and set myself apart from others.

When I felt I was taking risks and pushing at the traditional boundaries and pressures, I had moments when I wondered whether I was going to go over the edge and do my own brand of macho self-destruction, New Age style. Each time I'd worry that my intuitive sense would fail me, even though it *never* did. Things would always fall into place in a healthier way, though I rarely had the perspective on that until months or more passed by.

Sometimes I'd feel exhilarated and vindicated for trusting that deeper part of myself that pushed me along in spite of the negativity I'd get from some people—and even from myself. There were regularly times too, when I'd feel defeated, disillusioned, and deeply exhausted—and I'd have to be by myself for a while, and shut out the outside input to get the energy going again.

Then there were those times when, like an ex-alcoholic longing to get bombed, I'd want to give in to all the old conditioning—the macho stuff. It seemed simpler to be controlling and dominating, to treat women like sex objects, to hide what I thought and felt, to be tough on my kids Marine Corps-style to get them "ready for life" without worrying about showing compassion or understanding, and generally just play the game of life for the symbols and wins, and not give a damn about the means, or the how's.

Those were the times I felt it would be so much easier to go with the flow and stop messing with the deeper forces of society that move relentlessly on, no matter what any of us thinks or does about them.

Besides, I've also come to know that I'm not that strong. I can't really go too far away from the traditional stuff without getting real tense and scared. In my gut I'm the same as every other man and I try not to forget that I need the games men play just as much as the next guy. I know I'd be bored to death if most men started acting New Age and sensitive. Part of me gets a little ill at the thought.

Even though I know it's dead end and often destructive, part of me loves those macho attitudes—you know, "playing to win," "I'm right, you're wrong," "the truth is out there, let's find it," "money and power are reality—and will make you happy," "look at my expensive new toy," "let's talk about getting laid," "we're the good guys and they're the bad guys," etc. Those games have been going on a long time and so they must be needed—who knows—or maybe they're like training wheels needed temporarily to get us ready for the next stage, whatever *that* is.

Those are my dark moments—but at other times the opening up and letting go of the tight grip makes everything feel so alive and rich, I'd catch glimpses in those times of how it could be in my life.

The hardest thing for me still is to avoid getting caught up in believing that I'm on a mission or a quest for truth or righteousness and that there's an answer somewhere out there to discover that'll make everything fall in place, or that there's a *right way* for men to be and live. I know I'm way off target when it begins to feel like religious preaching.

The New New Man

This may seem unfashionable to state, perhaps even imprudent, but it is true: Men have changed. For the better. Some of them are finally, actually, getting it right. Well, not right—that would be absurd—but *almost* right.

The '80s man has evolved into what you might call the New New Man. This is a man who is too smart to be blatantly macho in the Clint Eastwood mode, too cool to be sensitive in the moist-eyed manner of Phil Donahue. He is beyond chauvinism, beyond earnest empathy. He has combined aspects of Neanderthal man and the painfully introspective "New Man" of the '70s in a way that works.

Karen Heller, *Mademoiselle*, August 1986.

As a practicing psychotherapist for twenty-five years and as a male who has been on a quest for growth and for discovering the deeper psychological realities and undertow that pulls us along, I am keenly aware of the resistances, fear, and self-deception that are part of the process of personal growth and change. In particular, I see the paradox in my profession of psychotherapy where those who are the most defensive, who need help and freeing the most, are the most vehement and combative in resisting and denying that fact. . . .

True change, among groups of individuals, therefore tends to begin with those who are already the most open, who perhaps "need it" the least, and then filters slowly toward the more defensive. We live in a complex time when the forces of growth and change and those that operate counter to it seem to be racing neck and neck. We are not as innocent and open as we used to be, but we are also more realistic in our expectations, and we have to acknowledge the profound complexity and subtlety of the problems we face.

Mapping Change

The psychological growth and evolution of the male ultimately will not be founded in external changes or the discovery of more answers, but rather will involve a lessening of the rigid externalized defensiveness that filters and distorts his internal experience and propels him toward disconnection. Change will mean greater flexibility of response and openness to experience—inner and outer, and social change will come from that. As men loosen up, the rigid self-destructive compulsions that are an expression and by-product of the tensions of externalization and disconnection will diminish. Men will reconnect with themselves and others, and *this process* of lessened defensiveness will transform the external reality.

As rebalancing and internalization occur, there will be a decrease in the need and use of biology for tension reduction, such as drinking, compulsive exercise, disconnected sex, and harmful eating habits that compel him by giving him momentary "excitement" or release. Nor will the need for sleep and the expression of passivity be repressed and remain unfelt in the service of defensive masculine overactivity. The passion and excitement of parental bonding will emerge, and men will be highly involved fathers not because they should be but because of the profound fulfillment it brings.

Furthermore, internalization will diminish the work compulsion (work to escape tension) and the use of TV sports and such to disconnect from personal tension. As the work and achievement compulsion diminish, the capacity to find pleasure and satisfaction in a simpler, more personalized lifestyle will develop; this lifestyle will be less dependent on mechanical toys or high levels of external stimulation for pleasure and escape from boredom.

As men and women rebalance and become capable of relating

to each other as people and friends rather than polarized genders, the need to escape from each other through ritualized, "serious" interaction with a focus on tension-relating distractions (such as ritualized eating, drinking, shopping, television, and "going out") will disappear. Instead, there will be greater capacity for pleasure in playfulness and interaction between them.

Overall, the *experience* of an undistorted reality will once again motivate the nonpolarized male. How things feel, not how they look or how they allow one to escape internal tension, will be the standard for making choices.

The Changing Male

Specifically, in summary,

1. The psychological evolution of the male is not a return to traditional role playing in the nostalgic belief that things were better then; nor is it a New Age fantasy of total male sensitivity, love, and gentleness and an idealistic ideology, Utopian vision, or pursuit of abstract truths.

Rather, it is a movement away from the defensive, rigid, insatiable conditioning that perhaps was once functional for men but now only serves to press them relentlessly into narrow, rigid patterns of behavior that produce their psychological or inner death in the service of a pursuit of an externalized fulfillment and satisfaction that can *never* happen.

New Freedom for Men

These are perilous times to be a man in America. There are forces afoot that have changed men's sense of themselves, blurring what once seemed clear-cut modes and models of manhood. John Wayne is dead, and we have not yet picked his stand-in.

In that state of affairs there may lie some new degree of freedom for men willing to seize the opportunity. As the hard-and-fast model of masculinity gives way, it makes room for a greater range of humanness.

Perry Garfinkel, *In a Man's World*, 1985.

---

2. *What* a man does, does not define him as "macho"; rather, the degree of the unconscious defensiveness that produces his disconnection defines him. A poet or humanist is as likely to be "macho" as a football player or policeman—only with a different surface manifestation or outward disguise.

It is this underlying, polarized defensiveness that ultimately makes the personal experience of all externalized men the same—be they workaholic, alcoholic, abstraction-fixated intellectuals, crusading "househusbands," brilliant scientists or physicians, or successful businessmen.

3. The lessened defensiveness of the male would connect him to his *experience* of life and make him less vulnerable to engaging in defensive, destructive pursuits that are superficially designed to validate him as a man but in deeper ways serve only to reduce the constant buildup of tension that occurs as the distance from the personal and internal increases.

The lessened defensiveness will diminish the power of the images and symbols of masculinity as motivators of his behavior.

Male/Female Relationships

4. As relationships between men and women become person to person, rather than polarized object to polarized object, it will become possible to see how the sexes equally generate and reinforce the behaviors in each other that they resent and feel victimized by.

Furthermore, as defensive polarization diminishes between the sexes, romantic attraction as a basis for entering relationships will lose its power—in fact will become anathema. Simply put, romance won't feel good because to be with one's polar opposite, once its reality is undistortedly experienced, will be unattractive if not repulsive. The roller coaster of romantically founded relationships, from romantic euphoria to boredom and then rage, will fade.

5. The lure of "excitement" that produces a lemming-like attraction in men for self-destruction and oblivion (the oblivion of drunkenness, disconnected sex, physical violence, attraction to symbolic experiences, the "thrill" of danger, etc.) because of the urgent and unconscious need to reduce the tension of internalization will diminish. Self-awareness and self-care in the positive sense of creating conscious control by allowing men to experience themselves without distortion will increase.

In the past, when disconnection approximated totalness, the hunger for excitement (distraction and tension release) in relationship and life-choices increased, as did the tendency to feel bored and numbed when the craving for release and stimulation was temporarily blocked. This unconsciously pushed men into their unstoppable self-destructive patterns.

Male Relationships

6. The psychological evolution of the male will alter the traditional way men relate to each other—guarded, self-protective, and distrustful. As masculine defensiveness declines, the distortions and projections produced by defensively externalized aggression and autonomy, which cause him to be distrustful and chronically "on guard," will diminish. It will become possible to separate out real danger from the projected danger that has motivated most men and that is a self-created, self-fulfilling prophecy.

7. Finally, it will become possible to avoid the "web of paradox" that characterizes the lives of traditionally conditioned men, such that the more they fulfill masculine expectations, the farther away the supposed rewards seem to be. Feelings of failure, disillusionment, and a sense of being defeated by the "lies of society," which constitute the inner experience of even the most successful of men who are out-of-touch with their defensive process, will diminish. Fulfillment and satisfaction will become controllable by-products, not wished-for elusive quests.

"It is not enough, anymore, to ask that men become more like women; we should ask instead that they become more like what both men and women might be."

Men Have Changed for the Worse

Barbara Ehrenreich

Barbara Ehrenreich is a feminist author who has written for numerous magazines, including *Ms.*, *The Nation*, *Mother Jones*, and *The New York Review of Books*. She is the author of *Hearts of Men: American Dreams and the Flight from Commitment* and *Remaking Love: The Feminization of Sex*. In the following viewpoint, she reflects on the changes she sees in men as a result of the women's movement. She states that many men have changed in the ways women wanted, and yet the changes may not be for the better. She views "the new man" as shallow, vain, and status-conscious rather than as the equal partner women envisioned.

As you read, consider the following questions:

1. What three traits characterize "the new man," according to Ehrenreich?
2. The "new man" described by Ehrenreich is primarily a member of the upwardly mobile, young, unmarried, professional class. Does she ascribe the same new-man qualities to men of other classes? Why or why not?

There have been waves of "new women" arriving on cue almost every decade for the last 30 years or so—from the civic-minded housewife, to the liberated single, to the dressed-for-success executive. But men, like masculinity itself, were thought to be made of more durable stuff. Change, if it came at all, would come only in response to some feminine—or feminist—initiative.

In the 1970's, for example, it had become an article of liberal faith that a new man would eventually rise up to match the new feminist woman, that he would be more androgynous than any "old" variety of man, and that the change, which was routinely expressed as an evolutionary leap from John Wayne to Alan Alda, would be an unambiguous improvement.

Today, a new man is at last emerging. . . .

I see a change in the popular images that define masculinity, and I see it in the men I know, mostly in their 30's, who are conscious of possessing a sensibility and even a way of life that is radically different from that of their fathers. These men have been, in a word, feminized, but without necessarily becoming more feminist. In fact, I do not think that those of us who are feminists either can or, for the most part, would want to take credit for the change. . . .

The Shallow New Man

For the most part, the new men one is likely to encounter today in our urban singles' enclaves (or on the pages of a men's fashion magazine) bear no marks of arduous self-transformation. No ideological struggle—pro- or antifeminist—seems to have shaped their decision to step out of the traditional male role; in a day-to-day sense, they simply seem to have other things on their minds. Stephen G. Dent, for example, is a 29-year-old member of a private New York investment firm. . . . Dent defines his goals in terms of his career and making money, "because that's how the score is kept." To this end, he rations his time carefully: More than 10 hours a day for work and approximately half an hour a day for calisthenics and running. Women definitely figure in his life, and he is pleased to have reduced the time spent arranging dates to an efficient five minutes a day.

Dent feels that "sensitivity is very important to being a man. It's easy for people to become so caught up in their career challenges that they don't stop to be sensitive to certain things." By that he said he meant "being able to appreciate things that girls appreciate. Like being able to window-shop, for example. An insensitive guy probably won't stop and look at a dress in a window." . . .

I do not think there is a one-word explanation—like feminism—for the new manhood. Rather, I would argue, at least a part of what looks new has been a long time in the making and predates the recent revival of feminism by many decades. Male resistance to marriage, for example, is a venerable theme in American culture, whether whether in the form of low humor (Li'l Abner's annual Sadie Hawkins Day escape from Daisy Mae) or high art (the perpetual bachelorhood of heroes like Ishmael or the Deerslayer). As Leslie Fiedler argued in 1955 in "An End to Innocence," the classics of American literature are, by and large, propaganda for boyish adventure rather than the "mature heterosexuality" so admired by mid-20th-century psychoanalysts.

The sources of male resentment are not hard to find: In a frontier society, women were cast as the tamers and civilizers of men; in an increasingly urban, industrial society, they became, in addition, the financial dependents of men. From a cynical male point

Charley Murphy, *Men Talk,* Vol. 12, No. 3, Twin Cities Men's Center News. Reprinted with permission.

of view, marriage was an arrangement through which men gave up their freedom for the dubious privilege of supporting a woman. Or, as H.L. Mencken put it, marriage was an occasion for a man "to yield up his liberty, his property and his soul to the first woman who, in despair of finding better game, turns her appraising eye upon him." After all, the traditional female contributions to marriage have been menial, like housework, or intangible, like emotional support. The husband's traditional contribution, his wage or at least a good share of it, was indispensable, measurable and, of course, portable—whether to the local tavern or the next liaison.

But before male resentment of marriage could become anything more than a cultural undercurrent of grumbling and misogynist humor, three things had to happen. First, it had to become not only physically possible but reasonably comfortable for men to live on their own. In 19th-century homes, even simple tasks like making breakfast or laundering a shirt could absorb long hours of labor. Bachelorhood was a privileged state, sustained by servants or a supply of maiden sisters; the average man either married or settled for boardinghouse life. As a second condition for freedom from marriage, men had to discover better ways of spending their money than on the support of a family. The historic male alternatives were drinking and gambling, but these have long been associated, for good reason, with precipitate downward mobility. Third, the penalties levied against the nonconforming male—charges of immaturity, irresponsibility and latent sexual deviancy—had to be neutralized or inverted.

Within the last few decades, all of these conditions for male freedom have been met. Domestic appliances, plus a rapid rise in the number of apartment dwellings and low-price restaurants made it possible for a man of average means to contemplate bachelorhood as something other than extended vagrancy. As Philip Roth observed of the 1950's in "My Life as a Man," it had become entirely feasible—though not yet acceptable—for a young man "to eat out of cans or in cafeterias, sweep his own floor, make his own bed and come and go with no binding legal attachments." In addition, that decade saw two innovations that boosted the potential autonomy of even the most domestically incompetent males—frozen food and drip-dry clothes. . . .

The Changing View of Being Alone

No sooner had the new, more individualistic male life style become physically possible and reasonably attractive than it began also to gain respectability. Starting in the 1960's, expert opinion began to retreat from what had been a unanimous endorsement of marriage and traditional sex roles. Psychology, transformed by the human-potential movement, switched from "maturity" as a standard for mental health to the more expansive notion of "growth." "Maturity" had been a code word, even in the professional literature, for marriage and settling down; "growth" implied a plurality of legitimate options, if not a positive imperative to keep moving from one insight or experience to the next. Meanwhile, medicine—alarmed by what appeared to be an epidemic of male heart disease—had begun to speak of men as the "weaker sex" and to hint that men's greater vulnerability was due, in part, to the burden of breadwinning.

The connection was scientifically unwarranted, but it cast a lasting shadow over conventional sex roles: The full-time homemaker, who had been merely a parasite on resentful males, became a potential accomplice to murder, with the hard-working, role-abiding breadwinner as her victim. By the 1970's, no salvo of male resentment—or men's liberation—failed to mention that the cost of the traditional male role was not only psychic stagnation and sexual monotony, but ulcers, heart disease and an early death.

New Men Fleeing from Commitment

The local newspaper headlined recently, "Surrounded by wimps who are lazy, unassertive and undependable, and always wanting you to take the lead." In her article, writer Deborah Laake defines a wimp as "a wormboy, someone who does not want to carry the ball. A wormboy watches his life like a movie and flees when it makes demands on him. He is passive. He cannot be depended on during tough times." She recounts a theme that I have heard recently from many women. "Men talk a good line. They seem like equal partners to the emerging "strong" woman. Yet when the relationship begins to touch on intimacy, these same strong men turn mushy, insecure and indecisive. If pushed, they tend to withdraw and flee from the relationship."

Jed Diamond, *Men Talk*, Fall 1988.

Today, the old aspersions directed at the unmarried male have largely lost their sting. Images of healthy, hard-working men with no apparent attachments abound in the media, such as, for example, the genial-looking bicyclist in the advertisement for *TV Guide*, whose caption announces invitingly, "Zero Dependents."

Perhaps most important, a man can now quite adequately express his status without entering into a lifelong partnership with a female consumer. The ranch house on a quarter-acre of grass is still a key indicator of social rank, but it is not the only one. A well-decorated apartment, a knowledge of wines or a flair for cooking can be an equally valid proof of middle-class (or upper-middle-class) membership, and these can now be achieved without

126

the entanglement of marriage or the risk of being thought a little "queer." . . .

The Myth of Sensitivity

Finally, there is that most promising of new male traits—sensitivity. . . . For more than a decade, sensitivity has been supposed to be the inner quality that distinguishes an educated, middle-class male from his unregenerate blue-collar brothers: "They" are Archie Bunkers; "we" are represented by his more liberal, articulate son-in-law. As thoughtful a scholar as Joseph H. Pleck, program director of the Wellesley College Center for Research on Women, who has written extensively on the male sex role, simply restates the prejudice that blue-collar men are trapped in the "traditional" male role, "where interpersonal and emotional skills are relatively undeveloped."

No one, of course, has measured sensitivity and plotted it as a function of social class, but Judith Langer, a market researcher, reports that, in her studies, it is blue-collar men who express less "traditional" or "macho" values, both in response to products and in speaking of their relationships with women. "Certainly I'm not suggesting that *only* blue-collar men show such openness," she concludes, "but rather that the stereotype of blue-collar workers can be limited."

To the extent that some special form of sensitivity is located in educated and upwardly mobile males, I suspect it may be largely a verbal accomplishment. The vocabulary of sensitivity, at least, has become part of the new masculine politesse; certainly no new man would admit to being insensitive or willfully "out of touch with his feelings." Quite possibly, as sensitivity has spread, it has lost its moorings in the therapeutic experience and come to signify the heightened receptivity associated with consumerism: a vague appreciation that lends itself to aimless shopping.

None of these tastes and proclivities of the new man serve to differentiate him from the occasional affluent woman of his class. Women in the skirted-suit set tend to postpone marriage and childbearing, to work long hours and budget their time scrupulously; to follow fashions in food and clothing, and to pursue fitness, where once slimness would have sufficed. As Paul Fussell observes in "Class: A Guide Through the American Status System," the upper middle class and I would include all those struggling to remain in the upper part of the crumbling middle class—is "the most 'role-reversed' of all." And herein lies one of the key differences betwen the old and the new versions of the American ideal of masculinity: The old masculinity defined itself against femininity and expressed anxiety—over conformity or the rat race—in metaphors of castration. The new masculinity seems more concerned to preserve the tenuous boundary between the classes than to delineate distinctions between the sexes. Today's upper-middle-class or upwardly mobile male is less terrified about moving down the slope toward genderlessness than he is about simply moving down-scale. . . .

Do Women Like the New Man?

The question for feminists is: Is this new man what we wanted? Just a few years ago, feminists were, on the whole, disposed to welcome any change in a direction away from traditional manhood. Betty Friedan, in *The Second Stage*, saw "the quiet movement of American men" as "a momentous change in their very identity as men, going beyond the change catalyzed by the women's movement," and she suggested that it might amount to a "massive, evolutionary development."

That was written in a more innocent time, when feminists were debating the "Cinderella complex," as Colette Dowling termed women's atavistic dependencies on men, rather than the "Peter Pan syndrome," which is how one best seller describes the male aversion to commitment. There has been a small flurry of feminist attacks on the new male or on assorted new-male characteristics.

The *Washington City Paper* carried a much-discussed and thoroughly acid article on "Wormboys," described by writer Deborah Laake as men who are "passive" in relation to women, who "shrink from marriage" and children, and "cannot be depended on during tough times." According to one woman she quotes, these new men are so fearful of commitment that they even hesitate to ask a woman out to dinner: "They're more interested in saying, 'Why don't you meet me for a drink?' because it implies so much less commitment on their part." I wouldn't exaggerate the extent of the backlash, but it has been sufficient to send several male colleagues my way to ask, with nervous laughter, whether I was writing a new contribution to the "war on wimps."

I don't blame them for being nervous. My generation of feminists insisted that men change, but we were not always directive—or patient—enough to say how. We applauded every sign of male sensitivity or growth as if it were an evolutionary advance. We even welcomed the feminization of male tastes, expecting that the man who was a good cook and a tasteful decorator at 25 would be a devoted father and partner in midlife. We did not understand that men were changing along a trajectory of their own and that they might end up being less like what we *are* than like what we were once expected to be—vain and shallow and status-conscious.

But . . . it is important to emphasize that if we don't like the new male, neither are we inclined to return to the old one. If the new man tends to be a fop, the old man was (and is), at worst, a tyrant and a bully. At best, he was merely dull, which is why, during the peak years of male conformity, when the test of manhood lay in being a loyal breadwinner, so many of us lusted secretly for those few males—from James Dean and Elvis Presley to Jack Kerouac—who represented unattainable adventure. In our fantasies, at least, we did not want to enslave men, as *Playboy*'s writers liked to think, but to share the adventure.

What Might Be

Today, thanks to the women's movement, we have half a chance: Individualism, adventure—that "battle with the world" that Friedan held out to women more than 20 years ago—is no longer a male prerogative. But if it is to be a shared adventure, then men will have to change, and change in ways that are not, so far, in evidence. Up until now, we have been content to ask them to become more like women—less aggressive, more emotionally connected with themselves and others. That message, which we once thought revolutionary, has gotten lost in the androgynous drift of the consumer culture. It is the marketplace that calls most clearly for men to be softer, more narcissistic and receptive, and the new man is the result.

So it is not enough, anymore, to ask that men become more like women; we should ask instead that they become more like what both men and women *might* be. My new man, if I could design one, would be capable of appreciation, sensitivity, intimacy— values that have been, for too long, feminine. But he would also be capable of commitment, to use that much-abused word, and I mean by that commitment not only to friends and family but to a broad and generous vision of how we might all live together. As a feminist, I would say that vision includes equality between men and women and also—to mention a social goal that seems almost to have been forgotten—equality among men.

"Everyone knew that men not only had freedom of choice but freedom to grant permission to women to make choices."

Men Have Not Changed

Sey Chassler

Sey Chassler is consulting editor to *Parade* magazine and vice president of the Child Care Action Campaign. In the following viewpoint, he reflects on his own attitudes and behavior toward women. He concludes that even with the supposed vast consciousness-raising of the past thirty years, not much has really changed. He believes that most men, like himself, may pay lip-service to the equality of men and women, but their actions betray their real belief—that women are men's subordinates.

As you read, consider the following questions:

1. The author asks himself, "Why did I have the choice of doing or not doing the dishes, while my wife did not?" What is his answer?
2. Chassler does not believe things will ever change: "The world belongs to men." Do you agree or disagree with him? What evidence from the world around you supports your view?
3. Do you think articles like Chassler's will make any difference to male readers' attitudes toward women? Why or why not?

One morning, about 20 years ago, my wife and I were arguing about whether or not I ever listened to her. It was one of those arguments that grow into passion and pain and, often, for me at least, into a kind of hysteria. This one became one of those that do not go away with the years. Suddenly, she threw something at me, and said: "From now on you do the shopping, plan the meals, take care of the house, everything. I'm through!"

I was standing in the kitchen looking at the shelves of food, at the oven, at the sink, at the refrigerator, at the cleaning utensils. At my wife.

I Could Not Do It All

My reaction was orgasmic. Somewhere inside of me there was screaming, hurting, a volcanic gush of tears flooded my head and broke down over me. I shook and sobbed. I was terrified. No matter what, I knew I could not handle the burden. I could not do my job and be responsible for the entire household. How could I get through a day dealing with personnel, budgets, manuscripts, art departments, circulation statistics, phone calls, people, agents, management, writers, and *at the same time* plan dinner for tonight and tomorrow night and breakfast and a dinner party Thursday night and shopping for it all and making sure the house is in good shape and the woman who cleans for us is there and on time and the laundry done and the children taken to the doctor, and the children taken care of? How could *any* one person do all that and stay sane? No one could do that properly. No one. Natalie simply watched me for a while. Finally she said: "Okay. Don't worry. I'll keep on doing it." She put on her coat and went to her office.

Despite her simple statement that she would go on doing it, I stood awhile telling myself that no *one* could do all of that. No one. There was a *click* in my head—and it dawned on me that *she* was doing it.

The Invisibility of Women

How invisible my wife's life was to me. How invisible to men women are.

Shortly afterward, in 1963 or 1964, not long after *The Feminine Mystique* was published, Betty Friedan and I were invited to speak to the nation's largest organization of home economists. As executive editor of *Redbook* magazine, I was asked to talk about the magazine's view of women. Betty was talking about the thesis of her book—that all American women were trapped in their homebound positions and that women's magazines, among others, put out propaganda to keep them trapped.

I had read *The Feminine Mystique*, of course, and felt I was fully prepared to answer it and, thereby, to defend not only *Redbook* from Friedan's attack but to defend American women, as well.

In mid-speech I proclaimed that, despite what Friedan had written, women, in this day and in this country, were free to be whatever they wished to be, that they were not children to be told what they might and might not do, that they could work at whatever profession they chose or whatever job, that they were free to be wives if they wished, and truck drivers if they wished, and mothers if they wished or homemakers if they wished. The list was growing longer and the speech was getting more and more impassioned in its proclamation of freedoms. I paused and waited for the applause. I had, after all, just proclaimed freedom throughout the land! I looked out at the audience. The hall was silent.

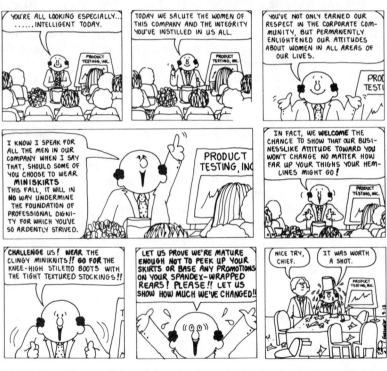

My pause became a dark empty cavern, and I could feel myself groping for a way out, wondering what had gone awry. I felt naked, stripped bare before 800 women. I could not understand what I had said that was wrong. Looking for comfort, I thought of my wife, and—*click!* I suddenly realized that my wife was a woman who was free to choose a career and *had*—but who also had delayed that career until her children—*her* children!—were in school. She was not as free as I thought, nor was any married woman. . . .

At home one night after dinner, I sat down to read the paper, as usual, while my wife went into the kitchen to do the dishes. I could see her in the kitchen. She looked happy, or at least not unhappy, there in the pretty kitchen she had designed—and she was probably appreciating the change of pace after a hard day as chief of service in a mental hospital dealing with a staff of three or four dozen employees and a hundred or more patients, some of whom threatened her from time to time. Yes, she was using the time well, since she had no hobbies to break the tension. I was feeling comfortably and happily married, when—*click!*—the view changed, and I saw a hardworking woman doing something she'd rather not be doing just now.

When my wife finished and sat down near me, I kissed her with a special tenderness, I thought. She didn't. As a matter of fact, she turned the other cheek. Something was going on in both our heads.

Male Choice

The next night *I* decided to do the dishes and she read the paper. At the sink, I began to think about male arrogance. Why did I have the choice of doing or not doing the dishes, while my wife did not? By the same token, why had she had to wait until our children were in school to exercise her "free" choice of working at her career? Our jobs were equally pressured and difficult (hers more harrowing than mine) and yet, if I chose to sit and read after dinner, I could. She could not, unless I decided she could by *offering* to do the dishes. . . .

I felt I had caught the edge of an insight about the condition of women and while I wanted to, I found I couldn't discuss it with men; it made them uneasy and defensive. They'd fight off the conversation. They'd say things like "But that's the way it is supposed to be, Sey. Forget it!" After a while, I began to feel like one of those people who carry signs in the street announcing the end of the world. Pretty soon I got defensive, too—and my questions produced terrific dinner-table fights with other male guests. The women almost always remained silent, seeming to enjoy watching the men wrestle. The men were convinced that I was a nut. And several, including my father, accused me of "coming out for women," because in my job as editor of a women's magazine that would be "smart" and "profitable."

I certainly couldn't talk to any woman directly, because I was embarrassed. I didn't believe women would tell me the truth—and, more important, I was not going to let them know I was worried or thinking about the matter or afraid to find the answer.

If you are one of those men who feel trapped by women, who think they are fine for sex but interfere with living, all of the above may not be very clear to you. Maybe the following will set some clicks off for you. . . .

Sexist Contests

As reported in *The Wall Street Journal* in December 1983, in a story on sex discrimination in law firms, King & Spalding of Atlanta had a company picnic. Initially proposed for the festivities was a "wet T-shirt" contest, but, in the end, the firm merely decided to hold a bathing-suit competition. It was open only to the company's women summer associates. A third-year law student from Harvard University won. While awarding her the prize, a partner of the firm said, "She has the body we'd like to see more of." King & Spalding is no small company. Among its clients are Coca-Cola Company, Cox Broadcasting Corporation, and General Motors.

The question here is: why would a Harvard law student parade around in a bathing suit for a bunch of rowdy male lawyers? It's easy to say she was looking for a job with a good firm. Since the bathing-suit competition incident, King & Spalding has promised it will not practice sex discrimination, and the student who won the contest has agreed to join the firm. But the question remains: why would she enter such a contest? . . .

Dominance. Male dominance. Someone calls the shots, someone else does as she is told.

Roles Have Not Changed

The labor market behavior on the part of wives has done little to change the differentiation of family roles or the attitudes of most families. Husbands are still seen as the breadwinners, or at least the primary breadwinners, while wives are still responsible for the home and children even if their role set has expanded. . . .

The changes in women's roles—particularly their employment outside the home—have not been matched by changes in men's roles.

Audrey D. Smith and William J. Reid, *Role-Sharing Marrriage*, 1986.

What men see when they look out and about are creatures very like themselves—in charge of everything. What women see when they look out and about is that the creatures in charge of everything are *unlike* themselves.

If you are a man, think of a world, your world, in which for everything you own or do or think you are accountable to women. Women are presidents, bankers, governors, door holders, traffic cops, airline pilots, bosses, supervisors, landlords. Shakespeare.

The whole structure is completely dominated by women. Your doctor, your lawyer, your priest, minister, rabbi are women. The figure on the cross is a woman. God is a woman. Every authoritative voice and every authoritative image is the image and voice of women: Buddha, Mohammed, Moses, Matthew, Luke, Paul, the guy who does the voice-over on the commercial and Ben Franklin—all are women. So are Goliath and David. So are the Supreme Court, the tax collector, the head of the CIA, the mechanic who fixes your transmission, the editor of your daily newspaper, the doctor who handed you to your mother. Jack the Giant Killer. Walter Mondale. St. Patrick. Ronald Reagan is a woman. Walter Cronkite is a woman. George Steinbrenner is a woman. Think of such a world. The Pope is a woman. JR is a woman. Casper Weinberger. Think of yourself in such a world. Think of your father in it. Think of *him* as a woman. Think about it.

Don't just brush it off, for Mary's sake—think about it.

What would you say to your boss if he announced that he was thinking of having a wet-jockstrap contest at the company picnic? Or if your best girl asked you to take your pants off, while you crawled under the car to have a look at the manifold? What would you say? If your wife asked you to stay at home with the baby or to meet the plumber or to do the shopping or to clean the toilet bowl some day, what would you say?

Click?

The Husband's Dominance

My wife and I have been married 41 years. We think of ourselves as being happily married—and we are. But the dominance is there. It means that in my relationship with my wife, I am almost totally the boss. When we have a discussion (that's marital-ese for argument), more often than not it is I who declare when the end of it arrives. If we make a plan together and she does most of the work on the plan, it is given to me for approval. If I do most of the work on the plan, I submit it to her for her information. If she agrees to the plan, she'll say, "Good, should we do it?" If *I* agree to the plan, I'll say, "Good, let's go." That doesn't mean that I make all the decisions, control all the funds, make all the choices, talk louder than she does. I don't have to. It simply means that I do not have to ask my wife for permission to do anything. Whether she does or says anything about it or not, everything my wife does is to a large extent qualified by what I think or will think. In effect, she must ask my permission. What's more, as husband, I seem—no matter how I try to avoid it—to assign all the jobs in our family. In effect, I win all the arguments—even the ones we don't have. That's emotional dominance—and it means that everything that occurs between us, everything we do together, is monitored by me.

135

Once during a lecture tour I was talking to undergraduates at the University of Indiana about the Women's Movement and how important it is. One of the women, a senior, asked a question and then she said: "I don't want to get married when I graduate. I want to be someone." *Click.*

That statement haunts me. I never had to say anything like that. I had always thought I would get married *and* be somebody. What's more, I took it for granted that my wife would be responsible for the family in addition to her job. I would love and care for my children, but I wouldn't have to deal with their phone calls at the office. They'd call my wife at the office. That's what mommies are for, aren't they? No one had to tell the children that. No one had to tell me that. No one had to tell my wife that. We all *knew* it. And everyone knew that men not only had freedom of choice but freedom to grant permission to women to make choices. . . .

Men Make the Moves

The Women's Movement has made some remarkable changes in our lives, but it hasn't changed the position of the male much at all. Men still make the moves. They are the ones who, in their own good time, move in. And in their own good time, move out. Someone makes the rules, someone else does as she is told. . . .

I was sitting with a man friend, when, in relation to nothing in particular, he said: "Guys get to be heroes. Girls get to be cheerleaders. Guys get to be dashing womanizers, great studs. Women get to be sluts."

Click.

A lot of us men think of these things and we hurt when we do. And a lot of us—most of us—simply don't think of these things. Or we think of them as something that will go away—the complaints from women will go away, as they always seem to.

Still, as men, we recognize Freud's question: "Good God, what do women *want?*"

To be heard.

My 89-year-old mother, married 65 years to my 89-year-old father, says to him, "Someday you'll let me talk when I want to." . . .

Will men ever appreciate fully what women are saying?

I don't think I will ever, fully. No matter what clicks in my head.

The world belongs to men. It is completely dominated by us—and by our images.

> *"Men gradually began to think of themselves as parents in their own right and not just substitutes."*

Men Are Enjoying
the New Fatherhood Role

Kyle D. Pruett

Kyle D. Pruett, a noted child psychologist, is a professor of psychiatry at the Yale University Child Study Center in New Haven, Connecticut. In 1982, he began a five-year study of families in which the fathers are the primary caretakers of the children. In the following viewpoint, he describes some of the findings from that study. Pruett's research, as well as his personal experience, have convinced him of the benefits, to both father and child, of the nurturing father.

As you read, consider the following questions:

1. Pruett argues that new research finds that fathers are just as "naturally" responsive to children as are mothers. Why then, according to Pruett, have fathers so rarely been the primary caretakers of the children?
2. According to Pruett, what are some of the ways active fathering and active mothering differ?
3. What are some of the benefits Pruett ascribes to active fathering?

In spite of all we feel we've accomplished as a society in encouraging men and women to evolve to their fullest humanity, the evolution continues at a glacial pace. Sacred stabilities still shape our views, social policies, habits, and expectations. They are unmistakably present in frequent, recognizable justifications like, "While it is fine, even wonderful, for women to work, their only *real* job is to be a mother" or "While it is fine, yes wonderful, for a man actively to father and raise his children, his only *real* job is to make money and support his family."

The time to change this message has arrived. . . .

Anthropologists and ethologists such as Konrad Lorenz have suggested that the very nature and appearance of the human infant elicits powerful nurturing responses in both men and women.

Differences Between Moms and Dads

If we can believe, as the research suggests we should, that men are not bad for or dangerous around babies (as was the prevailing wisdom twenty years ago) how then do they behave with babies? Here again the research speaks loud and clear. In a 1975 study, Parke and Sawin studied first-time parents and found intriguing, important differences in the way fathers and mothers handle their children. Mothers picked up their babies and held them intimately close to neck and breasts, handling and often talking in a gentle, soft, low-keyed manner. Fathers seemed to want always to *do* something with their babies when they picked them up. They were playful and provocative, tickling, nudging and roughhousing, somewhat more with their sons than their daughters, though not in every case. These findings were later expanded to include the observation that fathers used more play and games in general than did mothers. . . .

Babies Like Dad

Do the babies respond to their fathers' novel, complex, interactive style? You bet they do. There have been several studies of fathers and their infants which focus on the effect the baby and father have upon each other. A group of Harvard pediatricians, led by T. Berry Brazelton and Michael Yogman, have noticed that by the time babies are eight weeks old, they are already responding quite differently to fathers and mothers. At only six weeks of age, babies will hunch their shoulders and lift their eyebrows, as though in anticipation that "playtime has arrived" when their fathers appear. When the same six-week-olds see or hear mothers, they seem to expect more routine, serious, or functional business, such as feeding or diapering.

Fathers often notice such anticipations (or even invitations) in their babies, and they have a profound effect on them. These face-to-face differences in play, modulation, and verbal and physical contact are mutually appreciated by child, mother, and father, thereby justifying the father's feeling that there is something special afoot here. The infant's skill in evoking and shaping parenting may be more enduringly powerful than either inborn or biological parental predispositions.

The bottom line here seems to be that the father's involvement, undoubtedly promoted by such responses from his baby, has measurable positive effects in its own right on the development of the child. Intellectual competence is one observable effect. Frank Pedersen, psychologist at the National Institute of Child Health and Human Development, has found that the more actively involved a six-month-old baby has been with his or her father, the higher that baby's scores on certain tests of mental and motor development. Similarly, Ross Parke, examining children over the first eight weeks of life, has found that the more fathers were involved in the everyday repetitive (even boring) aspects of care, such as bathing, feeding, dressing, and diapering, the more socially responsive the babies were. In addition, Parke also found such babies were able to withstand stressful situations better. . . .

Fathers Get Involved with Their Kids

So, the babies were doing well. How about the fathers? Did they demonstrate the capacity to nurture another person adequately, to ensure its survival, and to assure its development as a human being? Could they "read" and understand their babies well enough to feed, change, nap, and comfort on time? Would their responses reasonably conform to the baby's needs?

In a word, yes.

Fathers and Children

Fathers are just beginning to understand what mothers have known for years—the wonderful gratification and utter adoration a baby can give, and how it's possible to fall head-over-heels in love with your child.

Ethel Persons, interviewed by Deborah Mason, *Vogue*, May 1988.

Though as a group they achieved the relationship at different rates, all the fathers had formed the deep reciprocal nurturing attachment so critical to the early development of the thriving human baby. The depth and rapidity of the attachment amazed even them. *How* it happened varies, of course, from man to man and baby to baby. . . .

The fathers as a group reported a similar progression of feelings as they gradually took charge of their babies' lives. Most of the families had an initial three- to eight-week period in which the mother was the primary, or at least coequal, caretaker of the infant. Afterward the mother returned to work, career, or school. This was a critical transition for both parents and babies. But a curiously consistent sequence of realizations was reported by the men.

At first, when the everyday troubles began with the crying or inconsolable infant, the father would think to himself, "What would my wife do?" No surprises here.

No Stand-In

The surprises came in the next stage. Anywhere from ten days to a few months later, these men had completely abandoned their mental portrait of themselves as being a "stand-in for mom." Unique caregiving styles flowed forth as the men gradually began to think of themselves as parents in their own right and not just substitutes standing "in loco matris" (in the mother's place). Most of the men kept this feeling to themselves as though they could not quite believe it, or trust it, or maybe shouldn't even have it.

The interactional impact of babies on fathers has, of course, intrigued other researchers. Some tried to find an expression that would adequately describe the father's fascination with his baby. "Engrossment," the word introduced in the early 1970s by psychiatrist Martin Greenberg to encompass the sense of "absorption, preoccupation and interest by the father in the new infant," seems a whispered understatement compared to these fathers' own descriptions of their experiences. These fathers had actively incorporated their infants into their whole lives. They were enraptured *and* enthralled with their babies. There appeared to have been a very literal "taking in" of these babies by their fathers as a profound emotional event.

The fathers also had difficulty believing that they had become so immensely significant to their own infants. A four-month-old girl in the first group stopped eating for two days and developed a week-long sleep disturbance after her father shaved off his beard. She became irritable and inconsolable and avoided her father's gaze when he attempted to comfort her. She would accept her mother's presence and comforting, but only briefly. Only after a neighbor failed to recognize him in the parking lot did it occur to the father that his daughter might be having the same problem. . . .

Changing the Way We View Dads

Changing the way we think of men as fathers is an enormous undertaking. . . . But one hears little hints, sees little clues that the beginning has started. Groups of boys who are popular and masculine bring their Cabbage Patch Dolls to school. Fathers' voices are heard on fast-food radio commercials. Men talk with their children about brushing their teeth on television toothpaste advertisements. Men are photographed with their children in respectful, nurturing, even affectionate poses in the *New York Times'* men's fashion section. Prime-time television sitcoms feature family men who make real decisions for their children, give real help, make real mistakes, and are unabashedly nurturing without being portrayed as powerless martinets. Such evidence, though subtle, is encouragement that profound change may not be impossible.

Men Can Be Good Parents

Of course, men *can* parent, and as well as women. . . .

Not only are more men discovering that they *can* parent, but they are also discovering their capacity for intimacy and affection with their children, the excitement of developing their very own parenting styles instead of miming the styles of their wives and mothers, their enjoyment of growing with their children.

Richard Haddad, in *Men Freeing Men*, 1985.

But the time has come for this change, and the solutions must be real and effective. People laughed at W.C. Fields' jokes about "dog and kid haters" because his humor reflected the diffidence men were supposed to adopt *publicly* toward their children. When it came to being a father in his own family, Fields sent loving letters to his children and longed for their company, writing his daughter after she had borne a son following a difficult labor, "It is impossible, Hat, to tell you how glad I am to know all the worry is over. You are well, ain't it great, Hat? You keep well now and get over this O.K. . . . I suppose all the worst is over, don't discharge nurse or Dr. too soon. . . . Tell me how it all happened, how you feel . . . tell ALL." *That* would not make many people laugh. But it's not funny any more. It's loving and nurturing. Times and fathers have changed.

The paternal child care we see about us reflects a basic change in traditional patterns. This change heralds a shift in values that is real and long overdue. Moreover, it's not just an individual issue for men and women who work out their personal child-rearing dilemmas in the privacy of their own homes. It is a strongly felt, compelling goal toward which our society must strive. Our schools, hospitals, politicians, governing institutions, artists, businesses, writers, grandparents, scientists all know this at some level and must be called upon to help to sponsor the solutions to the father problem.

"A father may not think he's very good at child rearing; . . . he may be right."

Men Are Uncomfortable with the New Fatherhood Role

Evan Thomas et al.

The following viewpoint appeared as a report in *Newsweek* magazine, describing the trend toward more involved fatherhood. The authors of this viewpoint argue that men are less than enthusiastic about their new role as nurturing parents. More often than not, these fathers are thrust into what feels like an unnatural role through circumstances of marital breakup, loss of job, or wife's career.

As you read, consider the following questions:

1. According to the authors, how does society view men who are heavily involved in caring for children?
2. What evidence do the authors offer to prove that the newly involved fathers are indeed reluctant?
3. What factor will force men to become more involved fathers, according to the authors?

David Ross is trying. The 38-year-old Los Angeles lawyer was away a lot while his first child, six-year-old Daniela, was an infant, and he doesn't want to make the same mistake with eight-month-old Alexandra. "I try as much as I can to be with the kids," he says, though his wife, Soraya, awards him a less-than-perfect performance rating. "He gets bored with them," she says. "That's not true," protests David. "I enjoy it." "You enjoy it," says Soraya, "but you have to be reminded." Confesses Ross: "I think taking care of a baby is a hard job. It's hard to clean up a kid and feed him six times a day. I never thought of it as something fun."

Robert Razowsky, 32, changes diapers, bathes his son and gets up for night feedings. He once dutifully went to a Dad's Sunday at his son's Moms and Tots class. But the gas-station owner from suburban Chicago is more likely to be found at a Bears game on weekends, and he suspects that a lot of his friends would also rather go to a ball game than bond with their kids. "If I had to take care of children 50-50, would I still want them?" he asks. "I don't know."

The modern father. His wife probably thinks he doesn't do enough. His boss probably thinks he takes this "kid thing" too far. His parents think he looks a little odd cleaning house and changing diapers. And the father himself? He may not be at all sure what kind of a father he wants to be.

Most fathers have become reluctant warriors in a social revolution. Now that even the most traditional women are going off to work, the pressure is on dad to help more—if not share equally—on the home front. He is supposed to be the new sensitive man, caring and warm. Yet most men were raised to succeed at work, not at home. When his role as breadwinner is undermined, often his ego is too. A father may not think he's very good at child rearing; lacking a proper role model, he may be right.

The Myth of Mr. Mom

Is Mr. Mom a myth? Yes, says Glen Palm, professor of child and family studies at St. Cloud State University in Minnesota. "We've been wanting to put men on an equal plane too quickly. There are very, very few men who belong there." Most men know they ought to do more to raise their children, but that doesn't mean they really want to. If it's hard for the new woman to "have it all," it's just as hard for the new man to be the close, caring father his own father probably never was.

Men do pitch in at home more than their fathers did, but still not nearly as much as their wives. Most studies show that women do two or three times as much housework and child rearing as their husbands. When men do play an equal role, they often avoid the drudgery of housework. "Men are helping out more, but they take the fun jobs. Cooking or giving a bath is a lot more fun than vacuuming," says Darla Miller, director of child care and development at North Harris County College in Texas. Admits one father, Houston investment banker Bruce Galpert: "I take my son Matthew to the park or out bicycling so that Celeste [his wife] can clean the house."

Government and business are slowly moving to make it easier for men to share the load. Even the macho Los Angeles Fire Department now permits men to bring babies to the fire station. Six states (Minnesota, Rhode Island, Connecticut, Maine, Wisconsin and Oregon) have passed laws requiring employers to give both mother and father time off when they have a new baby or seriously ill child. . . .

Doonesbury

BY GARRY TRUDEAU

But will men take the time off when it's offered? Some companies do report an increase in male employees requesting benefits that will allow them to spend more time with their children. Studies of 6,600 Du Pont workers showed a doubling of men's interest in flexible work schedules. In 1985, for instance, only 18 percent said they wanted the option of part-time work to allow them to stay at home with the kids. In 1988, 33 percent did. Still, men who stay at home for more than a week or so are in the minority. A 1986 study of 384 companies showed that while more than a third of the businesses offered unpaid paternity leave, only a handful of men took the leave.

Peer-group pressure has a lot to do with it. "They don't see other men asking for time off, and they don't think the culture sanctions it," says James Levine, director of the Fatherhood Project at the Bank Street College of Education in New York City. Another part of men's intransigence is purely economic: men on average still make more money than women. "Typically the father gets put to work because that's where his time can be most efficiently spent," says Professor Palm. "Until women's pay is equal to men's, they won't have an equal opportunity to develop parenting skills."

Family Duty

Not surprisingly, when it come to chores like changing diapers, many men are all thumbs, simply because they never received the child-care training many women get as teenagers. By the time a man becomes a father, "he probably has never baby-sat," says Yale psychologist Kyle Pruett. "He didn't read Dr. Spock, he probably doesn't think he can bathe a baby without hurting it." Most young fathers today grew up before women's liberation, back when their own fathers still felt their family duty was to bring home a paycheck and maybe take out the garbage. "My father looks at me with a little bit of a crossed eye," says George Berg, an accounts manager from St. Cloud, Minn. "He probably thinks I'm a wimp and that my wife has too much influence."

Fathers often feel like inept sluggards around the house. Michael Tiller, 35, of St. Louis recalls feeding his daughter a meal of peas as her first solid food. "She acted like her mouth was full of live fire ants," he recalls. His wife suggested sweet potatoes. It worked. "She didn't read that in a book," says Tiller. "She knew that and I didn't." Feeding skills aside, fathers feel clumsy emotionally as well. "These are guys who grew up under the old order of masculinity: the sturdy oak, the silent male," says Ronald Levant, author of a book on parenting, *Father's Day '89*. "They were told big boys don't cry. In athletics they were told to play with pain. There was a prohibition against sad, fearful, vulnerable feelings."

Some fathers are downright angry about having to get involved. Studies show that marriages are more volatile when the father is forced to help around the house because the mother has taken a job. A Penn State study that followed blue-collar newlyweds for three years found that fathers in dual-earner marriages quarreled with their wives more than fathers in single-earner families. Mothers, meanwhile, sometimes feel threatened by a challenge to their traditional role and reinforce the husband's role as odd man out by treating him like an employee. "Mothers tend to be the experts. There is a natural tendency for the mothers to take over," says Palm. "It's hard for the father to build confidence in himself as a parent." In a *Parenting* magazine survey, 64 percent of the fathers said mother knows best about daily child care. Only 1 percent said father knows best. Even when dad is involved, kids often naturally run to mother. "It drives me crazy sometimes," says Berg, a father of two. "It hurts a lot." . . .

Men Don't Really Understand

Being a parent is a serious job and it's a job for *both* parents. This message seems not to have entered many fathers' minds.

Most men aren't yet even trying to deal with the problems of family and work the way most women are. Men aren't searching hard for the right balance. They don't agonize; they don't feel guilty. It's not a topic of men's conversation, as it is for women, when they gather. Men aren't sticking out their necks as much in the attempt to balance work and family, aren't sacrificing their work and life-style to the degree women are. Although they may say they do, men don't really understand.

Deborah Fallows, *A Mother's Work*, 1985.

Sheer necessity will force more men to get to know their children. In 1950 only about 10 percent of mothers with small infants worked. Today more than half do. Still, it won't be easy for fathers to feel natural as caregivers until society regards them that way. "When men do become house husbands, we don't take them seriously. We still say, 'Aren't you cute?'" says Marie Oser, former vice president of Child, Inc., in Austin, Texas. When Kevin Davis takes care of his kids on the weekend, his friends sometimes say, "Oh, you're baby-sitting." "No I'm not," he replies. "I'm being their father."

"Men do not value friendship. Their relationships with other men are superficial, even shallow."

Men Do Not Have Strong Friendships

Michael E. McGill

Michael E. McGill is professor and chairman of the Department of Organizational Behavior and Administration at the Edwin L. Cox School of Business at Southern Methodist University in Dallas, Texas. In the following viewpoint, he expresses the often-held opinion that men are incapable of forming intimate friendships with other men.

As you read, consider the following questions:

1. According to McGill, what are some of the differences between male and female friendships?
2. McGill states that even men who have been "friends" for as long as twenty years do not really know each other. Why? Looking at the men you know, do you agree with McGill? Why or why not?
3. Does McGill believe men feel that "something's missing," that they *need* intimacy with male friends? If so, why don't they have it?

To say that men have no intimate friends seems on the surface too harsh, and it raises quick objections from most men. But the data indicate that it is not far from the truth. Even the most intimate of male friendships (of which there are very few) rarely approach the depth of disclosure a woman commonly has with many other women. We know that very few men reveal anything of their private and personal selves even to their spouses; fewer still make these intimate disclosures to other men. One man in ten has a friend with whom he discusses work, money, marriage; only one in more than *twenty* has a friendship where he discloses his feelings about himself or his sexual feelings.

The most common male friendship pattern is for a man to have many "friends," each of whom knows something of the man's public self and therefore a little about him, but not one of whom knows more than a small piece of the whole. These friendships are usually circumstantially contrived and constrained; most often, they are created in the context of common occupational or recreational interests and pursued very cautiously. Because of the lack of depth that comes from limited disclosure, these male friendships tend to be of the "fair weather" variety: men turn to them in neither celebration nor crisis, preferring at such times to be alone. In fact, men are rarely seen two by two unless the occasion is business or competition (some would argue convincingly that these are one and the same); most of the time, men are alone or in groups.

Female Friendships Are Different

By contrast, women typically have many friends who know everything there is to know about them. Theirs is an open, fully disclosing interaction, not constrained by circumstance or content. A woman is just as likely to become fast friends with the women sitting next to her in the doctor's waiting room as she is with her neighbor of many years. The same could never be said of men, who are not nearly so quick to decide on the potential that acquaintances have to become close friends, and who are seen to exercise the utmost caution in disclosing themselves to other men even after years of interaction. Perhaps the most telling difference between the friendships of men and those of women lies in the *uses* of friendship. Whereas men are fair-weather friends, it is in times of celebration and crisis that women most often turn to their friends to share the joy and the sorrow they experience. Their intimacy enhances the highs and softens the lows.

The friendship of two women is true friendship. Women's friendships represent the extension into adult life of the "buddy system" of children's-camp partnerships for mutual help and protection. Women bare themselves to one another and bear one another, they are bosom buddies. Men, who neither bare themselves nor bear one another, are buddies in name only. . . .

What Do Male Friends Talk About

In these exclusively male friendship groups, the teams may change but the topics remain the same. Sports dominate, both participant and spectator. If the buddies aren't telling stories of their own exploits, past and present, they are analyzing the performance of the local high school, college, and professional players. Among most buddy groups, the "Monday-morning quarterbacking" goes on all week. For younger, unmarried men, sex is almost as popular a topic as sports. Curiously, the two topics are discussed in much the same way, with anecdotes of past and present conquests and analyses of the players, but rarely a personal revelation. Among their buddies, men take a decidedly impersonal approach to even the most personal of topics.

Few would admit to it, but gossip is as common among men as it is among women. There are some slight differences. Men tend to talk about other men in terms of competence, performance, and achievement, rather than character. Men are more likely to discuss friends and enemies alike in terms of what they do (or don't do) than who they are. But by any definition it is still gossip. . . .

Insincere Friendships

Men's relationships with other men, which could be a true echo of their manhood, are generally characterized by thinness, insincerity, and even chronic weariness.

Stuart Miller, *Men and Friendship*, 1986.

Add business, politics, the weather, and events of the day to sports, sex, and gossip, and you have the script for conversations in male friendship groups. The focus is almost always on externalities, things that happen "out there." In the absence of any exchange of private and personal information, it is little wonder that these men who spend so much time together scarcely know one another at all. . . .

Humor is used by men both as a guise for intimacy and as a guard against it. This is particularly evident in the reaction of men to any attempt to introduce more personal disclosures into a friendship group. Anyone who tries to deal with traditional male friendship topics in a manner that would lead to the development of genuine intimacy, either by disclosing something of his own private or personal self or by probing for similar disclosures from others, is certain to be censured by his friends. Humor is the safest form of censure for males; the casual put-down of volunteered

149

feelings or intimate disclosures saves the volunteer from embarrassment by acknowledging that surely he was joking. At the same time, the put-down reinforces male friendship norms that hold that personal subjects are not to be injected into the relationship. The man who persists in pushing for intimacy among his friends in the face of these sanctions is likely to be ostracized. Man to man, the message seems to be "If we can't joke about it, we can't talk about it." . . .

Friends of Convenience

One of the things that has been found to be true about male disclosures is that they are often circumscribed by circumstance. By virtue of common occupation, recreational interest, or pure proximity, some public revelations are made and a kind of closeness is cautiously developed. The resulting relationships are constrained to these fragments of public information. So it is in male friendships that each knows a little bit about the other(s), but remove the circumstance, the reason for relating, and there is no adequate common knowledge of selves to sustain the relationship. This is one of the contributing factors to the fair-weather friendships so often seen between men. The relationships evolve cautiously in convenient circumstances. In the absence of any effort to get beyond circumstantial disclosures, there is no intimacy and no basis for conducting the relationship in times of crisis. What men mean by friendship is partial public knowledge of one another, without problems. If it is personal or problematical for a man, it doesn't have a place between friends. . . .

How Do Men Explain Their Friendships?

When questioned about the number and nature of their friendships, many men take an extreme view. They argue that men don't have close personal relationships because they don't need them. More simply put, men don't need friends:

• "I don't really belong to any groups at work or anywhere else. I would have to say that I don't have what you would call close friends, not even one or two. Frankly, I just don't see the need for them. I get along just fine on my own."

• "I have a lot of acquaintances, but no real buddies, so to speak. I've never really taken the trouble to develop any friendships, nor have I seen the need for them."

• "I don't have time for anybody but my family and my employees. As far as I'm concerned, friends are more of a burden than anything else. A close friendship is just not worth the bother."

• "I don't have any real interests outside my work, so there's not much opportunity for me to meet people. I don't know what I'd do with friends, anyway. I'm plenty busy with my job."

• "The way I see it, if a man can't make it on his own, he's not much of a man. Hey, I'm the first one to get a group of guys together to go hunting or fishing, but that's where friendship stops for me. I don't need anything more from it. I don't *want* anything more from it. I don't have anything to do with anybody who does." . . .

Men Are Poor Friends

In my opinion, men make poor best friends. Among ourselves, we men have functional friendships, alliances that serve specific purposes—tennis partners, business associates, drinking buddies. In those friendships we share no more of ourselves than the activity requires. We use interaction with one another to prove ourselves, following conventional rules of commerce and competition, ever aware that if we get too close, confide too much, it may be used against us.

Michael E. McGill in *About Men*, 1987.

Those few men who seem to understand the truly intimate character of women's friendships express envy that their own friendships with men lack this quality and the capability it affords women to deal with personal issues. The acknowledgment that women have something in their friendships that men lack and need or want typically comes when men and women face some shared personal crisis. At these times, men are made painfully aware of the absence of any aid and assistance from their own friendships. Confronted with the death of a parent, divorce, a problem with the children, men are left to their own devices, while women enjoy the company and solace of their friends. The intimacy of female friendships eases the suffering of women. The isolation of men intensifies their suffering. David Laster describes his traumatic introduction to the real limits of his buddy group:

"The four of us—Tom, Jim, Steve, and I—had been hunting buddies for ages. Every chance we got, we would go out for deer, ducks, birds; whatever the season, we hunted it, and almost always together. We had some great times together, the four of us, despite the difference in our ages. It didn't matter because we really hit it off well. I think each of us thought of the other three as our best friends. We often said how we felt—we could talk about anything we wanted to in the group. Even the wives got to know each other pretty well. Once or twice a year we'd get together as couples. But mainly it was just a good group of guys all the way around.

"I remember it was a Friday and we were all going to take off work at noon so we could drive out, set up camp, and be ready to go first thing in the morning. I had one of those four-wheel-drive trucks, so the plan was that I would pick everyone up. Steve

151

lived farthest out, so we always picked him up last. As it turned out, I didn't get away from work as early as I had hoped, and by the time I got Tom and Jim, we were running about an hour late. We pulled up in front of Steve's place and honked a couple of times. Usually he would have come running out, yelling and swearing about us being 'slow old farts,' but this time there was no sight of him. I saw his gear back by the garage, and I thought maybe he didn't hear us. Tom and Jim stayed in the truck while I went around to get him. He was in the backyard and he was dead. He had taken his shotgun, put the muzzle in his mouth, and with a piece of wood pushed the trigger and blown the back of his head away. He left a note near his body: 'I'm sorry. There is no one to talk to.'

"At first I was just terribly angry. I was really pissed off at Steve. This was not some teenaged kid crazed out of his mind on drugs, or some guy down on his luck. He was thirty-one when he killed himself. He had a good job and a super wife. They weren't rich, but they didn't have any big debts or anything. I just couldn't see that he had any reason for doing what he did. It seemed so selfish. I remember thinking, 'How could he do this to me? How could he say there was no one to talk to, when there was me?' I felt like I could have helped him, no matter what it was. We could talk about anything. At least I thought we could. Only later did it hit me that I didn't really know if we could talk about anything or not, because we never really talked about much that was personal.

Transference of Anger

"In the days following Steve's death, I transferred my anger from Steve to my wife and friends. I'm not saying that any of this was right or rational. I'm just saying it was how it was. I was pissed off at Steve's wife and my wife because at the funeral and all, it seemed like they could really let go of their grief with each other. They cried and hugged, they were really emotional in a way a man could never be. In the midst of it all, I had a sense that they were really helping each other. They were together, and being together helped them deal with Steve's death. As for me, I just had Tom and Jim. I knew that they were hurt by Steve's death, too, but for some reason we couldn't really share what we were feeling. While the women were together with each other, we men were together by ourselves, drinking, staring off into space, each of us full of grief. But for whatever reason, we chose to deal with it inside, each in his own way, instead of talking about what we were feeling. I was envious of the women's way with each other. I was angry that I couldn't be the same way, angry that my friends and I, who knew Steve best, didn't have the kind of friendship that we could draw on for help when we most needed it.

"After that I pretty much lost touch with Tom and Jim. We just sort of stopped doing things together. We never talked about why, but I think we all somehow realized that if our friendship couldn't help us through something as traumatic as Steve's suicide, then maybe it wasn't much of a friendship. I've spent a lot of time thinking about how much I was responsible for what Steve did because I wasn't the kind of friend he needed. I think I know now what Steve meant when he wrote, 'There is no one to talk to.' As close as I thought we were, I've come to see that we were never there for each other to talk to. Oh, we were there to do things with—hunt, fish, drink, play cards—but we were never there to talk about the things we were feeling, the things that might make you wonder whether or not life was worth living.

A Lack of Friends

My friends have no friends. They are men. They think they have friends, and if you ask them whether they have friends they will say yes, but they don't really. They think, for instance, that I'm their friend, but I'm not. It's OK. They're not my friends, either. The reason for that is that we are all men—and men, I have come to believe, cannot or will not have real friends.

Richard Cohen, quoted in *The Intimate Connection* by James B. Nelson, 1988.

"I think now that what we called friendship wasn't really anything more than a casual and comfortable kind of 'acquaintanceship' where we shared certain things certain times, but we never shared ourselves. Maybe all male relationships are like that. Lately I've really tried to be more open with people, especially men. I've tried to build the kind of friendship Steve needed, because I believe I need that too. So far, it hasn't worked too well. Men get anxious when you talk about feelings, and it seems like the harder I try to get close, the faster guys pull away. Maybe I'm going too fast. But hell, if you go too slow, you may never get there, or when you do it's too late, like it was for Steve." . . .

Men Need To Change

It is one thing for men to recognize that they need more intimate friendships, but it is quite another thing for men to behave in the ways necessary to develop those relationships. All of the same dynamics that are operating to keep men at a distance from their wives and families are in high gear where friendships are concerned. The man who would develop intimacy with another man must first overcome societal prescriptions about what it is to be a man and a buddy. He must then overcome his own prohibitions against self-disclosure. Finally he must find a receptive and responsive friend. . . .

Despite the unprecedented opportunity that modern times present for men to become close to other men, they are still constrained by conventional male inhibitions and prohibitions against self-disclosure. Those few men who do muster the courage to reach out to others by revealing themselves are more likely to be met with rebuke and even ridicule than with a responsive reception. Even in those circumstances, where the avowed purpose is for men to support one another and become closer, it is difficult for them to overcome all the barriers to interpersonal intimacy that they have erected over the years. . . .

Men do not value friendship. Their relationships with other men are superficial, even shallow. "Best buddies" reveal so little of themselves to each other that they are little more than acquaintances. There is no intimacy in most male friendships and none of what intimacy offers: solace and support.

"Intimacy often grows through shared pursuits and shared risks, rather than the shared disclosures of women."

Men Have Strong Friendships

Drury Sherrod

Drury Sherrod is a social psychologist associated with the Claremont Colleges in Claremont, California. He has done extensive research and writing on human relationships and is currently focusing on gender differences in friendships. In the following viewpoint, Sherrod acknowledges that male friendships do not have the same kind of intimacy that female friendships do. Nevertheless, he writes, men do develop strong and important bonds with their male companions. These friendships should be evaluated on their own terms and not in comparison with female friendships.

As you read, consider the following questions:

1. Sherrod argues that it is inappropriate to expect the same things in a male friendship as in a female friendship. Why?
2. According to Sherrod, although male friendships lack the strong intimacy of female friendships, they are nevertheless satisfying to males. What things do men get out of their friendships?
3. Sherrod anticipates that in the future, male friendships will become more intimate than they are presently. Why?

Excerpted from Drury Sherrod, "The Bonds of Men: Problems and Possibilities in Close Male Relationships" in Harry Brod (ed.), *The Making of Masculinities* (Boston: Allen & Unwin, 1987), 213-239.

Our culture has traditionally viewed male friendship as embodying the ideals of comradeship and brotherhood. Men have buddies, pals, lifelong ties—bonds of unspoken, unshakeable commitment—the kind of friends for whom one would "lay down one's life." Yet surveys find most men today name their wife as their closest friend. And the psychiatrist Daniel Levinson concluded in *The Seasons of a Man's Life* that "close friendship with a man or woman is rarely experienced by American men." Much research supports Levinson's conclusion, but thorny questions plague our interpretation of the research.

A difficulty in evaluating research on men's friendships is the question of an appropriate standard of intimacy. Should male intimacy be compared to female intimacy in its form, style, and goals? Or should the unspoken commitments of typical male friendships be evaluated by different standards than the easy verbal and physical intimacies of women's relationships? . . .

Numbering Friends

The simplest comparison between men's and women's friendships is to ask, "Who has more friends, men or women?" When the question is framed this way, the answer is deceptively simple. Sociologists have conducted several large surveys in different parts of America, and the number of friends claimed by men and women is fairly even. When all the categories of people—young and old, working and not working, blue collar and white collar—are taken together, men and women report roughly the same number of friends. For example, in a survey conducted in Nebraska, men and women each counted about 3 people among their closest friends. In the San Francisco Bay area, women claimed slightly more than 6 close friends apiece, while men reported about 5. Across northern California, the average man named 11 nonkin persons he could call on for help and advice, while the average woman cited 10. And among college students at the University of California, Los Angeles, young men and women said they had between 3 and 4 intimate friends each, and about 6 to 8 casual friends apiece.

Some gender differences emerge in these friendship surveys, but they are small, and they tend to reflect the different number of social contacts that age and occupation provide to men and women. For example, young working men sometimes report slightly more friends than women report, apparently because young working males have more opportunity for social contacts than nonworking women. In contrast, older retired males usually report slightly fewer friends than older women, as males lose access to their work-related contacts, while women retain their social networks with age. But, overall, as far as numbers go, both sexes report about equal numbers of friends. Both men and women name between 3 to 6 people they consider close friends, and up to 10 or 11 people they can call on for help and advice. The meaning of these numbers is unclear, however, because men and women seem to define friendship in very different terms.

Male Friends

I'm tired of hearing that male friendships revolve solely around the stuff of the outside world, and that the inner world of intimacy is reserved for women friends. . . .

Men do forge relationships centered around shared interests and hobbies. But women misjudge the depth of these relationships. Given the right chemistry and time, sports, work, family and the stock market merely become the canvas on which men paint the more subtle and intimate strokes of friendship.

Bill Lustig, *Glamour*, February 1987.

Robert Bell is a sociologist who has interviewed almost 200 men and women in the northeastern United States about their friendships. His interviews give us some idea of what friendships mean to men and women. For example, a 45-year-old woman described her friendships with women in the following way:

In my close friendships there is a high degree of giving and receiving. What I mean is that things that are important to each of us are expressed and reacted to by each of us. If I am really troubled or upset I can unload on my friends and they will understand and give serious consideration to my problems. Because we can deal with the really significant things in our lives our friendship is complete and revealing.

A 38-year-old man experienced his friendships in quite a different way:

I have three close friends I have known since we were boys and they live here in the city. There are some things I wouldn't tell them. For example, I wouldn't tell them much about my work because we have always been highly competitive. I certainly wouldn't tell about my feelings of any uncertainties with life or various things I do. And I wouldn't talk about any problems I have with my wife or in fact anything about my marriage and sex life. But other than that I would tell them anything.

These quotations sound extreme, but they accurately mirror the meaning of same-sex friendships to men and women. In a study conducted in St. Louis, young adult men and women held very different criteria for what made someone a best friend. Women sought a friend who could be a confidante, a friend who would help them "grow as persons." Men were more likely to seek a

157

friend with similar interests, someone "to have fun with.". . .

We generally think of close friendships as involving a good deal of disclosure about the intimate details of our lives. After all, a best friend is someone who accepts us as we are. Yet in the same way that men and women disagree about the meaning of close friendship, they also differ in the amount and kind of personal information they disclose to close friends. A striking example of the limits on self-disclosure among men is seen in David Michaelis's book *The Best of Friends*, subtitled *Profiles of Extraordinary Friendships*. Michaelis describes two middle-aged best friends who met as college athletes at Yale, later sailed a 20-foot boat across the North Atlantic, and have remained competitive yet committed friends for more than 20 years. Over the years, they evolved an unwritten code, a gentleman's agreement that their competition should never result in an affront to their friendship. As one of them observed:

> I often wonder why our friendship continues to bounce along the way it is, but I'm not going to try and alter it to serve some other god such as "progress-in-a-relationship" or what one calls "growth." This friendship is not trying to produce a family. This is not trying to satisfy the various ego needs of the participants, though it may do that anyway. It simply satisfies some sort of ultimate human regard: That you are highly regarded and that you regard another with the highest esteem. But I don't know if friendships do progress anywhere, I've often wondered why do he and I find it prefectly comfortable to continue playing these roles that have been comfortable for so long. I guess we return to that mode because it seems natural to both of us. . . . Plenty of serious discussions go on. But even those discussions are guided by the same limits. There definitely are limits.

A considerable body of research confirms the limits on self-disclosure in most close male friendships. In the typical research paradigm men and women fill out a "self-disclosure questionnaire," which asks them to rate on a scale from 1 to 5 the degree of information they have revealed about themselves in their most intimate conversations on a variety of topics. The topics range from trivial items, such as hobbies and favorite sports, to extremely intimate topics such as sexual fantasies, guiltiest secrets, and inferiority feelings. Women usually disclose significantly more intimate information about themselves than men do, regardless of age, region of the country, or social class. When the most intimate questions are analyzed separately, men disclose much less than women. . . .

Both Are Open and Trusting

Other research supports these consistent gender differences. A study in New Brunswick, New Jersey, examined the communication styles of men and women in their 20s and 30s. The subjects supplied detailed accounts of what they talked about with their best friends and how they related to each other. Consistent with other findings on self-disclosure, the New Jersey men talked with each other mainly about topical issues, such as work, sports, movies, or politics. The women talked about these issues too, but they were also just as likely to talk about personal problems, as well as their relationship with each other. Despite these major differences in men's and women's relationships, both sexes felt they were completely open and trusting with their best friend. As one of the men said about his best friend, "We are pretty open with each other, I guess. Mostly we talk about sex, horses, guns, and the army." . . .

The Value of Male Friends

Once we open our world to another man, we learn that we are not alone in our fears, insecurities, uncertainties, and desires. Nothing is "wrong" with us, as we might have secretly suspected. Through a friendship with another man, we affirm much that is good and strong in us as men. Frank and honest exchanges of experiences allow us to gain a fresh and clear perspective on ourselves.

Ken Druck, *The Secrets Men Keep*, 1985.

So far, we have seen that men and women claim about the same number of friends, that both sexes desire intimate friendship, and that both sexes describe friends as equally important in their lives. Also, both feel they are open and trusting with their friends, and among older adolescents, males seem to know at least as much about their best friends as females know about their best friends. Yet the meaning and content of male and female friendships are vastly different, on the whole: Men prefer activities over conversation, and men's conversations are far less intimate than women's conversations. . . .

If males generally fail to communicate intimacy with other males, are less satisfied with their friendships than women, and perceive less support from their friends than women do, may we conclude that men's friendships are less intimate than women's friendships? From one perspective . . . the question itself may be inappropriate. For most men, most of the time, the dimension of intimacy in friendships with other men may be irrelevant to their lives. According to the research, men seek not intimacy but companionship, not disclosure but commitment. Men's friendships involve unquestioned acceptance rather than unrestricted affirmation. When men are close, they achieve closeness through shared activities, and on the basis of shared activities, men infer intimacy simply because they are friends. . . .

America today is in the midst of a new economic and social revolution. Since 1979, more than half of the adult women in the United States have been employed outside their homes. So many mothers with small children work that only 5% of America's households fit the mold of a working father, a mother at home, and minor children. In America's cities, the divorce rate hovers around 50%. More Americans are delaying marriage, never marrying, and living alone than ever before. The structure of the family has been so stretched and torn by dual careers, divorce, and single life styles that the family may no longer be a reliable source of intimacy and emotional support for either men or women. Since many more men than women rely on their spouses for the intimate support of a best friend, the transformation of the family may have a profound effect on men's relationships. Quite simply, men may no longer be able to look to their wives for a best friend, for their wives may be physically and emotionally unavailable. . . .

Options for Men

How might men respond to a social environment in which they must look beyond their wives as their primary and often sole source of emotional support? There are several options. Some men may withdraw from intimacy altogether, retreating into the narcissistic self-preoccupation of the "new male" described by Barbara Ehrenreich. Other men may slump into the depression of the disconnected. But neither of these options satisfies the human need to be known and valued by another person. For this essential human link, many men, I believe, will look to other men. Here, in a shared sense of "maleness," men may find the kind of emotional support and intimacy from a male friend that men have traditionally enjoyed in other times and other cultures. . . .

Encouraging examples of male friendships are found in David Michaelis's *The Best of Friends*. What is striking about these extraordinary friendships, however, is the uniquely male nature of the relationships. These committed friends are not the kind of men who "wear their hearts on their sleeve," as one naval officer said about his long-time friendship with another officer. Yet he is eloquent about their friendship:

> I can't imagine going through life and not having someone like Mike. I don't know what those people who don't have a friend like Mike do. I almost find it hard to believe that everybody doesn't. I mean you gotta have somebody. And I mean a nonsexual friend. There's only so much that you'll tell your whoever, and at that point you need that kind of guy with whom you can just really be yourself. That's the purest kind of relationship. There's nothing asked, nothing expected, nothing to cloud it up. . . . I accept him as he accepts me. . . .

Many men feel a need for an intimate bond with another man, even though the forms of such a bond may be difficult to achieve. For many males, the path to intimacy with another man leads through a series of tests and challenges. Intimacy often grows through shared pursuits and shared risks, rather than the shared disclosures of women. Repeatedly, men have described their own friendships to me as "different" from the friendships of their wives or girlfriends. As one man said, about his best male friend, "We don't act the same way my wife acts with her friends, but it doesn't mean we don't care. It's just different. We express a lot through racquetball.". . .

One Example

I want to close with an example from my own life. I have a best friend of more than 20 years' standing. Although he lives across the country we manage to stay in regular touch. Several weekends a year we visit each other's homes, and each summer we have a tradition of camping in the mountains. We talk openly about our lives, and we spend a lot of time playing, appreciating our shared sense of humor. Over the years, we have accepted our friendship as a bond of love, distinct from romantic and familial love, but equally important. If our relationship is unusual in light of the research cited in this essay, it is not because we ourselves are unique, but because we have made an unusual commitment to our friendship. We have invested time, energy and resources; and we have made ourselves vulnerable and acknowledged our need for one another. In the same way, other men, too, can commit themselves to close male relationships. With commitment and persistence, men can learn to break through the bonds that confine them and rebuild the bonds that unite them.

Recognizing Stereotypes

A stereotype is an oversimplified or exaggerated description of people or things. Stereotyping can be favorable. However, most stereotyping tends to be highly uncomplimentary, and, at times, degrading.

Stereotyping grows out of our prejudices. When we stereotype someone, we are prejudging him or her. Consider the following example: Ms. Smith believes all men look down on women and discount their capabilities. Whenever she misses a promotion at her job and a man receives it, she believes she was not chosen simply because she is a woman. She disregards any other possible reasons why she did not get the promotion. Why? She has prejudged all men and will keep her stereotype consistent with her prejudice.

Several of the following statements are taken from the viewpoints in this chapter. Consider each statement carefully. *Mark S for any statement that is an example of stereotyping. Mark N for any statement that is not an example of stereotyping. Mark U if you are undecided about any statement.*

If you are doing this activity as a member of a class or group, compare your answers with those of other class or group members. Be able to defend your answers. You may discover that others will come to different conclusions than you. Listening to the reasons others present for their answers may give you valuable insights in recognizing stereotypes.

S = *stereotype*
N = *not a stereotype*
U = *undecided*

1. Men are incapable of forming intimate and lasting friendships with other men.

2. Some men prefer to have many different friends and keep their personal lives and feelings out of the friendships.

3. Men only like to talk about sports and sex with other men.

4. Women and men have roughly the same number of friends.

5. Many men prefer activities to conversations with their male friends. Women, on the other hand, often prefer conversations.

6. Men cannot talk about their thoughts or feelings with other men.

7. A woman's real job is to be a mother.

8. Surveys have shown that in most cases, women even if they work are still the primary caretakers of children. Men are still the primary breadwinners in their families.

9. Men are bad for babies.

10. The more involved with their babies fathers are, the more successful the babies are later in life.

11. Babies and young children bore men and men resent having to help with child care. Men only like doing the fun chores.

12. Many women when they are younger get more practice at taking care of children. Consequently, women feel more at ease taking care of children than men do.

13. Men want to be macho and dominate women.

14. Men have realized that the old macho attitudes prevent women and men from establishing close relationships. Men have abandoned these attitudes.

15. Traditional roles for men are passé. Men have moved beyond them to become sensitive, caring people.

16. Men have taken on feminine characteristics but have not become any more respectful or open to women themselves.

17. Men's roles have changed not because of heightened feminist consciousness, but because the traditional role was boring.

Periodical Bibliography

The following articles have been selected to supplement the diverse views presented in this chapter.

Joseph Alper — "Fear of Femininity," *Psychology Today*, June 1988.

L.M. Kit Carson — "Robert Bly Wants To Make a Man of You," *Utne Reader*, December 1984/January 1985.

Bryce J. Christensen — "Double Bind: The Redefinition of American Fatherhood," *The Family in America*, October 1988. Available from The Rockford Institute, PO Box 416, Mount Morris, IL 61054.

Rosalind Coward — "High Time Men Changed," *New Internationalist*, September 1987.

Maggie Gallagher — "What Men Really Want," *National Review*, May 12, 1987.

Pete Hamill — "Great Expectations," *Ms.*, September 1986.

Charles F. Hampton — "So You Think It's a Man's World," *Vital Speeches of the Day*, January 15, 1984.

David Hellerstein — "Multiplying Roles: The Next Stage," *Ms.*, October 1987.

Morton Hunt — "About Men: The Comfort of Pals," *The New York Times Magazine*, January 18, 1987.

Rita D. Jacobs — "Gut-Spilling Is Being Used by Men as a Shortcut to Intimacy," *Glamour*, March 1986.

Robert B. McCall — "Homemaker Dads," *Parents*, April 1987.

Samuel Osherson — "Finding Our Fathers," *Utne Reader*, April/May 1986.

Kay Richards — "Phantom Fathers," *The Progressive*, August 1987.

Richard Taylor — "About Men: A Fulfillment," *The New York Times Magazine*, March 29, 1987.

Michael J. Weiss — "Equal Rights: Not for Women Only," *Glamour*, March 1989.

How Does Work Affect the Family?

MALE/FEMALE ROLES

Chapter Preface

"Who takes care of the children?" This question has become the center of debate about the contemporary family and its future.

Today, more adults than ever before hold jobs outside the home. There are more single-parent families than at any previous time in our history, and there are more middle-class, dual-career families. What impact does this have on family life and, more specifically, on children?

The authors of the viewpoints in this chapter debate the benefits and drawbacks of working parents.

"It's my [working] mother who is my role model.... She's taught me so much about what it is to be a woman."

Working Parents Help Their Children

Anita Shreve

Anita Shreve is an award-winning writer and former editor for many publications including *Redbook*, *Newsweek*, and *US*. She has also written a book, *Remaking Motherhood: How Working Mothers Are Shaping Our Children's Future*, from which this viewpoint is taken. In the following viewpoint, Shreve discusses how working mothers influence their children in positive ways.

As you read, consider the following questions:

1. Name four differences between working and non-working mothers that Shreve describes.
2. Why does Shreve believe that children of working parents develop strong self-esteem and independence?
3. According to Shreve, what do children think of their working mothers?

Logically, one would expect working mothers to treat their daughters differently than do at-home mothers. First, the mother's time with the daughter is more limited than that of a traditional mother's, and so she may feel that when she is with the child, she must use that time not only for experiencing her daughter but also for instilling certain attitudes and values. "I have to have an impact on my daughter, who is four, when I am home, because I'm with her only three hours a day," said Elaine, the dentist. "I talk to her a lot. I encourage her to be independent." This sense of needing to have an impact may be intensified by the realization that the child, for many hours a day, is under the influence of another individual or set of individuals who may have values different from those of the mother.

Second, achieving self-esteem, autonomy and a feeling of mastery did not come easily to many of the women of the current generation of working mothers. If a woman has struggled to achieve these attributes, she may have a keener appreciation of them and, as a result, might consciously try to pass on these characteristics to her daughter. "I think I'm a positive role model for my daughter in that I'm letting her know that a woman just doesn't get taken care of in life," said Sue, the typesetter. "She really has to go out on her own and make her own life. She has to make her own happiness. She shouldn't depend on anybody to take charge of her. When I was growing up, I was raised to believe that you're going to meet Prince Charming and be swept away, and it's going to be okay just because you're in love. And you know, that's not the way it is, and it's very hard when you find that out. I don't want my daughter to grow up under that illusion."

Different Behavior

Third, a working-mother model behaves, by necessity, in ways that are different from the at-home mother. Going and coming to and from work; discussing one's triumphs and frustrations with one's spouse; sharing, of necessity, child-rearing tasks; and expressing certain attitudes about economic independence and assertiveness in the workplace to other adults cannot fail to impinge on a child's consciousness. "I think working mothers say things to their children that are very different from the things mothers who stay home say to their children," said Jayne, the architecture critic. "Children pick up on attitudes and characteristics subliminally just by noticing who you are and what you do."

And fourth, working mothers instill independence and autonomy in their daughters to a greater degree than do at-home mothers for the simple reason that the mothers aren't *there* for the daughters, in a physical sense, as much as at-home mothers can be. "I remember from the time my daughter, Elizabeth, was a very young child encouraging a certain amount of independence in her," recalled Celeste, the interior designer. "I did this both because I'd never had it as a child and wished I had, and also because I had just started working and I simply didn't have the time to hover over her." ...

The fostering of independence and autonomy has been among the clearest of the research findings on the effects of working mothers on daughters. In a survey published by Jeanne Bodin and Bonnie Mitelman in their book *Mothers Who Work*, the majority of mothers polled said that their children were more independent and responsible as a result of having a working mother.

In her definitive review of the literature on the effects of maternal employment on children, Lois Hoffman had similar conclusions: "The employed mother provides a model that is associated with competence and accorded higher status in the family. The children of employed mothers received more independence training, a pattern that is particularly valuable for daughters since they often receive too little in the traditional nonemployed-mother family. Other aspects of the employed-mother family—the involvement of the father, the greater participation of children in household responsibilities, and the more egalitarian sex-role attitudes—have all been linked to greater self-confidence and competence in girls." Hoffman also found that this fostering of self-reliance seemed to have a direct correlation with a mother's satisfaction with her work. When working mothers were happy with their decision to work, they were more likely to encourage their daughters to be independent.

At-home mothers, on the other hand, may unconsciously allow their children to become overly dependent on them because these mothers see their primary role as "mother" and may need to be needed. Indeed, many mothers who embrace this way of being are often compensating for not being needed in the world by anyone save their husbands and children, and often only in a service or "servant" role. "Mother-daughter relationships in which the mother is supported by a network of women kin and friends, and has meaningful work and self-esteem, produce daughters with capacities for nurturance and a *strong sense of self.*[Italics mine.] Mother-daughter relationships in which the mother has no other adult support or meaningful work and remains ambivalently attached to her own mother produce ambivalent attachment and inability to separate in daughters," writes Nancy Chodorow in *The Reproduction of Mothering.* . . .

Like mother, like daughter. Researchers have found that daughters mirror their working mothers' attitudes, particularly about appropriate sex roles. The more nonstereotypical the mother's attitudes about the roles of men and women, the more nonstereotypical the daughter's attitudes will be. More specifically, the presence of a working mother in the home results in fewer differences in perceptions of male and female roles by children. And if the mother's work is regarded as successful by the children, this will lead to more egalitarian sex-role ideologies as they mature.

Throughout the research, the link between mother and daughter is quite direct. Remember the studies that asked both boys and girls to list the things that men and women needed to know in order to function in the world? If you ask the daughters of working mothers those same questions, the answers are quite different from the answers of daughters raised in traditional families: Interestingly, daughters of working mothers don't just see women as having a wider range of behavior; they see women *and* men engaging in more cross-sex activities. In their responses they indicate that *each* sex is less limited than the traditional model, and they tend to describe both males and females as possessing a wider variety of traits.

As we have seen, girls acquire their sex-role identity by imitating their mothers. If the mother appears to have a role in the world similar to the father's (breadwinner as well as nurturer, for example), then this will broaden the daughter's concept of what is appropriate for women. Clearly, the parental division of labor and the parental division of child-rearing contribute to this concept. This only holds true, however, if the mother is content with her own sex-role identity; if she is conflicted about her sexuality and uncomfortable or guilt-ridden about her role as a working mother, then the daughter might be expected to be aware of this discomfort and come away with conflicting messages about working and mothering.

Parenting by Working Mothers

The easing of sex-role stereotypes appears to begin unconsciously right from birth and shows up as early as nursery school. One study discovered that working mothers played with their babies in a manner formerly seen mostly in fathers: The mothers handled their infants in a physically robust manner, suggesting that sex differences in parenting style may be a function of work roles. Another study noticed that mothers who had more egalitarian sex-role ideologies encouraged their daughters to play more and to be more active than did mothers with traditional ideas about sex roles. Nursery schoolteachers' comments on how girls' play has changed as a result of the presence of the working mother appear to confirm this. "Ten years ago, girls would not have been playing 'going off to work,'" says Dr. Nancy Close, a lecturer in child development and a day-care consultant at the Yale Child Study Center. "Today, however, they are packing up briefcases to go to the office just like Mom." Dr. Close has also noted changes in dramatic play among girls. "Girls are now taking on more of the superhero roles. They are playing at being Superman and Wonder Woman. Girls demonstrate more power than they would have in play situations ten years ago—and frankly, it's very nice to see." . . .

Ending Sex-Role Stereotypes

The advantage parents cited most often . . .was that the children would not be limited by sex-role stereotypes. They will not grow up as their parents did believing and expecting men to work outside the home while women work inside the home. From the role model that the parents present, their children will know from the beginning that women can have careers, men can cook and do housework, both can take care of children, and neither dominates the other.

Audrey D. Smith and William J. Reid, *Role-Sharing Marriage*, 1986.

For girls, the benefits of a more egalitarian sex-role ideology are impressive. Not only, as one would expect, do girls then have higher expectations for achievement, greater self-esteem and more ambitious vocational choices; they also have higher achievement scores. "Cross-sex behavior is associated with higher cognitive functioning and achievement motivation in middle childhood," writes Dr. J. Brooks-Gunn in her paper "The Relationship of Maternal Beliefs About Sex-Typing to Maternal and Young Children's Behavior." But she also discovered that daughters of mothers who professed more egalitarian sex-role ideologies had higher intelligence scores at twenty-four months of age than daughters of mothers with traditional sex-role ideologies—and this was true even when the intelligence scores of both groups of mothers were the same. These results appear to correlate with other studies of young children. One investigation of children in publicly funded New York City day-care centers discovered that children had higher I.Q. scores at eighteen months and at three years of age than did a comparable home-raised sample.

These higher I.Q. scores for the daughters of working mothers are partially the result, say experts, of easing sex stereotypes, but they may also have other origins. Studies of working mothers with young children indicate that these mothers are more verbally attentive to their daughters than at-home mothers are, and that infants of working mothers, even as young as five months, show higher rates of exploration and accompanying verbalization. Discouraging clinginess and, conversely, demanding independent and mature behavior have also been associated with higher intelligence scores and higher level of achievement in school. In a study conducted by the National Assessment of Educational Progress, 100,000 daughters *and* sons of working mothers in grades four, eight and eleven were found to have significantly higher reading scores than their classmates. Researchers engaged in the study speculated that working mothers tend to be better educated than at-home mothers and that children of working mothers attend nursery school at an earlier age than do the children of at-home mothers.

Working Mothers and Attitudes Toward Work

Like mother, like daughter. The employment status of the mother directly affects a daughter's perception of her vocational choices. Researchers have found that the experience of having a mother who works strengthens a daughter's interest and commitment to a career. Women attending college have a stronger career orientation if their own mothers worked, for example, and women who report that they have successfully combined career and family life also say that they had greater maternal encouragement than did their colleagues who failed to establish their priorities at an early age. In addition, the more supportive the mother is of the right to work, the more supportive is her daughter. Although a working mother can sometimes put too many demands on a daughter to succeed, most working mothers appear to encourage and support their daughters rather than provide an atmosphere of excessive pressure. "The daughters of working mothers have a larger set of expectations about what they can do," says Dr. Sylvia Feinberg. "Their sphere of what can be done is unquestionably broader." . . .

Susan Weissman, director of the Park Center day-care centers in New York City, has had a firsthand opportunity to observe how preschool girls begin to learn about the world of work from their mothers. "I can see that these girls all believe that they are going to be something when they grow up. They seem to have the confidence that they can do just what they want to do, that the world is really wide open to them. Recently we had the children make a book about what they wanted to be when they grew up. And every girl epitomized the life that her mother was living—although to the level of the child's cognitive ability. One of the mothers owns a chain of ice-cream stores, and her little girl said she was going to grow up and scoop ice cream. Another said that she wanted to grow up and write checks and pay bills—her mother has her own business. Another said she was going to write a book—her mother is a writer. They see themselves as working; working is just part of the given—like first you're a teenager and then you work. Not one of them expected to be 'just' a mother, and not one of them said they were going to be what their fathers were. They all took on the mothers' roles." . . .

Admiring Mothers

Both sons and daughters of working mothers tend to name their mothers as the more influential parent in the household, but girls, in particular, have a high regard for their working mothers, and, as a consequence of this, for their own sex in general. According to Lois Hoffman, "Daughters of working mothers . . . admire their mothers more." Adolescent daughters in particular are more likely than daughters of at-home mothers to name their mothers as the persons they most admire. "It's my mother who is my role model," said Rebecca, the student. "She's taught me so much about what it is to be a woman, and how different it is for me than it was for her when she was growing up."

> *"We may find the children of welfare mothers fared better than those shuffled off to day care during the most sensitive period of their growing up years."*

Working Parents Harm Their Children

Mary Ann Kuharski

Mary Ann Kuharski is a free-lance writer, homemaker, and mother of thirteen children, six of whom are adopted, handicapped, and of mixed races. In the following viewpoint, Kuharski argues that mothers who work when it is not absolutely essential to the family's survival do a great disservice to their children.

As you read, consider the following questions:

1. According to Kuharski, for what reason do the majority of working mothers work?
2. Why does Kuharski believe it is so important to mothers to be home with their children?
3. What are some of the dangers of day care, according to Kuharski?

Mary Ann Kuharski, "There's No Place Like Home," *Conservative Digest*, November 1988. Reprinted with permission.

I received a flyer the other day advertising care for "sick children." When I called to investigate, I was told that for $30 a day (for up to nine hours) my child would be well cared for in one of the following rooms: the "Sniffles Room" for those (six months to 12 years) with respiratory ailments, colds, and so on; or the "Popsicle Room" for the youngsters with diarrhea or vomiting (severe cases not accepted); or, the "Polka Dot Room" for those with chicken pox.

It made me recall the time I caught the chicken pox at age seven while visiting at my cousin's house. To this day my aunt often reminds me that all I kept crying was "I want my Mom," and that I was not satisfied until she came to get me. Are the little ones of today really any different in such vulnerable circumstances?

A front-page story in the *Minneapolis Star & Tribune* described some frantic parents who were willing to place their child "without first checking" a provider's credentials, environment, or services, so anxious were they to find child care for their infants and small children. Unfortunately, the "solution" to such dilemmas is a push for government-sponsored (meaning taxpayer-financed) nationalized Day Care.

Support for the struggling mom who is doing all in her power to provide for her family's needs is certainly a loving approach. She needs and is deserving of assistance. VCRs, new cars, Caribbean cruises, and exclusive dress shops this mother will never know. For those, however, who turn their babies over to hired sitters simply because they *want* to work, we owe no such allegiance. In fact, we do both mother and child a great disservice by offering tax incentives which would entice a nurturing mom *out* of the home. Moreover, we mislead millions into believing the role of stay-at-home parent is second class in nature.

Studies have conclusively demonstrated that a majority of working mothers send their young to day care because they are striving for those extra luxuries or they admit reluctantly that when it comes to a full-time commitment, career takes priority over child. We've all heard the reasoning of some of them: "I just wasn't cut out to be home all day," some say. "He's so much happier with children his own age," is another answer. Or "She's so bored when we're home." (So is Mom, no doubt.)

Early Attachment

This past summer I gave birth to a beautiful baby boy, joyfully welcomed by his 12 brothers and sisters. Among the "New Parent" classes offered by the hospital was one on "early development and parent/child relationships" presented by the hospital's Child Development Psychologist. It skillfully demonstrated how attached each newborn was to the sound of his own mother's and father's voice.

175

When my oldest daughter, Chrissy, who had not yet seen her new little brother, happened to come into the room where the session of parents with babies was being held, the psychologist suggested a test. She placed baby Joseph between herself and Chrissy. Then she told Chrissy to talk to the baby at the same time she talked to him. Up to that time his eyes and full attention had been on the instructor. However, the minute the baby heard his older sister's voice he immediately turned his head and eyes toward Chrissy. It was a beautiful sight to behold. He did the same thing when my husband and I talked to him.

"He recognizes your voices and is familiar with you because he heard those voices daily when he lived inside his mother," she told the class. The same thing occurred with other parents who were present.

The psychologist concluded by warning that "prolonged separation of baby from mother can be quite harmful, especially during the first year of his/her life, when close bonds should be developing." In speaking with her after the session she confided, "We see so many two-parent-career-Yuppies at this hospital, and I can only say so much. They don't want to consider the adverse effects on their young because if they do, they would be forced to make some vital changes in their careers." . . .

Necessity of Parental Attention

Clinicians are unanimous that a child needs the attention of his mother for at least his first year, and continuity in his personal caretaker for at least his first three years, if he is to have the best chance for satisfactory personal relations later in life.

Michael Levin, *Commentary*, August 1986.

Perhaps, in years to come, we may find the children of welfare mothers fared better than those shuffled off to day care during the most sensitive period of their growing up years to fulfill mom's career goals.

As news stories continue to verify, day care is scarce and the demand is great. An acquaintance of mine, a career-fulfillment mother seeking care for her two-year-old, summed up her problem by saying, "When we were looking for a new house to buy, I think we must have checked out almost 100 different places, and with each one we became fussier. But when it comes to finding day care, unfortunately availability takes priority. We just can't be that fussy." How will this young woman ever be convinced that full-time mothering is the most vital role she can choose— for her child's sake?

It may be a decade before the full ramifications surface about institutional mothering. But already there is a growing list of experts (including Drs. Lee Salk, Selma Fraiberg, and Burton White, an educational psychologist who heads the Harvard Preschool Project) who believe day care is a "disaster" because institutional environments are not appropriate for small children.

Dr. Urie Bronfenbrenner of Cornell University also suggests, "Families are strong things. You don't kill them easily. But one of the things that gets through and discombobulates even good families is stress in the workplace when both parents are working. If there's stress in the family, the most vulnerable members of the family are most affected. And the most vulnerable members are the smallest children."

Children and Daycare

Dr. Jay Belsky, a Penn State University psychologist who has been researching the effect of infant day care for a decade, says the increasing evidence regarding the harmful effects of early institutionalization on children can no longer be ignored. Risking the wrath of day-care proponents and the more militant feminists, he believes his views are supported by a silent majority of his peers. Belsky, a professor of human development, found in several recent studies that the rate of insecurity nearly doubles for day-care children. Babies who were placed in child-care facilities before 18 months of age, he discovered, were more likely to cry and misbehave at ages 9 and 10.

Dr. Lee Salk, a clinical psychologist from New York, flatly declares that "a child needs a full-time or nearly full-time parent most during the first three years of life." Salk, who writes a monthly column for *McCall's* magazine, suggests that the security of knowing that a parent cares enough to be with him every day is far more crucial to a child than learning how to play with blocks, using watercolors or crayons, or developing manual dexterity and social skills in day-care settings. Salk advises a parent (Mom or Dad) to postpone his or her job for at least the first three years of a child's life. This is a very important period, when the child's sense of security, trust, bonding, and love take root.

This would prevent situations like the one that happened to an acquaintance of mine. Her boy woke up with an ear-ache in the middle of the night, and when she went to comfort him he responded, "Not you! I want the *other* Mom." At age 2½, he had already sensed who cared the most. (She then quit her job and stayed home with him.)

A study released by researchers Deborah Lowe Vandell and Mary Ann Corasaniti (of the University of Texas at Dallas) reveals that children placed in non-maternal care at an early age are not only less cooperative, less popular, and less confident than their peers, but they also have poorer study skills and make lower grades.

Such institutional environments have further proven to be hazardous breeding grounds for viruses and respiratory ailments. This was acknowledged by Minnesota internists and state epidemiologists, whose findings were given front-page coverage in the *Minneapolis Tribune*. One doctor suspects the summer outbreak of viruses occurs because "children aren't getting a break from each other—so many are in close contact with each other during the summer because they are in day care year around." Public health officials in most areas are warning parents to have their children immunized in order to guard against what has become common day-care diseases. Most often included is the widescale spread of diarrhea, jaundice, and hepatitis A.

Substitute Parenting

Shortly before the 8:03 leaves our station, I see from my window a sleepy child, now about 8 months old, pushed in his stroller by one of his parents—they take turns—toward the home of the neighborhood sitter. The child will spend the next 10 hours in her care, and one may wonder how much one hard-pressed woman, however kindly her intentions, can do for a baby who is one of six children she takes in for local professionals who are parents.

Katharine Byrne, *America*, March 9, 1985.

On another, far more serious plane, there are growing numbers of news accounts of day-care abuse, which should send a chilling alarm. Such reports tell of physical assault and injury, as well as sexual exploitation, including the use of pre-school infants and toddlers for pornographic acts and other forms of abuse. The severe and life-long damage that is inflicted on these vulnerable children should never be underestimated.

Questions and Wrong Answers

If only every young mother would ask herself, "How critical is my need to work?" before turning her infant over to sitters-for-hire. If only each new father asked himself, "Can I support my wife in her effort to care for our baby full-time, putting off luxuries for later?" Perhaps then more American children would be spared the experience of day care and enjoy the love and building of relationships that comes so naturally to full-time parenting. Dr. Salk pulls no punches when he suggests that the child of working parents may think of himself as a burden, as someone who is "in the way" and causing problems for his parents.

The establishment of government or even church-subsidized day care, in practice, will further serve to demean and demote the already weakened role of mothering in society. While such institutions may come to the aid of those in real need, the mere presence of such facilities will encourage and entice yet more women— those who do not have to work—to choose an outside career over caring for a child. After all, they will rationalize, "if the church sponsors it, it *must* be okay."

Unfortunately, young couples today are bombarded by "me-first" career-oriented feminist propaganda and sympathetic secular media that advise finding fulfillment outside home and family. Many, like a Minnesota editorialist, have come to believe that "the issue of Day Care is America's Number One problem." Forget the federal deficit, threatened Social Security for the elderly, issues of health care and its rising costs, the growing rate of crime, national security and defense, and the most ignored "issue" of all—the murder of 4,000 preborn babies a day by abortion. Day care is supposed to be paramount!

Unless Congress hears from those opposed to subsidized day care, we will soon begin the same "advanced" path as Sweden and the People's Republic of China. . . .

Our Real Priorities

It's time we consider our real priorities—as parents and as a country. Parents of bygone eras made it through the Great Depression and two major wars and never shuffled their young off to institutional care. Yet we, their children and grandchildren, demand government-sponsored nurseries as a "right" and necessity.

We don't really need nationalized day care in this country. What we do need is a national recommitment to the family. Children need to sense, by the daily presence of a full-time parent, that they are so valuable—so very precious—that only under the most serious circumstances would an institution or stranger be permitted to care for their daily needs. Are not children our country's greatest natural resource?

"The available evidence shows that children in dual-career families are more independent and resourceful."

Children of Working Parents Thrive

Lucia A. Gilbert

Lucia A. Gilbert is a professor of educational psychology at the University of Texas in Austin. She is a parent and the author of numerous articles and books focusing on male-female issues. In the following viewpoint, she states that the children of working parents develop many positive qualities. She believes this results from the additional independence and responsibilities the children in such families have.

As you read, consider the following questions:

1. What are some of the positive things Gilbert believes children learn from their working parents?
2. What do children think of their working parents, according to Gilbert?

Lucia A. Gilbert, *Sharing It All: The Rewards and Struggles of Two-Career Families*. New York: Plenum Publishing Corporation, 1988. Reprinted with permission.

How well do children in dual-career families fare? Are they harmed by day care? Are they selfish and self-centered? Is it too soon to know? The available evidence shows that children in dual-career families are more independent and resourceful and have a wider range of role models than children raised in more traditional homes. They benefit from greater contact and interaction with both parents and less exposure to sex-role stereotypic behavior in the home. Those from role-sharing families report greater self-direction and a closer relationship with their fathers than peers from relatively traditional households.

Children in role-sharing families also do more around the house and accept some fair share of the domestic responsibilities. A colleague of mine aptly noted that many parents don't take the time to teach children what needs to be done and so end up doing it themselves. She and her husband painstakingly taught each of their two children, when they were around four years old and still thought it was fun, to vacuum, set the table, cook, make salad, and so on. Now, five or more years later, she reports that "it's a routine. We all pitch in so we can have more time together."

Children see both parents doing what they want to be doing and thus being happier and more content when they are with the family. Says a university administrator in her early 40s married to a history teacher and who has two sons, age 8 and 10: "We both work, we both want to work, and that's how it's going to be. Our philosophy is that children have to adjust to you just like you have to adjust to them. I am not worried about how they will 'turn out.' We have our ups and downs, but things generally work out."

Children Respond

What do the children say? In a recent survey of male and female adolescent and young adult children (aged 13-24) raised in dual-career families, respondents rated their families high in closeness. They especially noted feelings of mutual concern and support. We found similar results in a study of adolescent girls raised in dual-career families. The benefits frequently mentioned in both studies included children's perceptions of both parents as positive role models, their exposure to a broad range of values and experiences, the family's financial security, and the children's opportunity to develop independence; time constraints were the most frequently mentioned problem.

Several girls commented on the positive influence of parents, particularly mothers: "The decisions mom made seem like the best choices, the way I'd decide on my own probably." "My parents have shown me that a female should not have to take care of the house alone and work. There should be equal sharing of housework." A common theme was that "they want to make sure

181

I can live on my own." Many of their parents emphasized the importance of good education, responsibility, and setting goals to achieve.

My own daughter said she sometimes feels we don't have enough time for her or get too distracted by pressures at work. On these occasions she rates growing up in a dual-career family as a 4.5 (on a scale that ranges from not that bad, 1, to terrible, 10). Otherwise she rather enjoys it. When I asked her what she saw as the effects on her, the immediate response was "getting to go to a lot of places, knowing a lot of different people, and going to your and dad's offices." This was followed by learning good habits, the ability to communicate (especially with her children, should she ever have any), and the willpower to stick with things even when the going gets rough.

Working Parents and Sexism

I think her last point about willpower relates to experiences with sexism. She was distressed by a recurring situation at school. The boys assumed they were smarter and more skilled than the girls, even though evidence made the contrary seem obvious. Not even logic could alter their viewpoint. The biggest insult occurred in physical education, which was a coeducational class. She was by far the best soccer player in the class, but even her male teacher failed to recognize her ability. She sat out a good part of the class time and watched the boys play. It infuriated her (and us). . . .

Working Moms Encourage Independence

There are some studies that indicate that children of working mothers may actually have advantages over children of at-home mothers. The research seems to indicate increased self-esteem, maturity and sense of responsibility among children of working mothers. "Independence is an important factor," says Lois Wladis Hoffman, a psychology professor at the University of Michigan and an expert on working mothers. "Working mothers seem to encourage it more than mothers who don't work. This is good for children of both sexes, but it is especially good for daughters." Hoffman adds that at-home mothers may "do more for the child than is necessary and therefore delay the time necessary for the child to become independent."

Barbara Kantrowitz et al., *Newsweek*, March 31, 1986.

Many children from dual-career families become quite articulate and assertive about sexism and develop a sensitivity and awareness about sex-role issues. The comment of a son in his early 20s seems particularly poignant. He believes that the main advantage to him was seeing his mother, and therefore other women, as his equals. Witnessing parents' struggles with taking on non-traditional tasks helps children comprehend the power of sex roles. When mothers encourage and reinforce fathers' participation in traditionally feminine household chores, which is often the case, their understanding of how men are changing heightens. Moreover, a more egalitarian-type marital relationship gets modeled. . . .

Nonsexist child-rearing at this point has different implications for the upbringing of daughters and sons. Women in dual-career families pursued nontraditional paths and know the importance of instilling similar values in their daughters. Many parents in dual-career families, mothers in particular, want their daughters to grow up with both the proverbial "roots" and "wings." Roots, which girls traditionally developed, provide a sense of commitment and dependability and an ability to connect to and nurture others. Wings, traditionally reserved for boys, give them the strength to be independent, take care of themselves, and evince a sense of well-being separate from others. One father noted the changing times and the excitement he felt watching his daughter mature from a girl to an adolescent: "This little girl of mine is tough, with creative aspirations that challenge her to write ballets about swans while shedding sudden tears when a friend moves away. I look forward to watching her grow and mature." Toughness and tenderness fit for girls who grow up to be independent women who know how to nurture others. . . .

Parenting Is Complex

Parenting in dual-career families remains complex. Women have pushed for dual-career marriages, and they experience more stress and overload than men when it comes to caring for children. Affordable child care persists as a trying and burdensome problem. Yet most women see the situation as positive and would not change it for a career in full-time homemaking. Men are being nudged by the women they love to participate more actively in parenting, and they too see the rewards in terms of their expanded roles within the family.

"A child may suffer permanent emotional damage from an exhausted lifestyle when there is no full-time homemaker in the house."

Children of Working Parents Suffer

Cal Thomas and Phyllis Schlafly

Cal Thomas is a syndicated newspaper columnist. In Part I of the following viewpoint, he argues that children are emotionally damaged when both parents work. Part II is written by Phyllis Schlafly, a well-known antifeminist and outspoken defender of traditional family roles. She believes children need full-time parental care. According to Schlafly, when both parents work, their children suffer from the lack of attention.

As you read, consider the following questions:

1. What negative qualities do children of working parents commonly develop, according to Thomas?
2. According to Schlafly, in what ways do children of working parents suffer?
3. Which viewpoint did you find more convincing—this one or the one by Gilbert? Why?

I

"It can be hard because kids don't understand. When I'd leave, little Al would get mad and not talk to me. But I have to be happy too. I wouldn't be a happy mother if I was staying home as a housewife." That is Olympic gold medal runner Valerie Brisco-Hooks speaking to a *New York Times* interviewer. She is not alone in her belief that motherhood is a hurdle which must be jumped in order to find real fulfillment.

The Labor Department says that nearly half of the nation's married women with children one year old or younger are in the labor force. The figure jumped from 24 percent in 1970 to 46.8 percent by the end of 1984. Of married women with children under 18, three-fifths are now working, a staggering number which has brought with it a profound sociological impact.

While some of these women obviously must work in order to survive, others work for different reasons. Regardless of the reason, the impact on families, particularly children, is severe.

Psychologist Dr. James Dobson advises the White House and the Pentagon on family life. He has sold more than 4 million books on family relationships and his "Focus on the Family" radio program is heard on 640 stations in eight countries.

Permanent Emotional Damage

Dobson says a child may suffer permanent emotional damage from an exhausted lifestyle when there is no full-time homemaker in the house. Numerous studies have shown that children who are shuttled from one baby sitter to another are different than they would be otherwise. Research consistently has demonstrated that the mother-child relationship is especially vital during the first three years of life and that there is no substitute for the bonding that occurs between generations during that time. The Harvard pre-school study revealed that a child's future intellectual capacity and emotional security are largely dependent on the quality of mothering occurring when the child is young.

Numerous studies have found, notes Dobson, that children "thrown into group situations too early" incline toward peer-dependency and insecurity as they move through childhood.

Further, the households of two-income families tend to be more chaotic and less organized than those with a homemaker on duty. The stress level of every family member is increased in a home where time is limited for recreation and relaxed conversation.

Dobson believes there are several questions mothers who have a choice about whether to work should ask themselves: 1) To whom shall I submit the task of guiding the unfolding process of development during the years when dramatic changes are occurring in my children? 2) Who will care enough to make the invest-

185

ment if every day my husband and I are too busy for the job? 3) What group-oriented facility possibly can substitute for the individual attention and love my child needs? 4) Who will represent our values and beliefs and be ready to answer our child's questions during his peak period of interest? 5) To whom will I surrender the prime-time experiences of his day?

Steve Artley/Reprinted by permission of Artley Cartoons.

The 1909 White House Conference on Children had it right when it concluded, "Home life is the highest and finest product of civilization. . . . Except in unusual circumstances, the home should not be broken up for reasons of poverty." It was in the 1920s that a new ideology of "social parenting" began to take shape in America. This has led us to the "modern family," no better represented than in the movie, "Irreconcilable Differences."

In the film Casey Brodsky, age 10, is divorcing her parents. Says Casey, "If I'm not going to be totally nuts when I grow up, I'd better get out while I still have a chance." Mom and Dad are so involved with personal ambitions that they don't have the time and energy to give Casey the warmth and affection that all children need. In the end they realize this and make a new start. In real life not everyone comes to such a realization.

As we relentlessly pursue "happiness," we would do well to remember what C.S. Lewis wrote: "We have no right to happiness. We have only an obligation to do our duty." It is in doing that duty that ultimate happiness is to be found.

II

Not so many mothers are at home in the afternoon any more. Those who are at home are usually "moms" to latch-key children, too. Confronted with the prospect of going home to an empty house, children will usually, if they can, gravitate to the home of a schoolmate whose mother is at home.

Indeed, so-called experts are now instructing latch-key children to do exactly that. In a latch-key course for 9-to-13-year-olds, pupils are given a multiple-choice question. "You are walking home alone from school and you think a man in a car is following you. What would you do? (A) Stand still and see what he does. (B) Walk quickly home and lock yourself in the house. (C) Walk to a neighbor's home and stay there. (D) Other." The correct answer is (C) because "if you go home and lock yourself in the house, you could be followed, and there might not be anyone there to help you."

Brenda Hunter, author of *Where Have All The Mothers Gone?*, eloquently described her life as a latch-key child. "No matter how sunny the atmosphere outside, an empty house is always cold and dark and lonely. I always made a check under the bed and looked in the closets to make sure that no burglar had entered our home."

The liberated lifestyles which encourage wives and mothers to do their own thing have left children to bear burdens of loneliness, depression, and the empty home. Latch-key children are crying out for the love of moms who will subordinate their own career ambitions and desire for material things to the well-being of their children. . . .

The NBC News White Paper called "Women, Work and Babies" put an important subject out on the agenda for national discussion. Jane Pauley, America's most famous working mother of twins, posed the question "Can America cope?" with the phenomenon of mothers of babies who have full-time jobs.

The program was not about single parents trying to support themselves and their children. The program was about two-earner couples in which the wife (a) wants a professional career for her own self-fulfillment, (b) simply likes the extra money (to go on vacations, etc.), or (c) admits she can't stand being at home with her children and would rather be anywhere else.

Any successful lawyer knows that, if he can frame the question, he can often get any verdict he wants from judge or jury. The question really is not "can America cope?", but "can babies cope?" and "can husbands cope?" . . .

From the babies' point of view, "day-care diseases" are serious. Anyone who has watched flu bugs and other contagious diseases go through a family of several children at home must recoil in horror at the thought of 30 toddlers in diapers, all ill and screaming for their mothers. The NBC program admitted that day-care babies are 12 times more likely to get the flu than home-care babies.

Another major problem from the babies' point of view is the constant change of personnel. Babies don't adapt well to the high turnover rate of hired "care providers."

While babies are the biggest losers in any system of non-mother care, it was clear from the NBC program that husbands lose, too. When a woman has a baby and a career, the husband ranks third on her scale of priorities, and a poor third, at that, because she's simply too exhausted for anything else even if she has any extra time, which she usually doesn't.

The lifestyle sections of newspapers have had many articles in recent months about how men in their 20s and 30s are rejecting or avoiding marriage. Is it any wonder? What man wants to risk a financial/emotional commitment, buy a ring and assume a mortgage on a house, when he will rank only #3 in the heart of the woman he loves? . . .

New Child Abuse

Consider a conversation I had with a childhood friend, now a full-time financial analyst. She has two helpers for a newborn and a 3-year-old. "Are you home most evenings?" I ask. "As a matter of fact," she answers, "we're out every night this week from Monday through Saturday."

I have witnessed many examples of this disconcerting style of "parenting." What I see emerging is an entirely new category of professionals who spend little, if any, time with their children. There appears to be a new form of neglect on the part of the rich: absence.

Sally Abrahms, *The New York Times,* January 20, 1988.

The artificial world of primetime TV programming seems to have abandoned the traditional family and plunged into a world where there are almost no mothers. June Cleaver, Harriet Nelson, Lucy Ricardo, and other stay at home moms have vanished. They've been replaced by single women, divorced women sharing homes, and female detectives with unemployed husbands. Some mothers appear, but they are usually widowed, divorced, unwed, or their children are peripheral to the plot.

In the real world, however, the tide is going against feminism and toward motherhood. Every woman doesn't need a baby, but every baby still needs a mother.

"Nationally mandated infant care leave addresses a concern central to society's very existence: the well-being of the family."

Infant Care Leave Would Help Working Parents

Edward F. Zigler and Meryl Frank

Edward F. Zigler is a professor of psychology and director of the Bush Center in Child Development and Social Policy at Yale University. Meryl Frank is director of the Infant Care Leave Policy at the Bush Center. In the following viewpoint, Zigler and Frank argue that a federal infant care leave policy is necessary for the survival of the American family. They write that the US government must show its support for the family by legislating infant care leave so working parents can stay home with their babies during the crucial first few months of development.

As you read, consider the following questions:

1. Why is it essential for parents to spend a lot of time with their newborns, according to Zigler and Frank?
2. In the authors' opinion, how can employers and the government send the message that families are important to society?
3. Why do the authors argue it is the government's responsibility to promote a national infant care leave policy?

From *The Parental Leave Crisis*, Edward F. Zigler and Meryl Frank, eds. New Haven, CT: Yale University Press, 1988. Copyright © 1988 by Yale University.

The research [concerning parental leave] brings to the forefront for the first time many points that our grandmothers could have told us: that mothers need time to recover physically and emotionally from pregnancy and childbirth; that families need time to adjust to the arrival of a new family member; and that infants need time in a stable, caring environment. Our grandmothers' intuitions are supported today by a multitude of medical and social science research that provides strong evidence for the need to enact an infant-care-leave policy in the United States.

In effect, medical science has provided the rationale for policies of the past, such as a disability leave after childbirth. Research in the field of obstetrics and gynecology has shown that women require between six and eight weeks to recover physically from pregnancy and childbirth following a normal, safe, vaginal delivery. These six to eight weeks of postpartum recovery are necessary to allow the uterus to return to its normal size, and to allow the placental site to properly heal. A delivery that requires surgery, or is premature or abnormal, would require more recovery time. And given the high percentage of atypical births today, the average disability leave associated with pregnancy and childbirth is more likely to be approximately ten weeks. Yet even though medical science has provided a clear definition of the length of time needed for mothers to recover from their physical disablement, it would be wrong and even foolish to assume that the time needed for physical recovery alone also ensures a healthy and caring parent-infant relationship.

The Parent-Child Relationship

The evidence of social science adds to our understanding of the time parents need with newborn infants in addition to recovery time. Numerous studies in the field of psychology have concluded that time together in the first months of life is essential to the development of a healthy parent-infant relationship. D. Stern and T. Berry Brazelton, for example, demonstrate that parents and their infants need time to establish a pattern of interaction which will enable them to recognize and respond to each other's signals. This attunement to each other's rhythms provides an important foundation in the infant's developing sense of self. Through their interaction with their parents, infants come to realize that they can influence and affect their environment, and thus they begin to develop a sense of security and trust within the family relationship and environment.

In addition to the development of a general sense of security, time together during the early period of an infant's life is crucial to insure a secure attachment to the caregiver. This attachment, based upon the infant's trust in the continuity of physical care and positive emotional response, is essential if the infant is to feel comfortable enough to begin to explore and experience the world. The infant must be provided with an environment which is of good quality, one that is warm, nurturing, and stimulating. Although new parents may immediately cherish their infant, it takes time for them, as well as the infants, to develop the emotions that insure bonding and to learn how to establish the routines of continuity and security. All of these characteristics take time for parents to develop, and certainly additional time for parents to find and recognize in infant day-care arrangements.

Room for Family Life

Perhaps the most surprising thing about parental leave is that it has taken Congress so long to deal with the subject. The need for such laws has long been recognized by other advanced industrial nations. An overwhelming majority of them—countries such as Canada, Italy, Sweden, France, and Britain—have already passed laws dealing with parental leave. . . .

Few families can survive today without two working parents, whether they live separately or together. With the family at work, the workplace will have to stretch a little and make room for family life.

David R. Spiegel, *Vogue*, April 1988.

Research on the family system has highlighted the period immediately following birth as vital for the redefinition of family roles. During the first few months following birth, all family members—mothers, fathers, and siblings—need time to adjust to the presence of a new family member and to renegotiate their family relationships and roles. Each member of the family feels disruption at the entrance of the new baby. Time is necessary to allow for a comfortable transition and to regain family equilibrium. Although these relationships are dynamic and do continue to change, the period following the introduction of the newborn into the family is one of the most important transitional periods in a family's life, and therefore requires special attention.

Overburdened Families

It is also clear that families need infant care leave upon the birth of a new child. A large number of surveys report stressed, overburdened families who must contend with the conflicting pressures of work and family. Parents report guilt over leaving infants too early and in questionable care arrangements. These worries are not without foundation. As Brazelton and others have shown, many parents who are unable to spend time with their infants begin to distance themselves emotionally from too great an attachment to the infant.

The lack of regulations and quality in infant day care adds to the stress of the family as well. As research suggests, little is known about the effects of placing newborn infants in day care of varying quality, and high quality infant day care is rare, and if it is available at all, it is costly. What research tells us, however, is that a comprehensive approach must be taken when evaluating the outcome of infants in day care. An infant's environment must be considered in terms of many factors, among them: levels of stress at home; maternal and parental attitudes about working; the support the mother receives from the community; and the infant's temperament and individual characteristics. All of these elements will affect the infant's experience in day care and all of these elements may be closely tied to the time, opportunity, and inclination parents have to establish a responsive environment and to recognize one in an infant day-care arrangement.

Research, surveys, and experience all independently lead to the same conclusion: parents and infants need time together to adjust to the many changes a family experiences at birth and to grow together into a strong family system. Grandma's knowledge has come full circle: as a society, we should support a period of family togetherness in the early months.

Society and Support

When social structures and institutions support parents in their parenting role, especially with very young infants, the message is communicated that the development of the family is valuable to society, and that the family is essential to society's well-being. However, no current, truly national policy exists to support families when parents must work as well as care for and respond to a new infant. Research presents a convincing case that the first year following the birth of a child is becoming an increasingly difficult period in a family's life. More and more parents of both genders must work outside the home to provide for their families. Without a recognition of the special needs parents and their infants have, families have little hope for relief. The working mother's recovery from childbirth, the parent's adjustment to the entrance of a newborn, the kind of day care the infant is receiving, and even the availability of such care is viewed mainly as a private concern, rather than a larger social concern. We, as a society, need to recognize the conflicts parents face between their work and their family, and we need to help to strengthen families by resolving these conflicts.

To date, the necessary support, both in terms of time and money, has not been provided to most American families. Even where it does exist, and then only for a minority of the population, it is often inadequate. Independently arranged leave policies, instituted by too few of our nation's employers, do little to address the overall problem of recognition and support for the role of the family on a national level. The uneven and haphazard adoption of leave policies has the effect of discrimination, both internally within a business and externally between businesses. A business may extend time only to a favored employee or to attract talented employees away from competitors. However, the opposite is equally true: some businesses are unwilling or unable to provide a leave, without the knowledge that competitors are doing the same. This type of competition may be efficient in the marketplace, but it does little to contribute to the stability of the family and the total work force in the long run. Yet the existing practices of individual businesses are too informal and haphazard to meet the needs of most families. Most families, especially low-income and single-parent families, still must struggle to meet all the demands being made on their time. Inevitably, when the financial survival of the family competes with attention to its emotional growth, survival takes precedence. Many families at this time have no other option than to put their family's development on hold while they earn the wages to provide for material support that is absolutely necessary.

The Benefits of Family Leave

Fortune's survey of 400 working parents found that nearly 70 percent of mothers suffer from stress. Some 41 percent of parents lose an average one day's work in three months, and 10 percent lose five days or more to tend to a sick child or other family matters.

Child care is the single strongest predictor of absenteeism in job performance, the survey found. Onsite child care centers have been found to cut absenteeism in half or better, and flextime has been shown to raise productivity by as much as 50 percent.

A family leave policy is likely to lower the high turnover rates common in female-dominated jobs.

Rosemary Trump, Testimony before the Senate Subcommittee on Children, Family, Drugs and Alcoholism, April 23, 1987.

We are still far behind the other nations of the world, both in our recognition of the family-society relationship and in our efforts to strengthen that relationship. For many nations of the world, infant-care-leave policies were established to rebuild economic and human capital in the aftermath of war. These policies have been in existence for years and have proven viable through the test of time. Only the United States lags in its recognition of the importance of the family over short-term economic interests. Only the United States refuses to see that "it is in the best interest of society to support families and parenthood in whatever way possible," according to Joseph P. Allen. American society is slow to become aware of how drastic and influential the changing demographics of the work force are. Although we may want to preserve the illusion that all mothers are at home with their young infants and that those who do work wait until their children are toddlers, statistics paint a much different and more realistic picture. There can be no illusion that we will return to a nostalgic past; a changed work force is here to stay.

As the Bush Center's Advisory Committee has emphasized, "The infant-care-leave problem in the United States is of a magnitude and urgency such as to require immediate national attention." Government has a responsibility to create and enforce an infant-care-leave system of support. Whereas some employers may be individually motivated to do so out of a concern for their work force, only a national policy mandated by the federal government can ensure that uniform support is available to all families working in all businesses, whether private or public. In calling for a recognition of the need for an infant care leave and its implementation on a national level, we are asking for increased responsibility by all who should be involved—parents, employers, and government.

Employers must acknowledge that employees are family members with responsibilities outside the workplace—responsibilities that will affect their performance as employees, especially at specific times in their lives. The strength of the American workplace and work force is directly related to the strength of the family. One way in which employers may be able to meet both their needs and the needs of their workers who are family members is to provide flexible working arrangements to help both employer and employee bridge the time between childbirth and reentry into the workplace. . . .

A Two-Sided Benefit

Although infant care leaves may be aimed primarily at helping new parents integrate their family and career roles, it is not a benefit which is one-sided. Rather it is a part of the larger issue wherein society's well-being arises out of a more synergistic relationship between the family and the workplace. The ultimate benefit is a stable, dependable, and productive work force, supported by a strong American family system.

The leave policy recommended by the Yale Bush Center Advisory Committee on Infant Care Leave does not seek to side with the family over the workplace. Rather, it requires respect from each side for the needs of the other, and it requires compromises that need to be made by each. It calls upon employers to recognize that family concerns constitute a legitimate demand on an employee's time and attention. The workplace can benefit by respecting those demands and by helping the employee meet the responsibilities of both work and family. One responsibility should not displace the other. The Committee's work calls equally upon parent-employees to recognize the employers' demands on their time and commitment. An infant care leave does not mean that family concerns displace those of the workplace. Rather, the two concerns affect each other. An infant care leave would need to address the distinct character of the American workplace as well as of American families in order to find a balance between the needs of parents, of infants, and of employers.

A Concern of Society

The issue of a nationally mandated infant care leave addresses a concern central to society's very existence: the well-being of the family. It is an issue involving what the family needs in order to cope with the birth of a new child, and how parents who do work can meet obligations of both work and family. A society is only as strong as its components, who are family members. The family, in turn, is only as strong as the institutions of society permit it to be.

"*Parental leave legislation will hurt the traditional and the poor family.*"

Infant Care Leave Would Not Help Working Parents

Dick Armey and Elizabeth Kepley

Dick Armey, the author of Part I of the following viewpoint, is a Republican US representative from Texas. Elizabeth Kepley, the author of Part II, is the director of legislative affairs for the organization, Concerned Women for America. Armey and Kepley argue that federally mandated infant care leave will not help the average American family. They maintain that only wealthy couples who can afford to take unpaid leave would gain from a national policy.

As you read, consider the following questions:

1. Why does Armey argue that parental leave will aid only the wealthy?
2. In Armey's opinion, how are businesses already taking steps to insure medical leave?
3. According to Kepley, why would parental leave not help parents and children bond?

Dick Armey, "Parental Leave Act Is Just Yuppie Welfare," *The Wall Street Journal*, February 26, 1987. Reprinted with permission of The Wall Street Journal. © 1987 Dow Jones & Company, Inc. All rights reserved. Written Statement of Elizabeth Kepley, Director of Legislative Affairs, Concerned Women for America on The Parental and Temporary Medical Leave Act of 1987 before the Subcommittee on Children, Family, Drugs and Alcoholism and The Committee on Labor and Human Resources of the United States Senate. Reprinted by permission of Concerned Women for America, 370 L'Enfant Promenade, SW, Suite 800, Washington, DC 20024, (202) 488-7000.

Representatives Bill Clay (D., Mo.) and Pat Schroeder (D., Colo.) propose in the nicely named Family and Medical Leave Act that employers of 15 or more be required by federal law to provide new mothers and fathers up to 18 weeks of leave with health benefits intact and a guarantee of returning to their position at the same salary. The measure, which faced hearings before the House Subcommittee on Labor-Management Relations, also provides for a study of the advisability of mandating paid leave. The bill, according to its sponsors, would establish "important protection for the rights of workers and families," since "most employers have failed to adapt their leave policies to the needs of workers."

This appeal to workers is a twist on the traditional one from the Democratic left, which is usually aimed at blue-collar workers and what the left sees as an American proletariat pitted against big business. Instead, it is creating an issue, looking to incorporate the block of voters known as "yuppies."

Yuppie Welfare

Democrats have done well by exploiting the social programs evolved during the "Great Society" years to create new programs that give more voters a vested interest in the election of Democrats. But yuppies don't need the government's money and have an almost universal skepticism toward government involvement in their lives. Enter parental leave, or "yuppie welfare."

The median income for families in which both parents work is $34,560 (vs. $23,562 for families with a sole provider). People on the lower side of the median cannot afford the luxury of 18 weeks of unpaid leave to "bond" with their children. This bill would ensure only that professional couples at the higher end of the family income scale will be able to take extended vacations with their newborn children while the federal government ensures that their salaries and positions are retained.

And what of those couples who've chosen to forestall childbearing? These couples, along with single people and those who already have raised families, also would be required to carry a parental-leave policy, forcing them to relinquish other benefits, such as higher pay or a better pension plan. A mandatory parental-leave benefit would not increase the size of benefit packages, but rather limit the size and number of other benefits.

Representatives Clay and Schroeder write: "In 1970 less than 30% of women with children under two years old worked outside the home. Today, almost 50% of women with children under one year of age are working and the percentage is continuing to grow." These changing demographics, they say, demonstrate the need for their legislation. They miss the point that if hiring practices and benefits packages had not met the needs of families with both parents working, their numbers would not have nearly doubled in 15 years.

No Need for Leave

Parental leave is not a grass-roots issue born in response to irresponsible employment practices. Yuppies constitute a large portion of my constituency, but since the introduction of the Family and Medical Leave Act I've heard from only six constituents asking me to vote for it. Some of my more senior colleagues tell me they had never received a letter suggesting the urgent need for federal parental-leave legislation before groups inside the Washington Beltway began pushing it.

Requiring employers to offer parental leave would set a dangerous precedent in employee-management relations. Most employee benefits are not federally mandated. Employers are required only to provide workers' compensation, unemployment compensation and half of Social Security.

A survey of 1,000 firms by the National Chamber Foundation, a nonprofit, educational foundation affiliated with the U.S. Chamber of Commerce, found that 77% had formal or informal parental-leave policies. Of the remaining 23%, more than two-thirds said their employees preferred other benefits. Congressional proponents of the bill are choosing to ignore the positive steps already being taken, voluntarily, by American businesses in this area.

One Company's Experience

Our firm, as well as most of our clients, consider the mandatory parental and medical leave to be a very unacceptable alternative to the present system of mutual accommodation and cooperation between employer and employee. Finding replacement personnel on a temporary basis simply does not work in the professional and/or business environment for various reasons, not the least of which is the lack of incentive on the part of the temporarily hired employee.

Jack Hirsch, Testimony before the Senate Subcommittee on Children, Families, Drugs, and Alcoholism, October 13, 1987.

Say my colleagues Schroeder and Clay: "Despite this revolution in the structure of the family, the United States, alone among industrialized societies, has no national policy regarding parental and medical leave." This statement reminds me of my children wanting to do something wrong and justifying it with "but everyone else is doing it!"

Representative Schroeder argues that "Child-rearing experts agree that the early months of a natural or adopted infant . . . are an important time for the new family to cement its relationship." As a father I can agree with that. As a congressman, I cannot agree that it is my job to pass laws to induce "bonding." The negative effects of government attempts at social engineering are too many to ignore. And we ought not ignore the costs to those employees who have no need for or cannot afford to take advantage of the parental-leave option but would be required to carry the load for those who do.

Should parental leave in its current form become law, the points I'm making in opposing it now will be made by its advocates in a future Congress. But they will use them to push for *paid* parental leave.

II

I represent the national organization of Concerned Women for America with over 573,000 members across the country.

Our purpose is to preserve, protect, and promote traditional values through education, legal defense, legislative programs and related activities. Our membership is comprised of professional women, housewives, and college students, many of whom at one time or another have worked in America's marketplace. We have major concerns regarding a federal mandate on a parental leave policy.

First, we believe that the issue of Parental Leave is a worthy one and must be addressed. It will affect both married and single women. As more women face the decision of entering the workforce or staying at home, the relationships within the roles of parenting, the family unit as a whole, and the business world will become more closely intertwined. We wish to see viable, creative solutions implemented to meet the needs of both the housewife and the working woman and to strengthen the roles of the parent, the child, and the employer.

A Personal Responsibility

Concerned Women for America advocates the strengthening of the family unit, but we believe that responsible parenting can not be federally mandated. It is the personal responsibility of parents to fulfill this duty. The original intent of the proposed legislation was to encourage parents to bond with their newborn infants, but the actual effects of the legislation are quite different. Parent-child bonding occurs at the onset of the infant's life; yet the bill allows parents to take their leave anytime within two years of the birth.

Studies recognize the importance of maternal-child relationships, of bonding and subsequent attachment. However, a child's separation from its parents after only eighteen weeks of intimate bonding can actually be a traumatic, counterproductive experience.

In his 1969 study entitled *Attachment and Loss*, the preeminent psychiatrist Dr. John Bowlby writes: "The responses of protest, despair, and detachment that typically occur when a young child aged over six months is separated from his mother and in the care of strangers are due mainly to 'loss of maternal care at this highly dependent, highly vulnerable stage of development.'"

Freedom of Choice

The recent trend towards "cafeteria-style" benefit plans allows employers to offer employees a menu of benefits from which to select. Mandating specific plans will curtail employee benefits and employer flexibility. Employers have made advances in employee fringe benefit plans by offering flextime and benefit plans which allow employees to "bank" benefits. This has advantages for employers and employees alike. The employee is able to make choices to meet his or her individual needs while the company can control costs. . . .

Both as an employer and a father, I certainly recognize the need for voluntary parental and medical leave in today's society. But I believe our federal labor laws are intended to give employers and employees the freedom to negotiate labor/management issues, *not* deprive them of that freedom.

Zack Hinton, Testimony before the Senate Subcommittee on Children, Families, Drugs, and Alcoholism, October 13, 1987.

The bill will not prevent maternal deprivation nor will it provide the necessary time for the bonding process to occur. Maternal deprivation is a general term used to describe a child living at home who is deprived of his mother's loving care. According to Dr. Bowlby, the relationship between mother and child takes three years to mature.

Harms the Family

Secondly, we are concerned that parental leave legislation will hurt the traditional and the poor family. The latest U.S. Census Bureau statistics reports that the median income for families with the wife at home is $23,562. It is $34,560 for families with both parents in the labor force. The redistributive effects caused by possible passage of this legislation are regressive. Due to mandated benefits, the employee benefit package will favor those families that can afford to take the unpaid leave. It will be detrimental for those families who cannot afford to take the leave. They will pay for a federally mandated benefit that they can not use and lose other more beneficial benefit packages.

We believe that [parental leave] will hurt the economic potential of women. In countries where there are liberal parental leave policies, there is also a very high rate of unemployment among women of childbearing age from ages 20 to 34. For example, the policy in Denmark mandates 18 weeks of parental leave, 90% of which is paid. 2.2% of Denmark's women from the ages of 20 to 34 are unemployed. In Italy, the policy provides five months with an option for an extra six months of parental leave. There is a 4% unemployment rate among Italian women. Compare these figures with the 1.2% unemployment rate of American women. (U.S. Department of Labor, 1983.)

Finally, the ramifications of this legislation will hurt the women which it is trying to help—those women, married and single, who wish to progress in the workplace. Although discrimination is against the law in America, we believe that mandated parental leave policies will discourage businesses from hiring women of childbearing age. Companies know that women are far more likely to take parental leave than men.

Rob Peter To Pay Paul

How will this mandated policy effect single women, or women who are members of the two-person family unit comprised of a husband and wife? It will result in those women and men who have no need of a parental leave policy paying for the child care of their fellow employees. There is an old adage which says that one must rob from Peter to pay Paul. These employees will have fewer or smaller benefit packages offered to them as employers struggle to cover the cost for parental leave.

In conclusion, businesses must be encouraged in their search for creative solutions to providing parental leave policies that will meet the differing variety of employee needs. Women have achieved so much in our recent history thanks to our vibrant free enterprise system. It would be tragic if passage of mandatory parental leave stunts these advances.

a critical thinking activity

Understanding Words in Context

Readers occasionally come across words which they do not recognize. And frequently, because they do not know a word or words, they will not fully understand the passage being read. Obviously, the reader can look up an unfamiliar word in a dictionary. However, by carefully examining the word in the context in which it is used, the word's meaning can often be determined. A careful reader may find clues to the meaning of the word in surrounding words, ideas, and attitudes.

Below are sentences adapted from the viewpoints in this chapter. One word is printed in italics. Try to determine the meaning of each word by reading the excerpt. Under each excerpt you will find four definitions for the italicized word. Choose the one that is closest to your understanding of the word.

Finally, use a dictionary to see how well you have understood the words in context. It will be helpful to discuss with others the clues which helped you decide on each word's meaning.

1. Children pick up attitudes and characteristics *SUBLIMINALLY* just by subtly noticing who you are and what you do.

   SUBLIMINALLY means:

   a) immediately   c) irrationally
   b) unconsciously   d) objectively

2. All that talk about *EGALITARIAN* marriages in which the husbands share 50-50 in child care simply doesn't happen in practice.

   EGALITARIAN means:

   a) intellectual   c) adjustable
   b) equal   d) biased

3. Children's needs should be top priority. Latch-key children are crying out for the love of moms who will *SUBORDINATE* their own career ambitions to the well-being of their children.

   SUBORDINATE means:

   a) to make less important   c) to make more important
   b) to limit   d) to influence

4. One of the things that *DISCOMBOBULATES* even relatively stable families is heavy stress from the workplace when both parents are working.

DISCOMBOBULATES means:

a) improves   c) upsets
b) changes   d) cheers

5. The strong memory of our own pasts combined with the *TENACIOUS* belief in the benefit of traditional moms who stay at home makes it easy to forget that American mothers have always worked.

TENACIOUS means:

a) weak   c) angry
b) loose   d) powerful

6. When you work outside the home, you are teaching a child that she is not the center of the universe which sends a healthy signal to our *NARCISSISTICALLY* prone children.

NARCISSISTICALLY means:

a) cooperative   c) forgetful
b) independent   d) self-centered

7. I realized that my briefcase was always the *CATALYST* because as soon as I reached for it, my children would burst into tears.

CATALYST means:

a) something that causes change   c) something that causes confusion
b) something that controls   d) something that soothes

8. Achieving self-esteem, *AUTONOMY,* and a feeling of mastery did not come easily to many women of the current generation of working mothers.

AUTONOMY means:

a) independence   c) careers
b) control   d) forgetfulness

9. My daughter was by far the best soccer player in the class and when she had to sit out a good part of the game, it *INFURIATED* her. Complaining to the coach did nothing to solve the problem or calm my daughter.

INFURIATED means:

a) pleased   c) bored
b) angered   d) puzzled

Periodical Bibliography

The following articles have been selected to supplement the diverse views presented in this chapter.

Faith Abbott   "Mothers' Lib," *The Human Life Review*, Summer 1988.

Barbara Amiel   "Dilemma of the Working Parent," *Maclean's*, December 23, 1985.

Sharon Baker-Johnson   "Working and Parenting: Can We Do Both?" *Daughters of Sarah*, March/April 1988.

Barbara Berg   "The Guilt That Drives Working Mothers Crazy," *Ms.*, May 1987.

Allan Carlson   "Work and Family: On a Collision Course in America?" *Persuasion at Work*, May 1986.

Edith Fierst   "Careers and Kids," *Ms.*, May 1988.

Alix Finkelstein   "Parental Leave: A Policy for the Future," *Parents*, September 1987.

Gay Sheldon Goldman with Kate Kelly   "Choices of the Modern Mother," *Parents*, October 1988.

Phyllis A. Hall   "All Our Lonely Children," *Newsweek*, October 12, 1987.

Mary Delach Leonard   "The Toughest Choice," *Ladies' Home Journal*, October 1987.

Karen Levine   "The Satisfaction Factor," *Parents*, September 1988.

Wally Metts Jr.   "Home-Grown Kids Need a Full-Time Mom," *Christianity Today*, March 6, 1987.

Kathy Palen   "Family Leave: A Needed Guarantee," *The Christian Century*, April 22, 1987.

Robert J. Samuelson   "The Daddy Track," *Newsweek*, April 3, 1989.

Nadine Taub   "A Public Policy of Private Caring," *The Nation*, May 31, 1986.

Ruth A. Tucker   "Working Mothers," *Christianity Today*, July 15, 1988.

5 CHAPTER

What Is the Future of Male/Female Relationships?

MALE/FEMALE ROLES

Chapter Preface

Of all the questions concerning relations between the sexes, one of the most important remains: can men and women coexist in harmony and equality? Some writers think it is impossible, or, at the least, extremely difficult. In her book *Women and Love*, Shere Hite quotes a woman who says, "Single women should boycott men—have a national strike! All these games are so demeaning to women. . . .Women are the candies, treats for men—not people." Many women believe that men will never change their behavior so women should look to each other for solace.

Many men, on the other hand, find women demanding and are hopelessly confused about what women expect. "The moment you cross the barrier (of intimacy) and actually start to get committed, you find that she begins to feel that you are inadequate as a partner. You know then and there that you are never going to be able to satisfy her," says Alex, a man Herb Goldberg interviewed in his book *The Inner Male*.

Conversely, countless self-help books on how to save a failing marriage or find the right mate attest to others' belief that men and women can have positive relationships. Warren Farrell, in *Why Men Are the Way They Are*, writes that men and women will get along once they start working toward mutual goals and stop viewing each other as the enemy.

In this chapter the authors offer their views on how the future of male/female relationships can most effectively be improved.

"No single relationship satisfies your every
need. . . .Friendships with the opposite sex can
make you feel more whole."

Men and Women Can
Be Friends

Susan Foster Ambrose

In the following viewpoint, Susan Foster Ambrose examines the
benefits of friendship with a member of the opposite sex. She
maintains that opposite-sex friendships can help men and women
reduce stress, gain new perspectives, and hear objective opinions.
Ambrose is a social worker in New York who often writes about
health issues.

As you read, consider the following questions:

1. According to Ambrose, what makes opposite-sex
   friendships so comforting?
2. In the author's opinion, why do men often prefer the
   friendship of women?
3. Why can Ambrose tell her male friends things she cannot
   tell her husband?

Susan Foster Ambrose, "The Benefits of Being Just Friends," *Glamour*, August 1986. This
article was originally published in *Self*.

When I took my first job out of college, working as a legislative aide on Capitol Hill, I finally met the man of my childhood dreams. No, not the knight in shining armor I hoped to marry someday, but the big brother I'd always dreamed of having.

John and I worked for the same congressman, and we shared an office. Consequently, two-thirds of our waking hours were spent together, and we became very good friends. As a political neophyte, I often turned to him for advice in my job, and soon I sought his counsel on other matters as well. It was John who took me shopping for my first car, prodded me into learning basic household repairs, and coached me on the fine art of asking for a raise. In turn, I helped John shop for his suits, protectively passed judgment on the various women in his life, and provided an amused ear the night he practically came unglued after shaking hands with the Vice President of the United States.

A Different Perspective

Why was this relationship so valuable and important to me? It was more than the fact that I finally had an "older brother." Simply put, John offered a different perspective from the one I shared with my women friends. For the first time in my life, I had access to the male psyche. I was privy to such mysteries as the inner sanctum of male humor or men's startling insecurities about women. I finally had a male contemporary I could ask to explain MEN to me.

John was practical, and could help me from Point A to Point B better than any friend I'd had. He was also protective; I had a shoulder to cry on if I needed one, and a warm body to hug that hugged back. With John I had a terrific friendship that reinforced my femininity, yet was free of sexual complications.

Such opposite-sex friendships are increasingly common. Not only are they helpful in the workplace, but researchers say these friendships contribute to happier and healthier lives for those involved. Alfred Dean, Ph.D., professor of medical sociology at San Diego State University, and Nan Lin, Ph.D., professor of sociology at the State University of New York at Albany, have researched the role of friendship and its stress-reducing effect on our lives. In their study of more than one thousand subjects, they found that both men and women who had a confidant of the opposite sex experienced less anxiety and depression than people who didn't.

What makes these opposite-sex friendships so comforting? "The key," says Dr. Dean, "is the degree of intimacy and the strength of the bond. The more satisfactory the intimacy, the less vulnerable a person is to stress." The researchers found caring, trust, affection and a sense of mutual obligation to be critical in building that intimacy.

But such elements also are found in *same-sex* friendships. What gives opposite-sex friendships their added appeal? "Men and women are capable of providing different kinds of support," says Dr. Lin. "Men are more in tune with things that we call 'instrumental' in nature; they do things well. Women are more likely to engage in 'expressive' kinds of activities; they're better listeners. They enjoy more interaction for interaction's sake. These skills are complementary, so both men and women benefit from opposite-sex friendships."

Dr. Lin adds, "Of course there are men who are good listeners and there are women who do things well. It's a matter of differences in general." To dismiss these differences, cautions Dr. Lin, is to lose the essence of why opposite-sex friendships can be so effective.

A Relationship That Works

Friendships between the sexes are important indeed – not just for biding time, nor for quelling loneliness. Not because, in these perilous days, friendship is even safer than safe sex, nor because career women are too tired and involved for new romance. They're important because – in spite of the fact that society is still self-conscious about them – these relationships work.

Susan Margolis, *Working Woman,* June 1988.

Men as well as women often search for the warmth and intimacy of a platonic friendship. In fact, the research of Drs. Dean and Lin revealed that more men had opposite-sex friendships than women. Dr. Dean speculates that men seek women friends because they're looking for a give-and-take they don't usually find with other men.

A friend of mine, a single, thirty-year-old attorney in Chicago, says, "A few of my male friendships are very close and supportive, but when I'm really feeling troubled, I somehow always find myself seeking out a woman to talk to. I can more easily open up in her presence. I suppose somewhere in my subconscious is a parental message that emotion on a man's part is weak; I'm afraid my male friends will be more judgmental.

"All this analytical stuff aside," he adds, smiling, "it's very simple: I like women. I like talking to them. I like needing them, and I like their needing me. We each have something to offer the other."

Chemistry

Lisa Maxwell (whose name, like others in this article, has been changed), a twenty-four-year-old high school teacher in Arlington, Virginia, remembers a personal crisis that began when she learned that while she'd been out of town, the man she was living with had been seen having a candlelight dinner with another woman. Lisa tearfully confided in a close woman friend, who promptly criticized "the jerk," and suggested that Lisa pack her bags.

The next day, a male colleague sensed Lisa's quiet turmoil and invited her out for a drink after work. As Lisa related her story, the friend listened carefully, offered a gentle bear hug and some sensible advice: Had Lisa even asked her boyfriend to explain the dinner? After all, a logical explanation *was* possible. Did she have previous reason to mistrust him? If an affair were going on, what did she consider to be her options? His blend of sympathy and practicality gave her both comfort and a workable game plan.

There is, of course, another key factor in the appeal of male/female friendships: sexual attraction. "Face it—you're playing with a sexual component even in a platonic relationship," notes Sylvia Lambert, a twenty-five-year-old management consultant from Boston. "That's as basic as Adam and Eve. I was always one of those girls who had more male buddies than girlfriends, and it's true today in my job, where I'm working with men every day." Sylvia frankly enjoys the subtle chemistry of having men as intimate friends without the sexual complications.

"In any male/female relationship, there's going to be some sexual tension," says Marilyn Ruman, Ph.D., a psychologist in Encino, California. "It's one of the things that makes an opposite-sex friendship fun."

Sometimes platonic relationships evolve into sexual ones, and that changes the rules. If the change doesn't suit one partner, reverting to the previous status is difficult to do, and the friendship may not survive.

No Romantic Tangles

I was lucky. When my "big brother" John suggested one day that we go out on an official date, I balked. I explained to him that I needed him as my buddy, free of romantic tangles. John understood, accepted that framework, and our friendship continues to this day, even after we both found our true loves and are happily married. (John married my best girlfriend.)

To avoid potential sexual problems, Dr. Ruman advises against sending mixed signals from the beginning. Even if you're not sending out a sexual message, the other partner may at some point feel your platonic status is ready for a change. In that case, Dr. Ruman advises total honesty. "Say something such as, 'I really value you as a friend, and that's what I want our relationship to be,'" she suggests. An honest sentiment about the other person's importance to you may be the best way to ensure that the friendship continues.

Candor is especially important when one or both opposite-sex friends are involved with other partners. Many people feel that one's lover or spouse should always be one's best friend, so it can be annoying, if not threatening, to know that a mate is confiding in someone else. Increasingly, husbands are. In his two-year study of nearly two thousand men and women for a book on male relational behavior, Michael E. McGill, professor at the School of Business at Southern Methodist University, found that one of every three men knows a woman other than his wife with whom he feels he can "talk about anything." That woman might be his mother, sister, colleague or a friend.

Such confidants often can provide a safe outlet for venting ideas before springing them on a spouse, or provide the objectivity that a subjectively involved spouse simply cannot. For instance, I could tell my friend John that I'd signed up for a weekend seminar on charting astrological predictions, and he'd probably respond, "How interesting! Why do you want to learn that and what do you plan to do with it?"

Best of All Worlds

In the best of all worlds, friendship between a man and a woman is a rich terrain. She gets to indulge her mothering/sistering/nurturing instinct without the complications it might cause in a sexual relationship. He gets to be, in a sense, even more intimate than he might be with a romantic partner–able to show certain vulnerabilities that he knows can't be pulled out and used against him at home. They both get to "practice" relating to the opposite sex outside of a romance, where the stakes are bigger–as my friend Christopher says, "It's like shooting free throws before the ten thousand people come into the stands." And we all get to indulge our basically repressed polygamist instincts. It is hard to ask one man in your life to be your Robert Redford, your Mick Jagger and your Woody Allen, and it is equally hard to be Candice Bergen, Madonna and Bette Midler to him. Friendship with the opposite sex lets all of us expand our horizons.

Aimee Lee Ball, *Mademoiselle*, August 1985.

My husband Don, on the other hand, might react to my news with, "I know you love this sort of thing, Susan, but right now we can't afford to spend money so frivolously. Besides, I thought we were going to paint the dining room that weekend." The point is, a close confidant outside a marriage does not have a personal stake in what is said. He or she cares, but isn't threatened by the possible loss of hearth and home if we pursue a dream.

Fulfilling a Need

My friend Katherine Grant, who is single and a career State Department employee living in Washington, finds that most of her male friends are married. "I'm not a threat to their marriages," she states. "In fact, I think I'm good for them. I have a willing ear and an ability to empathize while acknowledging the woman's point of view. No single relationship satisfies your every need, and no spouse can share all your interests. Friendships with the opposite sex can make you feel more whole, and I think that helps you bring more to your marriage as a result."

Regardless of the type of relationship—married or single, platonic or intimate—opposite-sex friends are searching to fulfill a universal need to bond. Says Dr. Dean, "Bonding, intimacy and close ties are crucial for our life's course. Where there's trust, affection, reciprocity, where you're able to go to that person when there is an external source of stress—that truly is a state-of-the-art relationship."

"Although we are oriented toward the opposite sex for sex, for everything else we are gender loyalists. This is no accident. True friendship is rare between women and men."

Men and Women Cannot Be Friends

Letty Cottin Pogrebin

Letty Cottin Pogrebin, the author of *Growing Up Free* and *Family Politics,* is one of the founders of *Ms.* magazine. In the following viewpoint, Pogrebin argues that men and women cannot maintain true opposite-sex friendships because of social inequality. She writes that although love is possible between unequals, friendship is not because it demands that people be on the same social, cultural, and emotional level. According to Pogrebin, boys and girls are raised in such distinctly different environments that they cannot be friends later in life.

As you read, consider the following questions:

1. According to the author, why are men and women different?
2. What examples does Pogrebin give of what she terms sex separatism?
3. In the author's opinion, what long-lasting effects does sex separatism have on people?

Name one.

Name one famous friendship between a woman and a man — one admired, esteemed, inspiring, nonromantic, nonsexual friendship between a man and a woman in history or literature. It's not easy. In every culture, friendship between the sexes has been either inconceivable or forbidden. Inconceivable because women were universally considered men's inferiors; forbidden because each woman was chattel belonging to either her father or husband. Why would she be interested in any other man unless she intended to compromise her virginity or her virtue; why else would he be interested in her when all women were carnal creatures, meant for decoration, fornication, reproduction and domestic service?

No True Cross-Sex Friendships

Cross-sex relationships that contradicted these norms usually involved "deviates," Bohemians, artists, people of "lower rank," or offbeat unions that can be otherwise explained.

There was Jesus and Mary Magdalene, but she was a follower more than a friend. And Barak, the biblical warrior, who said to Deborah, the prophet and judge, "If thou wilt go with me, then I will go: but if thou wilt not go with me, then I will not go." Although this echoes Ruth's declaration of fealty to Naomi, Barak was on assignment from Deborah to defend the Jews from the Canaanites. Theirs was a work relationship, not a friendship.

Aspasia was "a woman of considerable intellectual stature who conversed with Socrates and taught rhetoric. . . . Her friendship with Socrates caused her to be remembered and written about by his followers." Plato says that Socrates claimed he could deliver a fine eulogy thanks to Aspasia, "for she who is my instructor is by no means weak in the art of rhetoric; on the contrary she has turned out many fine orators and amongst them one who surpassed all the other Greeks, Pericles." (Aspasia is thought to be the real author of Pericles' oration.) "Socrates himself would sometimes go to visit her, and some of his acquaintance with him; and those who frequented her company would carry their wives with them to listen to her. . . . What art or charming faculty she had that enabled her to captivate, as she did, the greatest statemen, and to give the philosophers occasion to speak so much about her."

But have you heard of this remarkable woman? Despite her friendships with these great men and her recorded brilliance, is she ever mentioned in the same breath as Socrates, Plato, or Pericles? No; what is known about Aspasia, if anything, is that Pericles fell in love with her and she became his lifelong mistress. The romance is remembered; the friendships are forgotten. . . .

Women are A, men are B. Men do X, women do Y. Some people still trot out their favorite sex differences to prove that the two sexes were never meant to be friends and shouldn't even try.

In my book *Growing Up Free*, I used hundreds of pages to argue against the notion of inborn differences. I tried to show how females and males are systematically programmed to be different; how, other than our reproductive complementarity, most of our supposedly implacable sex differences are literally "man-made." But I still have questions: Are the differences between the sexes – culturally imposed though they are – going to forever keep us apart? How long before women and men can be friends with each other the way each of us can be friends with someone of our own sex? Before struggling toward some answers, you might want to answer the following questions about the conditions of your own cross-sex friendships.

Power Struggles

I don't feel I can sit down and really have an honest conversation with a man, especially with many of the men I work with. They won't let you get in a word edgewise. They'll talk right over you. They'll interrupt you in mid-stream when you are trying to get a thought out. They'll cut you right off. I would deliberately do it to them and then say, "Oh, you don't like it, do you? It is okay when you do it to me, but I can't do it back." And then they say, "Oh, you're so defensive," and I say, "No, I'm not. I'm just trying to be a person."

Anonymous woman quoted by Helen Gouldner and Mary Symons Strong in *Speaking of Friendship*, 1987.

- If something wonderful happens to you today, which of your friends will you tell first?
- Who do you go to with your most personal problems?
- When you are recuperating in the hospital, what friend do you want to visit you?
- Who would you call if you needed someone to talk to at three o'clock in the morning?

The chances are that the people who came to mind in answer to these questions are women if you are a woman and men if you're a man. Although the two sexes love, live, and work together, when it comes to close friendship, each sex usually turns to its own. Given our society's near obsession with heterosexual relations and our persistent ambivalence about homosexuality, it is surprising how little attention is paid to the fact that heterosexuals are so homosocial.

Gender Loyalists

Although we are oriented toward the opposite sex for sex, for everything else we are gender loyalists. This is no accident. True friendship is rare between women and men not because we are innately incompatible but because sex separatism is so rigorously ingrained during childhood. Most parents rear male and female children as if preparing them to live in two different worlds—giving them different toys, books, chores, rules, tools, and boundaries and different messages about sex-appropriate emotions. Therefore, before they reach school age, girls and boys *have* become strangers to one another, with incompatible play habits, different ideas of fun, and few grounds for friendship. For a decade or more, says psychologist S.B. Damico, boys and girls establish "separate social systems," have "only limited contact with each other," and act as though "members of the opposite sex are 'horrible' and to be avoided at all costs."

In school, sex enmity can be exacerbated by lining up girls and boys in separate rows, pitting them against each other in spelling bees or dodge ball, and allowing gender ghettos to form in the playground or classroom. Children learn fast that to cross the lines of sex demarcation is to risk the invective "sissy," "tomboy," or worse.

Egalitarian separatism would be bad enough, but boys' exclusivity not only underlines their differences from girls but establishes their superiority. Any sixth-grade teacher knows that the best way to humiliate a boy is to put him wherever the girls congregate. If proximity pollutes, then boy-girl friendship is perilous indeed.

Contradictions and Name Calling

When my twin daughters were 12, they and another girl often dressed up in costumes and improvised scenes with a male classmate who also loved acting. (Eventually the four friends collaborated on a script and produced their own eight-millimeter movie melodrama.) One day the boy confided that he'd been called a "faggot" for playing with girls. He was proud of his answer: "I told the guy, 'If I'm the faggot, how come you're the one who likes boys?' "

It's crazy: To be thought heterosexual, a child must be homosocial, while the child who is heterosocial might be typed as homosexual. That contradiction doesn't seem to bother anyone. Some parents welcome homosocial separatism because they fear that girl-boy friendship could lead to early heterosexual experimentation. Others think mutual scorn between the sexes is cute, harmless, or "only natural." Their idea is that boys should be boyish together, girls should be girlish together, and in due time the call of the wild hormones will bring the sexes together.

But the alienation that accumulates during ten or twelve years of separatism and mutual contempt doesn't just disappear with the first adolescent crush. Future relationships between young men and women are distorted by casting them as strictly sexual. It is difficult to get together as adult friends because sex separatism has labeled friendship and fun homosocial and put only love and sex in the heterosexual column. After a decade of separation and enmity, we cannot just outgrow the feeling that when we are with the other sex, we are, as in our childhoods, in alien territory. That's why so many people continue to rely on members of their own sex for everything *but* sex. That's why the two genders traditionally divide up for conversation, sports activities, and so on. It is rare to find men and women who are not romantically involved who spend time together for fun. People double-date so that when conversation fails the men can talk business or sports and the women can mine the emotional terrain. Women and men sometimes cannot agree on where to vacation because they have diametrically different ideas of recreation and leisure. . . .

Inequality Makes Us Different

To allow "birds of a feather" to find each other under the layers of masculine and feminine posturing, friends have to shed the "opposites attract" ethos of heterosexual sex. And they have to disavow the sexism that props up gender hierarchy. They must see women as full human beings and men as people with feelings before they can see each other as friends. Yet they should not have to be "the same" to have similarities; they must have the freedom to be *different but equal*. . . .

A Game with No Rules

The whole idea of friendship with women as opposed to a sexual relationship is a puzzle. It's not codified; you don't know what the rules are. And it's not something that's celebrated as any ideal in movies or books or anything.

How do you get to be friends with a woman and not have to come on in any way? Friendship is almost in opposition to the love relationship game, which is what makes it so hard for men and women to be really good friends.

Anonymous man quoted by Lillian B. Rubin in *Just Friends*, 1985.

Because equality between the sexes has yet to be achieved, true and complete friendship between the sexes is still unusual – except among those who have nontraditional attitudes or nonsexist educational or work experiences. Until such new norms become commonplace, it is no surprise to keep hearing, "But men and women are too different to be friends."

> "You can relinquish control or you can take control....The choice is yours."

Women Must Become More Assertive

Toni Scalia

Feminists have assailed traditional families in which the husband has ultimate control while the wife acquiesces to his judgment. Toni Scalia, the author of the following viewpoint, argues that too many relationships are marred by these roles. Scalia writes that women must stop abdicating their power and must work toward self-respect and self-empowerment. She is a free-lance management consultant and adjunct professor of sociology at Brooklyn College in Brooklyn, New York.

As you read, consider the following questions:

1. How does Scalia redefine "bitch" to make it a positive term?
2. According to the author, what is "selective abdication"?
3. In Scalia's opinion, how does society keep women from being assertive?

I have written this for every woman who has had to force herself to move away from a relationship that did not satisfy her needs and wants; for every woman too afraid to fully exercise her authority as a parent; for every woman who has been worked over in the world of business. I have written it as well for every woman juggling a career and a lover, enjoying the appurtenances of a new image, free to come and go as she chooses – and yet feeling a nagging lack of satisfaction. My message to all of them is clear: You can relinquish control or you can take control. In my terms, you can be *abdicator* or you can be *bitch*. The choice is yours.

Harsh Terms

These terms seem harsh. They are. They did not come as the result of an intellectual exercise. They came from personal experience – my own, and the experiences of the many women I interviewed. And both terms are much more than an attempt to categorize behavior. They not only describe what we do but how we are perceived either consciously or subconsciously by others. The sad truth is that most men, even now, are more comfortable with abdicator behavior from women. The woman who deliberately challenges and provokes is still called a bitch. So, why not turn the term around? If to be a bitch means that a decent and fair person suddenly expresses her own needs and wants, then being a bitch is surely a goal worth seeking. Of course, it makes for certain problems. If *bitch* is now a positive term, what do we do with the old-fashioned Bette Davis kind of bitch? Do we call her the bad bitch as opposed to the good one I advocate? Perhaps, or perhaps we should just forget altogether the bad bitch for now. This is only about the good one. And still there are problems. What about the times when the good bitch must abdicate selectively? Are there such times? Of course there are, and we shall deal with them. There are always paradoxes. But even with the paradoxes, the choices and the options are very clear.

Abdicating Behaviors

From my personal experience, I learned that the ability to create alternatives and take advantage of options was much more under my control than I had either been led to or allowed myself to believe. And this was reinforced by the stories of the women who shared their experiences with me. What I found was that women who relinquished control did so as a result of certain patterns I call *abdicator behaviors*. When we abdicate, we do the following:

- We avoid confrontation.
- We complain to our friends about our lovers' behavior and vent our anger only where it's safe.
- We play nice guy at work and deny the realities of political power.

- We don't claim ownership of the money we make and keep ourselves financially immature.

As I began my own attempt to move from acquiescence to equality, a healthy anger – directed at myself for acquiescing and at others for insisting and expecting me to – replaced complacency. And self-pity was replaced by an unforgiving honesty. And again both my experience and my research demonstrated that acting out a changed response to the social restraints placed on women (and their acceptance of those restraints) results in the changed response being viewed as a *personal* aberration.

"That's an excellent suggestion, Ms Winthrop. We'll wait for one of the men here to make it."

From *Reflecting Men at Twice Their Natural Size* by Sally Cline and Dale Spender. Copyright © 1987 by Sally Cline and Dale Spender. Reprinted by permission of Henry Holt and Company, Inc.

What happens is that when just anger replaces complacency and when honesty replaces self-pity, the personal behavior that results is *challenged* before it can become challenging to the issue that made the behavioral change necessary. And the woman opting for this change is called bitch.

We no longer exhibit *weakness* – we demonstrate *strength* – and are called bitch.

We no longer comply – we insist on authority – and are called bitch.

I am not using the term *bitch* in the pejorative sense. I am using it to reflect the cultural label that is applied to women who, as they practice self-determination, behave in ways that are contrary to the behavior that is expected of them by their husbands and lovers, children and families, bosses and subordinates. Almost without fail, when a woman steps out of the role society has assigned to her, she is called bitch.

Since this is our cultural reality, I have redefined the term so that it carries a positive meaning.

> *Bitch*: An aggressive woman who stands her ground and speaks her piece; one who operates on a quid pro quo basis and who behaves in such a way as to receive in equal measure the love, nurturing, comfort, and understanding that she supplies in her love relationships and parenting; a woman who does not rationalize either her successes or failures in the work place and aggressively pursues her individual potential.

This definition and the following one of *abdicator* were borne out by my many interviews with women:

> *Abdicator*: A woman who surrenders and relinquishes her adult authority and personal dignity in areas over which she is both capable and deserving of control; one who, by her behavior, travels the pathway of self-denial.

Throughout the research and the writing of this I have focused on behaviors: behaviors that either prevent women from enjoying or allow them to enjoy satisfactory love relationships; behaviors that either prevent women from becoming adequate parents or allow them to exercise mature and nurturing parental judgment; behaviors that either render women impotent within their work affiliations or aid them in utilizing their talents and intelligence to further their careers and professions.

Contrasting Behavior

Those actions that inhibit us from developing our potential, prevent us from satisfying our needs, and allow others to determine and define who we are, what we are capable of, and what we should do, I have labeled *abdicator behaviors*. Those actions that permit us to grow, allow us to pursue aggressively the satisfaction of our needs, and let us determine for ourselves who we are and what we want to be, I have labeled *bitch behaviors*.

There are significant contrasts between these two behavioral categories:

- The abdicator acquires; the bitch earns.
- The abdicator avoids; the bitch confronts.
- The abdicator is halted in her development; the bitch grows.
- The abdicator is reactive; the bitch initiates action.
- The abdicator hides her discontent, thus relinquishing her needs; the bitch keeps her discontent in focus and gives voice to

her needs.

Certainly, I have drawn these categories along strongly polarized lines, and I have done so in order to make vivid the contrast between the two. There is a point, however, where the setting up of such stark contrasts can be misleading. And that point occurs in the link between abdication and trust. There are situations where *selective abdication* – abdication by choice – is a healthy and necessary expression of trust. Selective abdication occurs when we have honestly assessed our skills and abilities and make a thoughtful decision to turn over a task to someone we judge more capable than ourselves. And we do that in work and in parenting.

Self-Empowerment

Beyond the issues of equal pay for equal work, federally funded daycare, maternity and paternity leave, and job sharing, is the pressing issue of female self-empowerment. Legislation alone cannot achieve that; the battle also must be won within the psyches of women and men who wish to live happily together.

The solution to backlash isn't for women to become less ambitious or successful, but for them to claim their own power and honestly communicate their needs to their husbands, believing those needs can be met, prepared to take action if they are not. The friendship men and women need in their marriages can only take place between two equally powerful beings. There can be no friendship if, out of the same fear of abandonment, the woman allows herself to be intimidated and the man allows himself to become a psychic bully.

Bebe Moore Campbell, *Successful Women, Angry Men*, 1986.

Selective abdication – again the healthy kind – occurs when after honest and thoughtful assessment of our love partner's behavior toward us, we turn over part of ourselves to be cared for, to be nurtured, to be loved. We give our trust. However, most forms of abdication are nonselective – that is, we abdicate in response to someone else's wishes, not in response to our own. Such abdication is a form of self-betrayal. This betrayal, in turn, results in mistrust of self. Having withheld trust from ourselves, it can only be falsely given, half-heartedly given, or angrily given to others. Only by recognizing and understanding our abdicating behaviors can we begin the process of trusting ourselves. Only by practicing bitch behaviors can we willingly give trust to others.

I wish I could say that, having stumbled my way through these changes, I decided to use my formal training to research and write up the process. I hold a bachelor's degree in psychology from New York University and a master's in sociology from Washington

University, where I am now completing my doctorate. I wish I could say that, but that's not the way it happened. It happened because of a corporate reorganization, a change in company direction, my own classically scripted and very well-acted abdicator behavior – and the job loss that followed.

I have no idea whether the decision to write this is indicative of healthy self-confidence or supreme arrogance. And I don't care. The point is that I did it.

Personal Experience

Like many women in the work force, I have often been in the position of "being the only one." I was the only female faculty member in the Department of Administration of Justice of a midwestern university system; I was the only female associate director in an international training and development consulting firm headquartered in the Midwest. My position there required that I travel around the country and conduct management development seminars for several Fortune 500 firms. Participants in the seminars spanned organizational levels from chief executive officer to entry-level managerial and supervisory personnel. The seminars focused on behavioral solutions to problems encountered on the job. It took only two or three seminars to recognize that the problems encountered by women were far different from those experienced by men. Not only were the problems different, but the behavioral solutions that men and women were using to resolve them differed as well. In an effort to be as accurate as I could be in both my analysis and in the solutions I was offering, I began to keep a journal describing and detailing these differences. Where the men practiced either accommodating behaviors or "true grit" leadership roles, the women either gave in and abdicated or gave up their sainthood and assumed bitch roles. The journal that I kept became part of the research that I later incorporated.

When I was later hired as a training manager for a large retail chain operation, my role as counselor for solving on-the-job interpersonal problems provided me with additional and valuable material. After leaving the retail firm, I spent a year gathering additional data and formalizing my research. I then began to write full time. I renewed contacts I had made in past work efforts and held individual interviews and group discussions with women from New York to San Francisco. I collected responses from well over 250 women.

It was during my last year of research that another crucial difference between abdicating and bitch behaviors surfaced. It was quite apparent that those women who displayed abdicating behaviors at work were far less able to make a distinction between their corporate behavior and personal behavior than were their more aggressive sisters. This led me to expand the research to include a description and analysis of abdicating and bitch behaviors within the two primary areas of personal life: love relationships and parenting.

Fight Discrimination

It is ridiculous to tell girls to keep quiet when they enter a new field, or an old one, so the men will not notice they are there. In almost every professional field, in busines and in the arts and sciences, women are still treated as second-class citizens. It would be a great service to tell girls who plan to work in society to expect this subtle, uncomfortable discrimination — tell them not to be quiet, and hope it will go away, but fight it. A girl should not expect special privileges because of her sex, but neither should she "adjust" to prejudice and discrimination.

She must learn to compete then, not as a woman, but as a human being.

Betty Friedan, *The Feminine Mystique*, 1963.

Here again the contrasts and distinctions between abdicating and bitch behaviors were significant. These are some of the contrasts I found within the love relationship:
• The bitch initiates behavior in the face of fear and anxiety; the abdicator maintains the status quo through compliance and with depression.
• The bitch assumes personal responsibility for her well-being; the abdicator relies on others.
• The bitch seeks her own activities; the abdicator lives vicariously through the actions of others.
• The bitch creates choices and chooses; the abdicator does not think in terms of options or alternatives.
• The bitch tunes in to her subjective feelings, using them to filter her surroundings; the abdicator rationalizes her discontent in terms of "they," "it," and "society."
• The bitch views her mate as an individual who wishes support, as she does, who needs to be cared for, as she does, and who seeks a balance between freedom and responsibility, as she does; The abdicator views her mate as caretaker.
• The bitch relies on her authority as an adult; the abdicator asks permission as a child.
The bottom line is that the abdicators maintained unions that did not fulfill their needs, whereas those women practicing bitch behaviors either gained equality within their existing relationships or moved on to another that met their needs, wants, and desires.
Not surprisingly, many of the women carried their behaviors over into the realm of parenting. The abdicator is revealed as a mother

in name only, as she gives over her responsibility for child rearing to husband, lover, family, friends, and institutions. She exhibits reactive rather than proactive responses, and passive and easy-way-out actions such as bribing and guilt offerings. She compromises and behaves inconsistently with respect to the goals she has for her children and the behavior she expects of them. Ultimately, she offers her children limited need fulfillment and conditional affection.

A Winning Parent

The bitch as mother is revealed as a winning parent as opposed to a whining one. She offers unconditional love but conditional behavioral choices for her children, based on her assessment of both social values and the child's potential. She maintains a declarative, imperative "I'm the parent here" attitude, with the goals she has for her children serving as the sieve through which she filters their behavior.

In love relationships, role differences, homebody versus bread-winner activities, and the assumed and actual cultural differences between men and women can hide the distinctions between abdicator and bitch behaviors. In my individual interviews and group discussions, it was difficult and it took much time and effort to draw out these behaviors and to truly understand the consequences.

In parenting, there is the given that since you bear the title of parent you must be in control. Or that the incident being discussed represents "only a phase" that the child was in. Here again, the behaviors and consequences were difficult to ferret out in many of the histories and cases I researched.

This was not true in the work place. Here I could see woman versus woman, abdicator versus bitch. Role differentiation did not come into play. Gender was so obviously no longer an issue. The battleground was the work place. The lines were clearly drawn and the distinctions were clear:

• The abdicator chooses security; the bitch chooses risk taking.

• The abdicator monitors her behavior, so she is not seen as "taking advantage of situations"; the bitch uses her environment without feeling the need to apologize.

• The abdicator maintains a tunnel vision approach to her work; the bitch searches for relationships, analyzes processes, and synthesizes contrasting approaches.

• The abdicator refuses to become political or denies the existence of politics; the bitch enters political realities, sometimes with bravado and always with determination.

• The abdicator says "I can't be that way"; the bitch conditions herself to play the bastard.

• The abdicator maintains her idealism; the bitch chooses to renounce her sainthood, her misplaced idealism.

- The abdicator seeks justice through "by the book" compliance; the bitch seeks vengeance through excellence and success.
- The abdicator keeps bringing home her paycheck; the bitch often risks bringing in double or nothing.
- The abdicator chooses to make a living; the bitch chooses to make a life.

Achieving Control

As abdicator and as bitch, woman is perpetrator. As long as she acts against herself, she is excused. But the bitch is put on trial.

Submissive and acquiescent behavior has been judged acceptable feminine behavior by women, men, and society and its laws. Control, authority, equality, and strength when exhibited by women have been and still are subject to personal and public censure. Challenge is the rule when women leave the realm of acquiescence and achieve control over the direction of their lives. And it is when they react to this challenge that women are put on trial.

My primary emphasis is on helping women successfully manage the challenge and effect behavioral change. Behavioral change does not occur if we sugarcoat the consequences of existing behaviors and soft-sell the need for new behaviors.

"Assertiveness training is not enough. Men have to start to be accommodating."

Assertiveness Is Not Enough

Sally Cline and Dale Spender

Sally Cline lectures in women's studies at Cambridge University in Great Britain. Dale Spender is the author of *Man Made Language* and *Mothers of the Novel*. In their book *Reflecting Men at Twice Their Natural Size*, Cline and Spender maintain that women support, or "reflect," men's ambitions while men do not reciprocate. In the following viewpoint, Cline and Spender write that assertiveness training itself is not sufficient to overcome this injustice. They argue that assertiveness can fix small areas of women's lives, but it does not affect the major areas controlled by men.

As you read, consider the following questions:

1. Why must Rosie compromise at work when she doesn't at home?
2. According to the authors, why does assertiveness not work in many parts of women's lives?
3. In the authors' opinion, has assertiveness changed the overall status of women? Why or why not?

Assertiveness training, based on the premise that women are not skilled in stating their needs or in making their presence felt (especially when it would serve their interests best to do so), is more often associated with the genre of feminism which has developed particularly in the United States but which more recently has started to make a considerable impact in Australia, Canada, and the United Kingdom.

The idea that women should learn to act as if they believed in themselves as people with independent interests, desires and rights has been explored through a wide variety of skill-sharing work-shops aimed interestingly enough not merely at older women who, we might suppose, due to years of 'faulty' socialisation, have much to learn in this direction (and we speak as two of that still stum-bling, still struggling breed), but at young women, to ensure that they begin to kick the need for approval, particularly male approval, before that need becomes a lifetime's addiction. Indeed, as we write this, the Training Calendar of the British National Association of Youth Clubs, which offers as its leading event 'Being Assertive: A Workshop for Women', drops through the postbox. In this typically broadbased training arena, discussions, role play and practical exercises will be used to help women who want to iden-tify and explore situations which cause stress, embarrassment, frus-tration and deep suffering to women both in their personal and professional lives. Workshops such as these, which are in them-selves offshoots of successful books on related themes, are based on the underlying idea that women are so self-sacrificing that they risk becoming submerged, that they fail to develop because they fail openly to identify their aspirations, demands or necessary dues. Self-assertion courses attempt to show women that without being aggressive, manipulative or devious, they can state their exigent needs with plain speaking and straightforward action. The com-monsense notion about assertion has been to assume that if women begin to promote themselves with confidence, to make known their needs, then their wishes will be granted and, to a large measure, the problem will be solved.

Rosie: At Home

Before we discuss the extent to which this argument holds good and examine its defects or weaknesses, we should mention at least one strongly self-assertive woman whom we interviewed. For not *all* women reflect men. Rosie does not.

Rosie is a thirty-five-year-old American, popular college lecturer, the mother of a chubby two-year-old called May. She is deeply attached to May's father, Christopher, with whom she has had a nine-year relationship in which they agree that Christopher does a great deal of the nurturing while Rosie does ridiculously little.

This is strange. Anyone meeting Rosie would instantly remark on her gentle, caring manner, her way of building you up and her almost psychic sensitivity which lights on your badly concealed weak points and dispels them with a few comforting, practical remarks. After ten minutes conversation with Rosie one feels cosseted, protected and, somehow, rather important. People say that Christopher must be very lucky and Christopher admits his good fortune. What is unusual is that Christopher seems to be rarely reflected in this manner.

Assertiveness No Solution

It is extremely difficult for women to stand up for their rights. Social conditioning at home, and educational processes later, conspire to thwart women's power and self-esteem. And assertive women are typically subject to abusive treatment. It is no solution to tell a woman who is being systematically beaten to stand up for herself and demand her dues; this may well be how she came to be battered in the first place. Above all, many women are financially dependent on men. It does not serve their interests to demand caring treatment from an uncaring provider.

Getting to know Rosie a little better, one discovers that she has principles like iron rivets and a mind like jagged razor blades. 'Don't let her mild, melting manner fool you,' a friend said affectionately. 'Beneath the warmth she's like an intellectual steel mill.'

'I won't be ground down any more by the men I live with,' Rosie told us firmly. 'If I had to do more for my lover than he was prepared to do for me, it would be irreconcilable with my politics. So I don't.'

Mutual Encouragement

It is not that Rosie despises the process of reflection. Far from it: 'I think a behaviour pattern which makes as a priority not making people look small in public, not humiliating people, not embarrassing people, allowing others to keep their dignity, making them feel wanted and proud of themselves is deeply important,' she said. 'I see reflection as part of a human compassion which must be preserved. The trouble is that, firstly, women have that compassion more than men and, secondly, they use it almost solely on men and for the benefit of men.'

Rosie should know. In her first marriage, she was not the strongminded woman she is today but a soft girl overbrimming with tenderness which she used up on making her husband feel bigger and better.

'Of course he never did anything like that for me. I had very little confidence in myself in those days. Felt I was smaller, inferior to almost everyone. I was easily put down. My husband had no trouble at all reducing me to some wretched inferior servant. I complained a little. Then he ran off with my best friend, leaving me feeling I hadn't treated him well enough. I lived alone for a long time. I learnt to survive. I learnt to wean myself off reflecting men. My confidence shot up. I became truly tough within myself.

'Having learnt that I can live without a man, I choose to live with Chris because he has never demanded that I bolster him up. He has always encouraged, protected and helped me professionally and personally in ways that women traditionally help men.' . . .

Rosie: At Work

Rosie's self-assertive behaviour is heartening. Within her personal context Rosie's results are optimistic. But this is only half of the story. 'My forceful determination not to reflect men works domestically but becomes woefully exposed as mere bravado in the job situation,' she admitted. 'Many of the things I refuse to do for Chris, I find myself constrained to do for Tom, the liberal head of department at my college.

'Tom is my oldest colleague. We started together fifteen years ago. When we began work, we were equals and friends. He was always more insecure than I was. I gave him my support readily and tried to boost his confidence. Academic institutions are hard, competitive arenas to work in and protectiveness and solidarity, although unusual, are greatly needed. In the early days it was more of a reciprocal process. Then Tom got promoted. As a principal lecturer he has a great deal of power. Yet in some ways he is still fundamentally unsure of himself. Like many men, he is very conscious of his own dignity, very sensitive about being shown up or being humiliated, and he relies on me for support. I protect him a lot. Why? I protect him a little bit for old times' sake, for the warmth and friendship we once had, but more I protect him because he has power over me.

'It is important for my own job security that I do not irritate him. Therefore although I take him on directly in terms of battles over students' needs and treatment, or how courses should be taught, it seems politic and useful not to take him on over day-to-day things that matter to his ego. For instance, when there is a staff meeting and someone suggests that a change is made in one of Tom's courses, I choose not to take him on then and not to give that other member of staff justified support. Tom would become defensive, take it as a personal criticism and he would make a feeble attempt to retain his course. I would know the argument was flaky, I know I could tear it to shreds, but I don't. What I do is very unassertive and very indirect. I put a lot of hard work and time in trying to deal with the problem in a roundabout way so that he doesn't feel shown up or threatened. I spend hours working out alternative structures to that course, then I try and persuade him that it's his idea and that it's a good one. I put in all the work he should have put in, simply to protect him. Of course Tom isn't grateful. He feels my behaviour is his due.'

Making Compromises

Most of the women we interviewed reflected men because they were unable to avoid the varying sanctions that were imposed if they refused to do so. Rosie was unusual in that at least in her social and personal life she managed to stand up for herself, speak up for other women and survive. However, even her self-assertive attitudes became toned down, moderated and marginalised outside the home. Indeed she fell into the kind of deceit and manipulation which Anne Dickson, author of the best selling *A Woman in Your Own Right: Assertiveness and You*, attempts to steer women away from.

The story of Rosie, the woman who cannot afford to compromise at home but cannot afford *not* to compromise at work, pinpoints one of the problems in the self-assertiveness philosophy in terms of its usefulness in resisting the impulse to reflect men.

Assertiveness training is supposed to help women who lack control over their own lives. But many women have no control over vast areas of their lives. Rosie is luckier than many but her situation highlights certain deficiencies in the self-assertiveness theory. Even the National Association of Youth Clubs, having outlined the advantages of self-assertion in their Training Calendar, are forced to admit that, 'Assertion is not aggression nor is it necessarily getting what you want, but it can lead to more open, honest and rewarding communication with others at home and at work.' Even Anne Dickson is obliged to recognise that although the newly confident woman has acknowledged 'that she is in charge of her actions, her choices and her life.... Choosing to behave assertively may mean not getting exactly what you want but having to negotiate a compromise instead.' For although the assertive woman persistently states her right to be treated as an equal human being, and Anne Dickson stresses that 'this principle of equality is one of the most important hallmarks of assertive behaviour', when women are faced with someone 'who for one reason or another has more power or a higher status than we do, it can be difficult to assert our rights as an equal'. Anne Dickson rightly states that 'given our prevailing culture, women are, with obvious exceptions, in less powerful positions than men'. Although she acknowledges that this crucial point 'can be made into an overtly political issue', this is not the purpose of her book and she fails to explore the issue.

Assertiveness-training procedures are undoubtedly effective in helping some women to live more powerfully. When women like Rosie use these confidence-boosting tools to stop reflecting individual men, they are often rewarded with personal success and achieve a measure of control over their domestic lives. However, this remains essentially an individual solution to a widespread problem; if assertiveness training is considered in relation to the social phenomenon of male reflection, confidence-improving techniques have neither affected nor altered the overall status of women in our society to date.

There are two major flaws in the assumption that if women start to assert themselves the problem of male reflection will be solved. Firstly, it puts the pressure on women to change when, as we have seen, it is precisely women who do not have the power (economic, sexual or political) to change their environment.

It is extremely difficult for women to stand up for their rights. Social conditioning at home, and educational processes later, conspire to thwart women's power and self-esteem. And assertive women are typically subject to abusive treatment. It is no solution to tell a woman who is being systematically beaten to stand up for herself and demand her dues; this may well be how she came to be battered in the first place. Above all, many women are financially dependent on men. It does not serve their interests to demand caring treatment from an uncaring provider. When men have financial and physical power and are prepared to use it, no advice to women about the kind of nurturing they need is necessarily going to work.

Where self-assertion does work, however, is in terms of women's self-respect and self-esteem. Confidence in ourselves, a full sense of our own worth, enables us to see that our needs are as important as those of our husbands, our boyfriends, our fathers. In the same way that the slogans 'black is beautiful' and 'glad to be gay' aimed to cultivate dignity, so the slogan 'sisterhood is powerful' aimed to invest women with the inner strength necessary to continue to struggle for liberation. However, all three slogans were less about asserting rights than about establishing values.

Men Must Help

This brings us to the second flaw in the self-assertiveness strategy: it urges women to be more like men. But the evidence gathered makes it clear that it is not women's behaviour which is wrong; rather, it is the fact that this behaviour is not reciprocated. Reflective behaviour is congenial, useful and productive. It is a method of achieving harmony. It is the key to making people believe they can stretch themselves beyond their most daring dreams. There is nothing wrong with considering others, putting them at their ease, managing their emotions to make them feel good, expanding their confidence, extending their abilities, improving their performance or nurturing their spirit. *What is wrong is that women do it for men and men do not do it for women.*

232

In our view, there should be more rather than less of this behaviour. It is the asymmetry which is at fault: an asymmetry which profits men at the expense of women. Who looks after women? Who helps women to expand? Who gives wives, girlfriends, mothers, daughters and sisters the self-confidence and protection that is their due?

For women to become self-assertive may be a necessary defence in the patriarchal society within which women struggle to survive but it is not the whole answer. Assertiveness training is not enough. Men have to start to be accommodating. Men have to learn to provide emotional support.

"If men today can allow themselves to feel dependent without feeling threatened. . . then tomorrow they may find they can relate to others more intimately."

Men Need To Make Commitments

Herbert J. Freudenberger

Herbert J. Freudenberger is a clinical psychologist and a psychoanalyst with a private practice in New York. In the following viewpoint, Freudenberger argues that a man's role in modern society has become ambiguous, causing him to seek power and wealth for himself while abandoning family commitments. Freudenberger contends that men must put the same amount of effort into personal relationships that they put into work. Only through this commitment, he states, can men hope to find intimacy and stability.

As you read, consider the following questions:

1. What reasons does the author give for men's general lack of commitment?
2. In Freudenberger's opinion, how have society's morals been eroded?
3. According to the author, what must men do to improve their relationships?

Herbert J. Freudenberger, '"Today's Troubled Men," *Psychology Today*, December 1987. Reprinted by permission from *Psychology Today* magazine. Copyright © 1987 (PT Partners, L.P.).

As we approach the 1990s, many men find themselves on new and historically peculiar terrain, where one of the main problems they face is that of being male. Men's sexual relationships with women, their commitments to marriage, family and work and their sense of self have all become ambiguous.

I would like to explore why this has happened and offer a few guidelines as to how men might deal successfully with these problems. My observations are based in part on my work with patients, but I believe their concerns and feelings represent, in intense form, the experiences of many men today.

These problems have several major sources: changes in sexual stereotypes and norms, the emphasis on material achievement, the rise of feminism and women's liberation, the lack of man-to-man intimacy and the scarcity of acceptable mentors for men to emulate. There is greater freedom but also greater confusion as men seek new ways of dealing with the many changes that have taken place over the last two decades.

In regard to sex, there has been a major shift in roles and rules. Men now feel more responsible for pleasing their partners as well as themselves. But they often experience this responsibility as a loss of control, as a source of vulnerability rather than a possibility of greater intimacy. The man performs sexually, but what does he feel as he performs? Since he no longer can be intimate in the old, in-control way, the price of greater intimacy seems too high.

Avoiding Commitment

The men who seek my help as a therapist often speak about getting into sex too quickly and wonder how long they can remain interested sexually in a particular woman without becoming bored. I see both issues as parts of the same problem: a desire to avoid commitment, a wish not to be held accountable in a relationship.

Many men distinguish sharply between responsibility and accountability on the job and in personal relationships. At work, accountability is measurable and gratification is relatively immediate. Society expects men to succeed at work. Responsibility on the job is a given, something one lives with, perhaps even lives for.

But responsibility in a relationship is often seen as unpleasant, an obligation to be avoided. "A woman relies on me," one man told me, "and expects me to make her my top priority. But I have other priorities, such as getting somewhere in life." Another said, "I fought hard, very hard, to be successful at work. I'm not going to jeopardize all that by committing to her right now." A third man explained that, "Giving in to a woman, as far as I'm concerned, is giving up of myself."

These men view personal commitment as being boxed in, being put in a position where they are exposed and vulnerable to their partners. Making plans for the future in such uncertain relationships seems frightening. In contrast, having a sense of future in their careers seems imperative, an integral part of their lives.

Selfish or Selfless?

They see real commitment to a woman as being totally selfless and therefore frightening. Lack of commitment is seen as a selfish but safer way to live. I think a substantial number of men today are coping with the questions of how to be selfish without being considered wholly self-interested and how to be selfless without running the risk of losing their sense of self. They bring these same fears to relationships and marriage. As one man put it: "That legal piece of paper. It really means I have no way to get out." Or a second: "Having a child just adds responsibility to my life. I don't want to feel that kind of obligation because it means feeling trapped and being taken over."

The Cement of Commitment

Relationships that are without the cement of commitment suffer from a sad irony: The lack of commitment causes stress, problems, and dishonesty, and then the stress, problems, and dishonesty reduce the likelihood of commitment. It is a vicious circle in which many spend their whole lives. This ironic pattern is true on a cultural level as well: Few people are willing to make serious commitments because they see that relationships are in such bad shape, but relationships are in bad shape precisely because there is such a widespread aversion to commitment.

Susan Page, *If I'm So Wonderful, Why Am I Still Single?* 1988.

I see many men like these in my practice—men who not only guard against feeling vulnerable and exposed but against feeling rejected. In my experience, their fears of abandonment and feelings of inferiority are nearer the surface than they like to admit. To guard against the fears, the men never really become involved with anyone. Some wander from relationship to relationship, always searching for evidence that proves they should be moving on.

Even when they live with someone, they are often really living alone. They don't share their thoughts and intimate feelings for fear that their partner might use what they expose against them. They keep themselves busy at work or become so involved in other activities—golf, tennis, exercising—that there isn't much time or energy left for intimacy.

Such men misjudge relationships because they approach intimate situations from an essentially self-centered, self-involved point of view, suspicious of others and overly protective of themselves.

These feelings may reflect the isolation, loneliness, depression, extramarital relationships or even abandonment the men have experienced during the years of social change.

Younger men may have felt a sense of abandonment as children as both their parents chose to pursue more activities and interests outside the home. But whatever the reasons, for these men issues of power, success and control usually associated with work have come to permeate their personal lives.

It is here that feminism and women's liberation enter the picture. For as women have moved to the center of their own lives, developed their own value systems and felt freer to follow their own desires and wishes, relations between the sexes have become more openly concerned with power and control. The traditional norms and stereotypes – man in charge, woman submissive to his decisions – often no longer apply. Many men, and women, simply don't know how to handle the situation.

In my practice, I hear men and women struggling with what they should feel in their intimate relationships, as opposed to what they actually do feel. The men no longer even know where they fit on the "Macho-Wimp" scale or how to make sense of new roles and life-styles. This seems to be why so many men burn out, why they seek gratification so intensely in work and play, where they feel a greater sense of power and control.

Changing Values

These conflicts often lead them to abandon the central values upon which our society has been built. Family commitment, interpersonal relatedness, responsibility to others – for many men these are less important than the peripheral values of acquisition, power and competition. This confusion of values has contributed, sad to say, to an erosion of social ethics and morality that has affected all our lives.

Where can these confused, vulnerable and uncomfortable men turn for help? At one time, men had older male role models and mentors to emulate. But that route is no longer tenable. Many older men are themselves confused and troubled by the social changes and often the only kind of man-to-man relationship men perceive, or are comfortable with, is one of competitiveness and rivalry, in sports and elsewhere. Intimacy between men continues to be as uncertain as intimacy between men and women.

Indeed, many men today are intimate with no one, including themselves. And here, it seems to me, lies the heart of the problems I have outlined, as well as the beginnings of a solution. Men must first learn to become intimate with their inner selves. They must once more learn to feel inwardly secure. To do this, they must again learn to trust themselves.

An important first step in achieving this is to take some time out, to step back and reflect: What are my priorities? Where am I going if I continue on this road? Where will I be 5 to 10 years from now? Do I really want to remain alone or continue showing only minimal concern for my loved ones and my community?

Men must learn how to open up to feelings, how to admit to and talk about their feeling of vulnerability and fears of abandonment. They must be helped to see others, men and women, as more than simply competitors and to see themselves as loving collaborators in personal relationships. Men must learn to really hear and understand when their friends and relatives tell them things such as, "You've changed in the last few years," "You're always working" or "You never seem to listen, you're always talking about yourself."

Working on Relationships

Men need to recognize that they may be approaching life in a rigid way, measuring relationships strictly in terms of immediate success. Because they take an adolescent-like approach, many men fantasize what a relationship ought to be, and if it doesn't measure up to their expectations, they leave.

Commitment Improves Life

The right kind of commitment keeping makes good sense because it is the only way to keep good human relationships alive. And good human relationships make everybody's life better. Commitments are worth the effort and, sometimes, the sacrifice, because, when all is said and done, people are almost always better off because of them. If we keep them the way they are meant to be kept—with care as well as with consistency—we are laying the foundation for the only kind of life fit for human beings. This is ultimately why commitment keeping is worth a try.

Lewis B. Smedes, *Caring and Commitment,* 1988.

Instead, they should view relationships as changeable situations wherein they may feel hurt, disappointment and anxiety as well as joy, gratification and satisfaction. Relationships need to be worked on with the same patience and energy that men traditionally invest in work. It is self-defeating to concentrate on the negative, and if things start going wrong, to use this as a reason for leaving a relationship.

A man needs to build time for relationships into his daily life, as well as time for work and exercise. He needs to learn to enjoy himself and devote enough time and energy to allow relationships to grow. Learning how to balance a life is an important requisite for happiness.

If men begin to recognize that they can gain far more by

legitimately caring, loving and collaborating, they may find less need to combat, compete and overpower each other. I find it interesting that in the psychiatric diagnostic manual, DSM-III-R, male sexual dysfunction is associated with "excessively high subjective standards of performance." Sexually dysfunctioning men seem to be more interested in what the penis does, not in what they feel during the act of doing.

Change is not easy. Under the best of circumstances, emotional needs often contradict intellectual understanding, and even when new roles and life-styles make sense, adapting to them usually involves conflict and struggle. But I am convinced that if men today can allow themselves to feel dependent without feeling threatened, can accept themselves as they are, with their strengths and weaknesses, then tomorrow they may find they can relate to others more intimately, joyfully and trustfully. Then, once again they will find the earth secure under their feet while they go about their lives as lovers, husbands, fathers and friends.

"Healthy commitment emerges as a natural outcome of a relationship. . .; it is not a goal of the relationship."

Commitment Should Not Be Forced upon Men

Herb Goldberg

A common stereotype maintains that men want sex and women want commitment. According to Herb Goldberg, the author of the following viewpoint, these conflicting goals are manipulative. He believes society exonerates women for seeking commitment and condemns men for pursuing sex. Goldberg, a practicing psychotherapist and professor of psychology at California State University in Los Angeles, argues that women unjustly pressure men for commitment before it is appropriate.

As you read, consider the following questions:

1. How does Goldberg equate the pressure for sex with the pressure for commitment?
2. According to the author, what happens when men are threatened into commitment?
3. What does Goldberg mean when he says commitment is the by-product of a good relationship?

Feminine pressure for commitment from a man in a relationship is the counterpart and equivalent to the traditional masculine pressuring of a woman for sex. Just as the unconscious defensiveness of masculinity produces an obsessive sexual preoccupation vis-à-vis the woman, so does the unconscious feminine defensiveness produce an obsessive relationship compulsion and obsession toward men.

Women choose men on the basis of their eligibility as commitment objects and often reject men who are potentially more compatible as partners in the same way as men choose women who are "sexy" and reject women who are potentially more suitable as partners but are not sexually appealing enough.

In proportion to the strength of their femininity and these compulsions, women are "irrationally" driven by this need and urgency for commitment, and it causes them to be temporarily blinded to objective reality in the same way as a man's sexual hunger impairs and intrudes on his better judgment. That is, it often causes them to make inappropriate, pain-producing, "self-destructive" choices. The preoccupation, soon after meeting a man, with whether or not he has "commitment potential," is as defensive and distorted as the man's premature pressuring for sex when he first meets a woman and hardly knows her as a person.

Different Criteria

What a man will share with his friends about a woman – what he will feel good and excited about – will be that she really turns him on sexually; she has a great body and she is beautiful. The things the woman will rush excitedly to tell her friends about an attractive man she has met will be that he says he loves her, he says he can't get along without her, and he wants to make a commitment to live with her or marry her. This will take the man out of the category of being "flaky" or "just like most other men."

The sex-focused male will end or threaten to end a relationship with a woman if she won't go to bed with him because, despite what *she says*, to him no sex clearly means she is not attracted and does not love him. A woman feels the same way about a man who resists commitment. Indeed, for most women to remain in a relationship that "is not going anywhere" is as emotionally impossible as remaining in a relationship with no sex is for most heterosexual men. Suddenly, he is transformed and is no longer attractive to her and she loses interest in him.

Unconsciously they enter into a bartering stance where instead of engaging in genuine loving and spontaneous giving, freely offered as one does with a friend or anyone one truly loves, each party is focused on his or her own defensive need satisfaction, doling out whatever payment is needed to prevent the ending of the "relationship." It may impel her to "give sex" to hold him even though genuine desire is absent, in the same way that he will "make a commitment" he really doesn't want because he knows he will lose her otherwise.

Obsessed with Commitment

In proportion to the degree of gender polarization (masculine/feminine) in a relationship, the undertow or defensive cravings in a man and a woman respectively masquerade as true love and interest in one another as people. Similarly, a traditional woman with no committed relationship in sight becomes as obsessed with commitment as men do when deprived of sex. She builds up a commitment tension that is just as obsessive, powerful, and unbearable as his sexual tension when he feels deprived. The undertow may push them surreptitiously into an unfortunate, defensive, demanding, and rigid involvement that moves from romantic illusion to mutual intimidation. Because of a deeper sense of being "used" after commitment, she may hold back her true self by becoming sexually "frigid," thereby "punishing" him for not *really* loving her, while he will hold back his true self by becoming emotionally withdrawn and detached, thereby responding similarly.

A Loss of Freedom

For [my girlfriend and I], the thought of commitment is real scary. I think one reason we get along is because we both have one foot out the door.

To me, relationships always seemed very stifling. They change your whole life around and don't allow you a lot of freedom to roam. Not roam to pick up women. Just roam to do stuff.

Chuck Cherney, quoted in *The New York Times Magazine*, November 15, 1987.

When a man dates a woman because he wants to have sex and because he considers her a "sure thing," that is considered a low level, dehumanized, and sexist motivation. If, however, a woman dates a man because he is a likely prospect for commitment and marriage, that is considered acceptable—a realistic, even smart motivation. *In both instances, however, there is sexism and dehumanization, the use of the other as an object for the fulfillment of gender defensive needs and compulsions that are beyond conscious awareness* and therefore largely denied. That is, he is an "object" in her eyes and is no more perceived as a person than she is by the macho, object-oriented male. Both are out-of-control and driven by unconscious, irrational, and damaging drives.

The unconscious feminine motives in these relationships, however, are interpreted more positively than the masculine ones because they seem to be more humanized, loving, and acceptable:

242

reflective of society's "values." This falls right into line with the distortions in understanding and interpreting gender motives generally.

Gender Defenses

It is a subtle, elusive phenomenon, but it is crucial to see beyond these illusions created by gender defenses and to recognize how the sexes are merely polarized, distorting the same phenomena (aggression, assertion, autonomy, and sexuality) in opposite directions, thus mutually reinforcing and perpetuating each other's distortions and defensiveness.

For example, repressed aggression in females makes girls seem "sweet and nice," while defensive overaggression in boys causes them to be seen as dangerous. In fact, both are flip sides of the same coin, acting out the same phenomenon of defensiveness in opposing directions. Indeed, who *is* more aggressive – the violent football player or the cheerleader who finds him attractive and reinforces him with her love because he's a "winner"; the man who fights for the woman's "honor" or the woman who passively and indirectly goads him on by not dealing with a situation she *could* handle herself and who will hold him in contempt if he doesn't fight on her behalf?

The feminine unconscious moves in the inner direction of the personal and creates an obsession with relationship and closeness. It gives the appearance of being positive, loving, and personal. She becomes a symbol of home and family and traditional values. Society supports her orientation and "values" and gives her its stamps of approval. It is hard to see how this can be "bad" or damaging. The feminine unconscious, however, makes women as out of balance and destructive as masculine defensiveness or being macho does to men, only in the opposite direction.

The problems created by the feminine unconscious are much more difficult to deal with and potentially more damaging because they are disguised by a "nice" veneer. Thus it is difficult to see and transform the damage it does.

When a woman breaks off with a man because he is "not marriage material" or "won't commit," however, the dehumanization is evidenced by the fact that this is the very same man that she previously wanted as the central human being in her life and supposedly "loved." Now she won't talk to him and accuses him of being the cause of her great pain. . . .

A Valid Response

We need to reinterpret the so-called male fear of intimacy and the male fear of commitment and see it instead as a valid response within the context of the defensively polarized relationship where he becomes as much an object as she, and his "frigidity" or withholding is personal, while hers is sexual.

A woman asking a man on or before a first date, or asking another woman, about a prospective man's capacity for intimacy and openness for commitment is setting up a damaging and dehumanizing context for herself and the man. I am reminded of a woman who was involved with a man for a long time, a man who really cared about her. They were best friends, great lovers, and enjoyed each other's company immensely. He didn't feel ready for marriage, however, though he also didn't rule it out altogether in the future.

She broke up with him to go out with a man she knew wanted to be in a committed marriage relationship with her. Consequently, she entered into a miserable marriage that lasted only a short time, in order to satisfy defensive, "irrational" needs. Any attempt to talk her out of marrying this man would have fallen on deaf ears. She was under the spell of her compulsions, the deeper feminine cravings.

Intimacy and Commitment

The man she married wanted commitment only because he felt challenged and competitive with the other man in her life. Many men will suddenly be "ready" for commitment when they are threatened, but that does not mean anything in terms of their genuine desire or capacity to be close or their ability to love. They want possession of the woman and validation of their masculinity, or are acting out of fear of losing her, and so they "make a commitment" just as women in challenging situations will use sex to gain control. It took the experience of a painful three-year marriage to allow her to see she had made a mistake. Subsequently, she divorced, and fortunately her real love was still unattached. She resumed her original, intrinsically satisfying relationship and finally married him.

When a woman criticizes a man for being incapable of commitment and intimacy, she is revealing her own defensive unconscious and usually is as out of touch with herself as is the man who accuses the sexually resistant woman of being "frigid" without seeing how his pressure is closing her up. A woman reveals her defensive feminine unconscious when she makes a statement such as, "Men are incapable of intimacy or commitment," or "There are no men around who really know how to be intimate." She is not recognizing how her own unconscious needs are creating a pressure that is an important factor in causing him to be resistant or incapable of "closeness."

Men have been taught to feel guilty about their resistance to "niceness" and a woman's desire to be close. The guilt prevents men not only from respecting and accepting their feelings of resistance as valid and feeling comfortable, but also from respecting their protective quality. Instead, men are told and come to believe, "You have a problem with closeness and intimacy and *you* had better overcome it." A man learns to see this as his problem solely. His guilt, self-doubt, and lack of self-awareness prevent him from properly translating the meaning of his resistance, and he begins to respond against himself.

Misused Terms

Commitment and intimacy are terms that are often misused and misunderstood. The prevailing tendency is to give these concepts a life of their own, just as with sex, where people speak of their "sex lives" as if they had little or no relationship to the rest of their involvement. A couple will say, "We are struggling with our intimacy and our efforts to get close to each other." They have to "struggle" because there is unconscious resistance, just as they have to struggle to make defensively motivated, unauthentic sex work. Such couples never seem to get it quite right, because they are unaware of the defensive polarization causing the problem.

In an authentic, loving relationship, the commitment is just there—a by-product, not an entity in itself—as in a best friendship. With a loving friend you *want* to be committed because you care about the person. If friends are in trouble, you are eager to be there for them not *because* you've made a commitment. If they want to talk, you *want* to talk to them or you feel free to let them know without guilt or a threat to the "commitment" that you can't. You don't have to work on it. The trust and the safety are there if it's a friendship built on genuine love and caring. Nondefensive relating, like nondefensive sex, is a process that emerges from two people feeling safe and good with each other. "Working at it" indicates a lack of safety or genuineness.

Thus, when a woman instructs a man to let down his barriers because he can "trust her and feel safe with her," she may actually believe she is trustworthy and means what she says. However, it is much like a man saying to a woman, out of *his* sexual need, "You can trust me—just let go and I know you'll enjoy the sex. I guarantee it." That will do nothing to make her *feel* safe.

Undue Pressure

When we pressure a man to commit by implying he has not grown up, we become like the coach who calls a man "sissy" to egg him on to perform. Maybe commitment is just the modern word for pressuring men to perform.

Warren Farrell, *Why Men Are the Way They Are*, 1986.

Most women feel vulnerable when they have sex without a commitment. A woman will say, "You are pressuring me for sex, and if I have sex with a man, I get very attached to him. It makes me feel very vulnerable." Men feel equally vulnerable when there is early pressure for commitment. They get scared, just as women get scared when they are pressured for sex by a "relative stranger."

When she says, "I love you, but if you don't marry me, I'll leave you, and don't want to see you anymore because it hurts too much," that is obviously not authentic love or friendship she is talking about. It is the fulfillment of her defensive need. She is being driven by a compulsion she must act out, and both she and he are usually beyond seeing that defensive obsession is propelling her. . . .

Women will be better able to understand men's obsession with sexuality when they grasp the irrational nature of their own obsession with commitment. This awareness in both men and women would be a major first step to a new humanization between the sexes. . . .

Healthy commitment emerges as a natural outcome of a relationship that is comfortable and nurturing; it is not a goal of the relationship. It does not have to be pressured for, worked on, thought about, or deliberated over. It will emerge out of the process, comfortably for both, when the individuals involved are not driven by defensive, polarized needs.

a critical thinking activity

Ranking Priorities in Relations Between the Sexes

This activity will allow you to explore the values you consider important when establishing relationships between the sexes. While your answers may differ from those of other readers, these disagreements mirror the reality of male/female relations. People often change their opinions about relationships according to their age, marital status, and career objectives. For example, high school students may have different priorities in their relationships than do adults in their thirties.

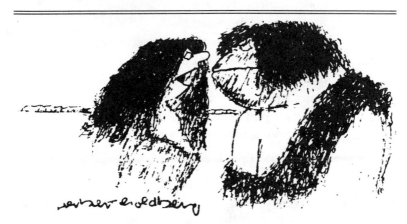

"Even though we've learned to talk we don't speak the same language."

From *The Wall Street Journal* - Permission, Cartoon Features Syndicate.

The authors in this chapter offer several suggestions on how relations between the sexes may be improved. Some people believe, as the cartoon illustrates, that men and women must learn to effectively communicate with each other before other problems can be solved. Others suggest that communication is not the problem, that it is unrealistic expectations that cloud male/female relations. Other potential priorities in male/female relations are listed below.

Part I

Working individually, rank the priorities listed in order of their importance to you at your present age. Use the number 1 to designate the most important priority, the number 2 for the second most important priority, and so on.

_____ dating someone with similar interests

_____ open communication with your partner

_____ dating someone who is attractive

_____ having children

_____ finding someone who supports equality between the sexes

_____ dating someone with the same religious and philosophical values

_____ finding a good husband/wife

_____ supporting your partner's career ambitions

_____ dating a wealthy person

_____ finding someone supportive of your life's goals

_____ being free to date a variety of people

_____ finding a partner who will be a good parent

_____ finding someone who is a good cook

_____ finding someone who will be a good provider

Part II

Step 1. Imagine what your priorities in a relationship might be ten years from now, and rank the priorities as though you were ten years older.

Step 2. The entire class should discuss the following questions.

1. What priorities in male/female relations are most important to you now?

2. What priorities in male/female relations did you believe would be most important ten years from now?

3. Do you think these priorities will continue to change throughout life? Why or why not?

Periodical Bibliography

The following articles have been selected to supplement the diverse views presented in this chapter.

Mary Kay Blakely   "The Tender Trap," *Ms.*, June 1988.

Vincent Bozzi   "Assertiveness Breeds Contempt," *Psychology Today*, September 1987.

Connell Cowan and Melvyn Kinder   "Fear of Intimacy: Not for Men Only," *Glamour*, October 1987.

Sandra M. Gilbert and Susan Gubar   "Sex Wars: Not the Fun Kind," *The New York Times Book Review*, December 27, 1987.

Priscilla Grant   "What Men Fear About Strong Women," *Glamour*, April 1986.

Leanne Kleinman   "Do Men Make Good Pals?" *Health*, November 1987.

Alfie Kohn   "Making the Most of Marriage," *Psychology Today*, December 1987.

James Maas   "Men Without Men," *Utne Reader*, April/May 1986.

Peter Mehlman   "And How Do Men Feel Now About Monogamy?" *Glamour*, July 1988.

Lesley Jane Nonkin   "Dreaded Bliss: Fears of the Almost-Husband," *Mademoiselle*, September 1988.

Patricia D. Perry   "Assert Yourself!" *Parents*, September 1988.

David Seeley   "Boys' Night Out," *Mademoiselle*, May 1986.

Michael Stetz   "Best Friends," *Utne Reader*, April/May 1986.

Peter Trachtenberg   "The Ultimate Seducer," *Glamour*, April 1986.

Robert J. Trottier   "The Three Faces of Love," *Psychology Today*, September 1986.

Claudia Wallis   "Back Off, Buddy," *Time*, October 12, 1987.

Paula Weideger   "It Takes Two To Tangle," *Ms.*, January/February 1989.

William H. Willimon   "Risky Business," *Christianity Today*, February 19, 1988.

Ira Wolfman   "The Closer You Get, the Faster I Run," *Ms.*, September 1985.

Organizations To Contact

The editors have compiled the following list of organizations which are concerned with the issues debated in this book. All of them have publications or information available for interested readers. The descriptions are derived from materials provided by the organizations. This list was compiled upon the date of publication. Names and phone numbers of organizations are subject to change.

Catalyst
250 Park Ave. S.
New York, NY 10002-1459
(212) 777-8900

Catalyst is a national research and advisory organization that helps corporations foster the careers and leadership capabilities of women. It publishes a wide variety of reference tools, manuals, and reports, including *Beyond the Transition: The Two-Gender Work Force and Corporate Policy* and *New Roles for Men and Women*. It also publishes the *Career Series* for women who are searching for their first job, and a monthly newsletter, *Perspective*.

Catholics United for the Faith (CUFF)
45 Union Ave.
New Rochelle, NY 10801
(914) 235-9404

CUFF supports, defends, and advances the teachings of the Roman Catholic Church. Its members do not object to women in the work force, but believe every effort should be made to allow women who wish to stay home to do so. It publishes the monthlies *Lay Witness* and *Bulletin*, in additon to books and pamphlets.

Center for Research on Women
Clement Hall
Memphis State University
Memphis, TN 38152
(901) 678-2770

The Center conducts, disseminates, and promotes research in the field of women's studies focusing on southern women and women of color in the United States. It operates a computerized information retrieval service called the Research Clearinghouse which contains more than two thousand entries of books, journal articles, unpublished manuscripts, and multimedia materials. The Center publishes a *Newsletter*, as well as *Southern Women* and *Research Clearinghouse Publications* two times a year, and *Research Papers* three times a year. It also publishes the book *Selected Bibliography of Social Science Readings on Women of Color*.

Child Care Action Campaign
99 Hudson St., Suite 1233
New York, NY 10013
(212) 334-9595

The Campaign's goal is to establish a national system of quality, affordable child care. It provides advocacy, education, and information for corporations, child-care organizations, and the media. Its publications include a bimonthly members' newsletter *Child Care Action News*, as well as various fact sheets, including *Who's Caring for Your Kids?—What Every Parent Should Know About Child Care* and *Child Care—The Bottom Line*.

Clearinghouse on Women's Issues
PO Box 70603
Friendship Heights, MD 20813

The Clearinghouse is a nonpartisan organization made up of members of other women's groups. It disseminates information on women's rights, particularly on issues of discrimination on the basis of sex or marital status, by holding luncheons featuring various speakers. It publishes a monthly *Newsletter*.

Coalition of Free Men
PO Box 129
Manhasset, NY 11030
(516) 482-6378

The Coalition is an educational organization that believes men are victims of discrimination. It fights discrimination, which it sees in the fact that only men are drafted and in evidence that men are given the most dangerous jobs in society. It works to promote friendships between men. The Coalition publishes a bimonthly newsletter, *Transitions*, and brochures such as *Men's Movement: A Perspective*, *Sex Discrimination in Language Against Men*, and *How To Conduct Men's Studies*.

Commission on the Economic Status of Women
Room 85, State Office Building
100 Constitution Ave.
St. Paul, MN 55155
(612) 296-8590

This legislative advisory commission was established to study the economic status of women. It has found that divorce laws, discrimination in employment, and child-care costs contribute to poverty among women. It conducts research, holds public hearings, and publishes reports such as *Employment Rights* and *Parental Leave and the Legal Rights of Pregnant Employees*.

Concerned Women for America
370 L'Enfant Promenade SW, Suite 800
Washington, DC 20024
(202) 488-7000

This group works to strengthen the traditional family according to Judeo-Christian moral standards. While it acknowledges that many women need to work for financial reasons, it believes that ideally all women should be at home with their families. It publishes several brochures, including *Come Help Save America*, and a monthly *Newsletter*.

Eagle Forum
Box 618
Alton, IL 62002
(618) 462-5415

The Forum is a politically active group that advocates traditional family values. It opposes any political forces that it believes are anti-family, anti-religion, or anti-morality. Its members believe that mothers should stay at home to raise their children. It publishes the monthly *Phyllis Schlafly Report*, as well as various brochures, including *Will 'Comparable Worth' Freeze Your Wages?*

Family Research Council of America, Inc.
601 Pennsylvania Ave. NW, Suite 901
Washington, DC 20004
(202) 393-2100

The Council is a research, resource, and educational organization. Its purpose is to ensure that the interests of the traditional family are considered and respected in the formulation of public policy. It publishes numerous reports from a conservative perspective on child care and other issues affecting the family. These reports include *The Importance of the Family to Society* and *Infant Day Care: A Cause for Concern*. It also publishes a bimonthly newsletter, *Family Policy*.

Free Congress Research and Education Foundation
721 Second St. NE
Washington, DC 20002
(202) 546-3004

The Foundation believes that men and women should follow traditional roles and that traditional families are best. It conducts research on public policy and issues that affect the family. It publishes the weekly *Political Report*, the monthly *Family Law and Democracy Report*, and the quarterly *Journal of Family and Culture*, in addition to papers and monographs.

Human Life Center
University of Steubenville
Steubenville, OH 43952
(614) 282-9953

The Center teaches conservative Roman Catholic moral values regarding marriage and the family. It opposes divorce and women working outside the home. It publishes two quarterlies, *International Review* and *Human Life Issues*.

Male Liberation Foundation
701 NE 67th St.
Miami, FL 33138
(305) 756-6249

The Foundation believes that men and women have biological and psychological differences that should be accepted. It argues that men are discriminated against in many ways—for example, it believes that most women between the ages of 15 and 25 are in a better financial position than men of the same age, yet men are still paying for dates. It supports paternity leave for fathers. The Foundation also seeks to protect homemakers from "screaming radical feminists." It publishes a monthly newsletter, *Male Liberation Foundation*, and *The First Book on Male Liberation and Sex Equality*. It also publishes position papers on current court decisions which involve discrimination against men.

Men International
3409 Hyde Park Dr.
Clearwater, FL 33519
(813) 787-3875

Men International believes current divorce and custody laws discriminate against men. It works to strengthen the traditional male image, particularly in the role of the father. It serves as a clearinghouse and resource center through its computerized *Men International Information Network*.

Men's Rights Association
17854 Lyons
Forest Lake, MN 55025
(612) 464-7887

The Association works to restore the dignity of the male, which it believes has been tarnished by feminism. It offers attorney referral services to men who believe they have not been given equal rights with women. It publishes many pamphlets, including *The Men's Manifest, Men's Movement Philosophy and Organizational Manual,* and *The Rape of the Male.*

Men's Rights, Inc.
PO Box 163180
Sacramento, CA 95816
(916) 484-7333

Men's Rights, Inc. believes that men are oppressed by divorce and custody laws which favor women. Its members oppose feminism. It publishes the newsletter *News Release.*

National Federation of Business and Professional Women's Clubs
2012 Massachusetts Ave. NW
Washington, DC 20036
(202) 293-1200

The Federation is a research, education, and lobbying organization that works for equity and self-sufficiency for working women. It provides financial assistance to women seeking to improve their employment and education opportunities. It maintains an extensive library on issues relating to women and work, including *Jobs for the Future,* and publishes *National Businesswomen Magazine* six times a year.

National Organization for Changing Men (NOCM)
794 Penn Ave.
Pittsburgh, PA 15221
(412) 371-8007

NOCM is an organization of men and women devoted to supporting positive changes in men. They are pro-feminist and support gay rights. They encourage men to have non-sexist relationships with women, to develop a more sensitive and involved role as fathers, and to relate better to other men. NOCM has many task groups which deal with such issues as male/female relationships and fathering, and which publish their own newsletters. It publishes a newsletter *Brother.*

Rockford Institute
934 N. Main St.
Rockford, IL 61103-7061
(815) 964-5053

The Institute seeks to educate the public on issues relating to religion and society, including family issues. It works to return America to Judeo-Christian values and supports traditional roles for men and women. It believes mothers who work or place their children in child care harm their children. It publishes a newsletter, *Mainstreet Memorandum,* and the monthly *The Family in America* and its supplement, *New Research.*

Select Committee on Children, Youth, and Families
US House of Representatives
385 House Office Building Annex 2
Washington, DC 20515

The Committee was created by the 98th Congress in 1983 to conduct an ongoing assessment of the condition of American children and families and to make recommendations to Congress and the public about how to improve public and private sector policies. It publishes reports and transcripts of hearings it holds on family issues.

Tradeswomen, Inc.
PO Box 40664
San Francisco, CA 94140
(415) 821-7334

Tradeswomen, Inc. offers peer support, networking, and advocacy for women in nontraditional, blue-collar jobs. It publishes the quarterly *Tradeswoman Magazine* and the monthly *Trade Trax* newsletter.

Women for Racial and Economic Equality (WREE)
198 Broadway, Room 606
New York, NY 10038
(212) 385-1103

WREE is a political activist organization. It strives to end racism and economic inequality through the enactment of a Women's Bill of Rights. WREE publishes the bimonthly journal *WREE-View of Women*.

Work and Family Center of the Conference Board
845 Third Ave.
New York, NY 10022
(212) 339-0356

The Center is a national clearinghouse of information designed to meet the needs of the business community, government agencies, and other organizations concerned with changes in work and family relationships. It supports research on child care, parental leave, relocation policies, and other related issues. It publishes *Family Supportive Policies: The Corporate Decision* and the *Bibliography on Work and Family Issues*.

Bibliography of Books

Franklin Abbott, ed.	*New Men, New Minds: Breaking Male Tradition.* Freedom, CA: The Crossing Press, 1987.
Barbara Hilkert Andolsen, Christine E. Gridorf, and Mary D. Pellauer, eds.	*Women's Consciousness, Women's Conscience.* San Francisco: Harper & Row, 1987.
Francis Baumli, ed.	*Men Freeing Men: Exploding the Myth of the Traditional Male.* Jersey City, NJ: New Atlantis Press, 1985.
Beryl Lieff Benderly	*The Myth of Two Minds.* New York: Doubleday, 1987.
Barbara R. Bergmann	*The Economic Emergence of Women.* New York: Basic Books, 1986.
Lynda Birke	*Women, Feminism, and Biology.* New York: Methuen, 1986.
Jeanne H. Block	*Sex Role Identity and Ego Development.* San Francisco: Jossey Bass Publications, 1984.
Joel D. Block and Diane Greenberg	*Women & Friendship.* New York: Franklin Watts, 1985.
Dee Brestin	*The Friendship of Women.* Wheaton, IL: Victor Books, 1988.
Judith Briles	*Woman to Woman: From Sabotage to Support.* Far Hills, NJ: New Horizon Press, 1987.
Harry Brod, ed.	*The Making of Masculinities: The New Men's Studies.* Boston: Allen & Unwin, 1987.
Linda Burton, Janet Dittmer, and Cheri Loveless	*What's a Smart Woman Like You Doing at Home?* Washington, DC: Acropolis Books, 1986.
Bebe Moore Campbell	*Successful Women, Angry Men.* New York: Jove Books, 1986.
Annie Cheatham and Mary Clare Powell	*This Way Daybreak Comes: Women's Values and the Future.* Philadelphia: New Society Publishers, 1986.
Kim Chernin	*Reinventing Eve: Modern Woman in Search of Herself.* New York: Times Books, 1987.
Stephanie Coontz and Pete Henderson, eds.	*Women's Work, Men's Property.* London: Verso, 1986.
James Dobson	*Dr. Dobson Answers Your Questions.* Wheaton, IL: Tyndale House, 1988.
Colette Dowling	*Perfect Women: Hidden Fears of Inadequacy and the Drive To Perform.* New York: Summit Books, 1988.
Ken Druck with James C. Simmons	*The Secrets Men Keep: Breaking the Silence Barrier.* New York: Doubleday, 1985.
Alice Hendrickson Eagly	*Sex Differences in Social Behavior: A Social Role Interpretation.* Hillsdale, NJ: L. Erlbaum Associates, 1987.
Lisa Eichenbaum and Susie Orbach	*Between Women.* London: Penguin Books, 1987.

Cynthia Fuchs Epstein	*Deceptive Distinctions: Sex, Gender, and the Social Order.* New Haven, CT: Yale University Press, 1988.
Warren Farrell	*Why Men Are the Way They Are.* New York: McGraw-Hill, 1986.
Rona M. Fields	*The Future of Women.* Bayside, NY: General Hall, 1985.
Rita Freedman	*Beauty Bound.* Lexington, MA: Lexington Books, 1986.
Perry Garfinkel	*In a Man's World.* New York: New American Library, 1985.
Edith Gilson with Susan Kane	*Unnecessary Choices: The Hidden Life of the Executive Woman.* New York: William Morrow, 1987.
John M. Gottman and Jeffrey G. Parker	*Conversations of Friends.* Cambridge, England: Press Syndicate of the University of Cambridge, 1986.
Roberta L. Hall, ed.	*Male-Female Differences: A Biocultural Perspective.* New York: Praeger Publishers, 1985.
Sarah Hardesty and Nehama Jacobs	*Success and Betrayal: The Crisis of Women in Corporate America.* New York: A Touchstone Book/Simon & Schuster, 1986.
Beth B. Hesse and Myra Mary Ferree, eds.	*Analyzing Gender.* Beverly Hills, CA: Sage Publications, 1987.
Alanson B. Houghton	*Partners in Love.* New York: Walker and Company, 1988.
Mark Hunter	*The Passions of Men: Work and Love in the Age of Stress.* New York: G.P. Putnam's Sons, 1988.
Michael S. Kimmel, ed.	*Changing Men: New Directions in Research on Men and Masculinity.* Beverly Hills, CA: Sage Publications, 1987.
Irma Kirtz	*Man Talk: A Book for Women Only.* New York: Beech Tree Books/William Morrow, 1986.
Philip Kitcher	*Vaulting Ambition.* Cambridge, MA: The MIT Press, 1985.
Edward Klein and Don Erickson, eds.	*About Men: Reflections on the Male Experience.* New York: Pocket Books, 1987.
Robert A. Lewis and Marvin B. Sussman, eds.	*Men's Changing Roles in the Family.* New York: The Haworth Press, 1986.
Tara Roth Madden	*Women vs. Women: The Uncivil Business War.* New York: Amacom, 1987.
Eva Margolies	*The Best of Friends, the Worst of Enemies: Women's Hidden Power Over Women.* New York: Doubleday, 1985.
Eva Margolies and Louis Genevie	*The Samson and Delilah Complex.* New York: Dodd, Mead & Co., 1986.
Maxine Margolis	*Mothers and Such.* Berkeley, CA: University of California Press, 1984.
Megan Marshall	*The Cost of Loving: Women and the New Fear of Intimacy.* New York: G.P. Putnam's Sons, 1984.
Rosalind Miles	*Women and Power.* London: MacDonald / Co., 1985.

Elizabeth C. Mooney — *Men and Marriage: The Changing Role of Husbands.* New York: Franklin Watts, 1985.

Ann M. Morrison, Randall P. White, Ellen Van Velsor, and The Center for Creative Leadership — *Breaking the Glass Ceiling: Can Women Reach the Top of America's Largest Corporations?* Reading, MA: Addison-Wesley, 1987.

Steven Naifeh and Gregory White Smith — *Why Can't Men Open Up? Overcoming Men's Fear of Intimacy.* New York: Clarkson N. Potter, Inc., 1984.

Peter Nelson — *Real Man Tells All.* New York: Penguin Books, 1988.

Nancy R. Newhouse, ed. — *Hers: Through Women's Eyes.* New York: Villard Books, 1985.

John Nicholson — *Men and Women: How Different Are They?* New York: Oxford University Press, 1984.

Carol Orsborn — *Enough Is Enough: Exploding the Myth of Having It All.* New York: G.P. Putnam's Sons, 1986.

Ethel Spector Person — *Dreams of Love and Fateful Encounters: The Power of Romantic Passion.* New York: W.W. Norton, 1988.

E. Jerry Phares — *Introduction to Personality.* Columbus, OH: Charles E. Merrill Publishing Company, 1984.

Stephen Price and Susan Price — *No More Lonely Nights: Overcoming the Hidden Fears That Keep You from Getting Married.* New York: G.P. Putnam's Sons, 1988.

Janice G. Raymond — *A Passion for Friends: Toward a Philosophy of Female Affection.* Boston: Beacon Press, 1986.

John Rowan — *The Horned God: Feminism and Men as Wounding and Healing.* New York: Routledge & Kegan Paul, 1987.

Maggie Scarf — *Intimate Partners: Patterns in Love and Marriage.* New York: Random House, 1987.

Barry Schwartz — *The Battle for Human Nature.* New York: W.W. Norton, 1986.

Lynne Segal — *Is the Future Female? Troubled Thoughts on Contemporary Feminism.* New York: Peter Bedrick Books, 1987.

Morton H. Shaevitz — *Sexual Static: How Men Are Confusing the Women They Love.* Boston: Little, Brown & Company, 1987.

Stephen A. Shapiro — *Manhood: A New Definition.* New York: G.P. Putnam's Sons, 1984.

Evelyn Shaw and Joan Darling — *Female Strategies.* New York: Simon & Schuster, 1985.

Audrey D. Smith and William J. Reid — *Role-Sharing Marriage.* New York: Columbia University Press, 1986.

Judith K. Sprankle — *Working It Out: The Domestic Double Standard.* New York: Walker and Company, 1986.

Carol Tavris and Carole Wade — *The Longest War: Sex Differences in Perspective.* San Diego: Harcourt Brace Jovanovich 1984.

Rosemarie Tong — *Feminist Thought: A Comprehensive Introduction.* Boulder, CO: Westview Press, 1989.

Index

divorce
  enslaves women in poverty, 73, 74
  frees women, 96, 97-98, 100
Dobson, James C., 17, 185
Dowling, Colette, 128
Doyle, James A., 31
Druck, Karen, 109
Druck, Kenneth, 104, 105, 159
Duncan, Riana, 220

economics
  determines gender roles, 40-47
education
  equalizes men and women, 68, 69
  con, 74, 75
Ehrenreich, Barbara, 122, 160
Ehrhardt, Anke A., 28
Ehrhart, Julie Kuhn, 75
emotions, 19-21, 22
Epstein, Cynthia Fuchs, 59

Fallows, Deborah, 79, 81, 82, 146
family
  infant care leave and
    is needed, 189-195
    con, 196-201
  traditional
    economics creates, 44-46
    con, 73, 74
  working parents and
    help children, 167-173, 180-183
    con, 174-179, 184-188
Farrell, Warren, 246
Fausto-Sterling, Anne, 55
Feiffer, Jules, 244
Feinberg, Sylvia, 172
feminism
  degrades motherhood, 78, 80-81
  exalts motherhood, 84-86
  has improved women's lives, 66-70
  con, 71-76
Ferber, Marianne A., 40
Fiedler, Leslie, 124
Fields, Suzanne, 77
Fields, W.C., 141
Fraiberg, Selma, 177
Frank, Meryl, 189
French, Marilyn, 86
Freud, Sigmund, 28, 81, 136
Freudenberger, Herbert J., 234
Friedan, Betty, 86, 91, 128, 129, 131, 224
friendships
  men and women can have, 207-212
  con, 213-217
  men do not have, 147-154
  con, 155-161

women have, 148-149
Fussell, Paul, 127

Garfinkel, Perry, 119
gender roles
  biology determines, 17-23
  con, 24-30
  brain structure determines, 48-54
  con, 55-60
  economic roles create, 40-47
  socialization creates, 31-39, 215-216
Gilbert, Lucia A., 180
girls
  working mothers benefit, 168-173, 181-182
Goldberg, Herb, 115, 240
Goldman, Renee, 103
Goleman, Daniel, 48
Gorski, Roger, 54
Gouldner, Helen, 215
Gray, Jeffrey, 56, 57
Greenberg, Martin, 140
Gross, Jane, 106
Guerra, Stella G., 66
Guisewite, Cathy, 50, 132, 144, 169
Gutentag, Marcia, 107

Haddad, Richard, 141
Hansen-Shaevitz, Marjorie, 81
Hardesty, Sarah, 68
Harragan, Betty, 69
Heller, Karen, 117
Hernandez, David, 21
Hewlett, Sylvia Ann, 71
Hines, Melissa, 52
Hinton, Zack, 200
Hirsch, Jack, 198
Hite, Shere, 94
Hoffman, Lois, 169, 173, 182
homosexuality, 215, 216
Hoyenga, Katharine, 36
Hoyenga, Kermit, 36
Hunter, Brenda, 187

industrialization
  creates gender roles, 44-46
intelligence
  having a working mother improves 171-172
  men and women are equal in, 59-60
  con, 51-53

Jacklin, Carol Nagy, 60
Jacobs, Nehama, 68
Jennings, Joyce, 37
Jong, Erica, 86

259